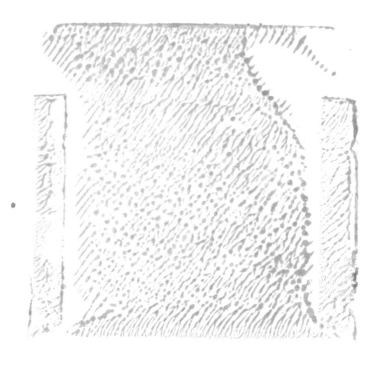

The
End of
Privacy

■

Also by Charles J. Sykes

Profscam

The Hollow Men

A Nation of Victims

Dumbing Down Our Kids

The
End of
Privacy

■

Charles J. Sykes

St. Martin's Press ❧ New York

Production Editor: David Stanford Burr
Book design by Donna Sinisgalli

Library of Congress Cataloging-in-Publication Data

Sykes, Charles J.
      The end of privacy / Charles J. Sykes.—1st ed.
          p. cm.
      ISBN 0-312-20350-0
      1. Privacy, Right of—United States. I. Title.
JC596.2.U5S95   1999
323.44'8'0973—dc21   99-15919
                                       CIP

First Edition: October 1999

1 2 3 4 5 6 7 8 9 10

Contents

PART 1

■

The
Attack on
Privacy

1

■

Prologue and Introduction

Before breakfast, a businesswoman signs on to the Internet, checks her e-mail, and orders flowers. Even before she has signed off, her on-line movements have left a trail of data that has been added to her profile, including the fact that the recipient of the flowers is a thirty-two-year-old man who lives in the next suburb. Her phone records indicate a number of late-night calls to the man's residence. While she was on-line, every icon she clicked on was tracked and recorded. Someone was learning about her. Several discreet "cookies" are left behind on her hard drive.

Later that week, her purchase of the flowers will be matched and merged with the fact she vacations in Aruba, buys lingerie from Victoria's Secret, uses a high-end hair color, and drives a late-model car. Her name will be sold to marketers looking for consumers who fit that profile. The same marketers have a dossier that already runs to more than eighty-five pages about her spending habits. Every time she uses the smart card at her grocery store, the profile expands, including her recent purchase of hemorrhoid medication, contraceptives, and her preference for cabernets. She is unaware that her ex-husband's attorney has just obtained a copy. Others will be interested to learn that she logged onto an Internet message board for patients with breast cancer for the fourth consecutive day. The next week, she will unexpectedly be denied a new home mortgage.

As she leaves her apartment, the security cameras capture her departure. She seldom notices them anymore, but the cameras keep record of her comings and goings as well as those of her guests. It makes for amusing viewing at the security staff's Christmas party.

The e-mail she read before breakfast was from a coworker, who told her he planned to quit. Writing back, she expressed her own ambivalence about her bosses. Their supervisor, who will be waiting in her office, read both the message and her reply. Once in her car, she makes a call on her cell phone, which instantly allows her location to be pinpointed exactly (the FCC has approved new rules that require cell phones to be trackable by law enforcement); and as she speaks her conversation can easily be heard on a nearby scanner. As she passes through a tollbooth, her presence is electronically recorded by an intelligent transportation system, whose cameras snap her license plate number, recognizing it as the same car that passed the checkpoint two days earlier at 2:30 A.M.

She flips on the radio, which reports that Chelsea Clinton has broken up with her boyfriend and has checked into a clinic with stress-related symptoms. Later that day, she has her own appointment with her psychologist, who at the moment is meeting with a representative of her HMO, which is undertaking a "utilization review," a procedure that requires the doctor to turn over all of his patient files. As she drives to work, a representative of the company is reading her therapist's notes about her night terrors. She occasionally wonders about the mail she receives advertising new antidepressants, but it does not occur to her that her pharmacy has been selling her name.

Privacy is like oxygen. We really appreciate it only when it is gone. The death of Princess Diana, the political convulsions over Bill Clinton's sex life, celebrity complaints about the predatory media give the issue prominence. But it is not the violations of the famous that make the battle over privacy the preeminent issue of the Information Age. It is the erosion of privacy in our everyday lives.

Snoops have always been with us. From time immemorial, gossips, nags, governments, and journalists have tried to listen in our conversations, follow our comings and goings and hunt for grist for their endlessly turning mills. What's new, however, is the tools they now have at hand to watch, listen, and record. Technology makes the fears of the paranoiac of the past seen Pollyanna-ish compared with the realities of the present and the prospects of the future. If it remains true that everyone is famous for at least fifteen minutes, it is also true that the average citizen now experiences the loss of privacy once reserved for the famous and infamous.

Questions of privacy touch us in nearly every aspect of our lives, from our relationships with our doctors, to our ability to communicate on the Net, to the intimacy of our personal relationships.

At the end of the century, the challenge to privacy comes from many fronts:

- Modern technology has made it possible to create vast new dossiers of extraordinary detail and specificity about our tastes, habits, and lives. Every time you apply for a job, subscribe to a magazine, call a mail-order catalog, use a credit card, dial a phone, seek credit, fly on an airplane, buy insurance, rent an apartment, drive a car, pay taxes, get married or divorced, sue someone, see a doctor, use a smart card, apply for government licenses or benefits, you become part of the dataweb, which has proven far more powerful than the paper trails of bygone years.

- People are increasingly anxious about the erosion of their personal privacy. In a 1998 Louis Harris poll, 88 percent of Americans said they were concerned about their privacy, while a majority (55 percent) said they were "very concerned."

- The Internet has rewritten the rules of private and public life, providing an illusion of privacy in a realm that actually is a fishbowl.

- Even as the private sector develops new techniques for tracking us, new government databases ranging from information about newly hired workers to airline passengers threatens to create a seamless dataweb that blurs the lines between government surveillance and commercial marketing.

- The National Research Council has warned that the medical records of millions of Americans are vulnerable to abuse, noting that "today there are no strong incentives to safeguard patient information because patients, industry groups and government regulators aren't demanding protection."* The federal government continues to move toward creating a single universal medical identifier that will track every visit to a doctor's office, every treatment, and every prescription for every patient from cradle to grave.

---

*Warren Leary, "Panel Cites Lack of Security on Medical Records," *The New York Times,* March 6, 1997.

- In politics the personal has become the political, shrinking the zone of privacy, making the lives of politicians—and the rest of us—fair game. Both the Nannies of the welfare state (in the name of compassion) and the Grundies of the right (in the name of virtue) continue to narrow the zone of our lives that is no one else's business. The loss of privacy has, in effect, become a tax on involvement in public affairs.

- Fueled by our penchant for therapy and sharing, Americans share their intimacies and dysfunctions with therapists, casual acquaintances, and national television audiences. Although the effect is numbing—does anything shock us anymore?—the pressure grows for the rest of us to join in the orgy of self-exposure lest we be suspected of unhealthy repression or concealing guilty secrets.

- The hypercompetitive media continually revise their standards downward as the line between the tabloids and the mainstream press is erased. Salacious gossip in tabloids that would have once been trash-canned with scarcely a comment, now is fodder even for the gray ladies of the establishment press. The Internet is rapidly breaking down whatever barriers between rumor and news that may have survived.

- Workplaces continue to be no-privacy zones, where employers read the e-mail, listen to the phone calls, electronically monitor, and videotape employees. One survey found that nearly three-quarters of large corporations collect information about their workers beyond what employees provide voluntarily; more than two-thirds report hiring private investigators to check into the background of their workers. More than one-third use medical records to make decisions about employees.

- Anxious to protect its own secrets, the government remains jealous of the ability of citizens to keep their own. Law-enforcement and intelligence agencies want to deny the rest of us the ability to encode our own communications to prevent their easy interception or reading.

It is easy to see what it at stake:

The greatest barrier to the growth of commerce on the Internet is not technological. The Net will realize its potential for hypergrowth only when it resolves concerns over the privacy and the security of information transmitted through cyberspace. Privacy may be worth uncounted billions of dollars.

Perhaps even more urgently, concerns over privacy threaten to erode many of the advances in medical science, including those involving genetic therapy. Fearful that certain information could damage their ability to obtain insurance or jobs, patients are already avoiding tests and even doctors altogether.

Already the political landscape is being laid waste by the assault on the private lives of public and private figures alike. At the heart of the cultural, political, and legal schism over the fate of President Bill Clinton was the question of privacy, an issue that threatens to spill over and poison public life as a whole. Ironically, an age that is obsessive about delving into the private lives of individuals is inevitably dominated at one extreme by the Puritan and the other by the pornographer. The zeal of the neo–Puritans in exposing Sodom and Gomorrah is at least equaled by the zest with which their opponents search out "hypocrisy," that gravest of all modern sins. In the campaign to explode privacy, what begins with piety ends with pornography. The Moral Majority meets *Hustler.*

But the greatest threats—obscured in debates over sexual McCarthyism, media intrusion, and technological snooping—go to the heart of our self-identity. Some commentators suggest that privacy is the essence of being human; but, in fact, it is quite possible to be human without privacy. It is more accurate to say that privacy is essential to being a *free* human being.° As Justice Louis Brandeis suggested more than a century ago, privacy—the right to be let alone—is the most valued, if not most celebrated, right enjoyed by Americans. Neither the Founding Fathers of the eighteenth century nor Brandeis of the nineteenth century thought that privacy was optional. How much less so in the twentieth and twenty-first centuries, when others have the power literally to watch us through walls.

°The preamble to the Australian Privacy Charter declares: "A free and democratic society requires respect for the autonomy of individuals, and limits the power of both state and private organizations to intrude on their autonomy . . . Privacy is a key value which underpins human dignity and other key values such as freedom of association and freedom of speech . . . Privacy is a basic human right and the reasonable expectation of every person."

BALANCING ACTS

The truth is that as much as we deplore the erosion of privacy—and we can be quite eloquent on the subject—many of us accept the violations in the name of a wide range of equally attractive virtues and interests. To paraphrase Jane Austen, privacy is a value that everyone speaks well of, but no one remembers to do anything about. No one disparages privacy to its face. They simply choose to emphasize the public's right to know, national security, personal safety, conveniences, economic opportunity, politics, ideology, or the pursuit of virtue. Privacy may be all well and good, but the economics of direct marketing are often far more compelling, the hyper-competitive environment of the new media makes reticence seem an unaffordable and archaic luxury, and, anyway, what are you trying to hide? Indeed, attempts to protect privacy are frequently regarded with suspicion. "There is not a crime," thundered Joseph Pulitzer, "there is not a dodge, there is not a trick, there is not a swindle, there is not a vice which does not live by secrecy."

The early privacy advocate E. L. Godkin, once told the story of a traveler in a Western mining town who "pinned a shirt across his open window on the piazza while performing his toilet; after a few minutes he saw it drawn aside roughly by a hand from without, and on asking what it meant, a voice answered, "We want to know what there is so darned private going on in there?"[1] The question still makes us uncomfortable.

These days, privacy is whipsawed from both the left and the right. As incompatible as their various agendas might be, virtucrats of all stripes are united in believing that the "personal is political," a slogan that now sounds grimly ironic in the post–Lewinsky political world. Originally used by feminists, to argue that issues like day care should be matters of public concern, the personalization of politics represents a deeper shift in the political debate. Whatever the original intent of the slogan, describing the personal as the political shrinks the zone of privacy while expanding the areas of our lives that are seen to be "everybody's business." Public debates center increasingly not around issues of great moment, but around various aspects of personal life and conduct, including what we eat, what we drink, what we smoke, how we recycle, and how we bond with our kids—tearing down the walls that once divided the public from the private realms.

In some respects, this focus reflects the temper of the times. Having lost faith in their ability to solve big problems, modern do-gooders have turned to small ones. Frustrated at their failure to fix society, they have turned to fixing one another and the rest of us, as well. As strangers show an ever-increasing enthusiasm to hector their neighbors and intrude into their lives, nagging has virtually become a national pastime.

Unfortunately for privacy, this means a two-front war. If liberals seem anxious to intrude into private lives in the name of "compassion," conservatives often act as if they want the state to be the arbiter of community and personal morality. While the left has supported the proliferation of government-run social-welfare databases, the right has championed the demands of law-enforcement agencies that want a back door to our personal communications. Conservatives object to government intrusions such as a national ID, but are reluctant to support any restrictions on the growth of massive private-sector data dossiers, even though they increasingly blur lines between government and private information-gathering. The left has a proud tradition of defending civil liberties, but therapeutic liberalism has waxed especially enthusiastic over the notion that it takes a whole village to raise your children.

SHUT UP, WE EXPLAINED

The political and ideological threats are dramatically magnified by the more general spirit of the age. We are not the first culture to revel in gossip, but our distinctive contribution is not gossip, but exhibitionism. Having perfectly soundproof walls, we have become a society that cannot shut up. The classical belief that the unexamined life was not worth living has been replaced by our modern conviction that the unpublicized, unexposed life that has no socially redeeming value.

Not only does the love that dare not speak its name now never shut up—no one else does either. The result is a society of way-too-much-information.

Richard Rhodes assaults us with the details of his sex life with a specificity that goes beyond excruciating. Kathryn Harrison feels compelled to publish accounts of her incestuous affair with her father. Joyce Maynard seeks to claw her way upward from mediocrity by exposing her relationship with the intensely private and reclusive J. D. Salinger. Dr. Laura's ex-boyfriend sells nude pictures of the virtues maven for posting on the Web. Dr. Jack Kevorkian and *60 Minutes* team up for a televised episode of euthanasia. Even the most famous privacy victims, Princess Diana and Bill

Clinton, found it necessary to share details about their most intimate affairs with worldwide audiences. Perhaps this is inevitable in a postmodern celebrity culture that has traded achievement for publicity; restraint for exposure; reticence for "authenticity"; and decency for self-revelation. Daytime television has become a national town hall of confession, peopled with a class of individuals willing to endure any humiliation or pay any price to escape their privacy. Unable to achieve fame through accomplishments or actual celebrity through other means, they offer their privacy as the kindling for their moment of pseudo-celebrity, especially on television. Television may be the ideal forum for the modern culture of confession because it provides the illusion of intimacy without the accountability and messiness of real relationships. For many Americans, it seems that reality is such a fragile concept that they are not really sure anything is real unless it is on television. Since nothing is fixed or sure, the virtual reality of television actually becomes more real than "real" life—untelevised life. Privacy is worse than irrelevant.

It is what nobody sees; there is no there there.

This has profound consequences for families, especially since we no longer have secrets from one another, or from our children. The young are no longer the uninitiated or the innocent. They no longer have to pass through various stages as they are socialized and introduced to the secrets of adulthood. All the veils are down. Any child who watches television, author James Twitchell notes, "sees things that only adults would have known of in a pre-electronic world."[2] On the Internet they can find out about things that adults do that even many adults have never imagined.

Of course, despite all of the claims made on its behalf, the explosion of sex-talk has demonstrably not made us healthier or wiser in matters sexual. Nor has the orgy of self-exposure and confessionalism made us more insightful. There is little evidence that the prurient press has appreciably raised our moral standards. Reading the peccadilloes and private quirks of celebrities and pseudo-celebrities has not had the cautionary effects its advocates would seem to claim for such intrusive journalism. Yet, the culture of full disclosure does not seem likely to wither away. It has however, established a cultural climate of disdain for privacy and distrust of those who avoid exposure or insist on keeping their private lives to themselves. That, in turn, influences the cultural, political, and legal climate for privacy.

∎ ∎ ∎

But it is not the freakish or the abnormal that is most alarming: it is the routine, the habitual, the almost numbing regularity with which others intrude on our private life. At times it may be possible to ignore the implications of all of this. We believe that we can chip away at others' privacy, but keep our own intact. All the while, we are changing the standards of what is private and what is public, shifting the lines depending on our moods, our politics, or the light. Perhaps the best example is how we feel about sex.

Is sex our most private or our most public activity? Starting in the 1960s, the courts have carved out a special zone of constitutionally protected privacy for almost all matters sexual, from the reading of pornography, to the right to procreate, to contraception, and even abortion. But if sex is private, one would not know it from going to the movies, reading the papers, or watching the typical prime-time sitcom. In modern culture, sex is as private as any other national pastime, and it gets higher ratings than baseball. Nor is this simply a matter of culture: sexual-harassment law has turned some of the relations between men and women into matters of law and political debate. We have found, however, that the loss of privacy, like any once-released genie, is very, very difficult to put back into the bottle.

THE PRIVACY PARADOX

Having said all of this, defenders of privacy need to confront several difficult questions: If there is a genuine concern for personal privacy, as public opinion polls consistently indicate, then why do so many people behave as if they did not care about their privacy? Why do people tell pollsters they are alarmed about the loss of privacy, but then blithely give out their credit-card numbers over the Internet? Or sign consent forms that allow sensitive medical information to be seen by dozens of eyes? Even granting the institutional power of the antiprivacy forces, why has the political support for privacy protections been so ineffectual?

First, few Americans have anything but the vaguest idea just how much of their lives is transparent, or how vulnerable they are to the new technologies and instruments of surveillance and monitoring. But even among those who do have some idea that their privacy is in jeopardy, many feel powerless to do anything about it, perhaps seeing it as an inevitable by-product of the information age.

But there is another explanation as well. Privacy is not an absolute; like free speech, or any other right, it must be weighed in the balance against such values as freedom of information, free trade, national security, and the public's need to know. Indeed, there are so many competing claims that privacy can hope to survive the balancing tests only if it is well established and well understood as a basic principle. But it is neither. Its legal status is confused, at best. And among the lost arts of our age is the ability to gracefully tell another, "It's none of your business." In part, that is because we forget too often why privacy matters.

2

■

Why It Matters

What Privacy Is—and What It Is Not

For some of us, privacy is simply the right to be let alone; but having said that, what precisely does it mean? Is privacy simply a matter of protecting our solitude? Is privacy something we can expect only when we are by ourselves, when no one else can see us, or gain access to us? Or does privacy extend beyond solitude to our relations with others—our family, friends, and associates? Are there times we can expect a modicum of privacy even when we are in public or engaged in public affairs? Is privacy the right to control information about ourselves? If so, what information? Can we really hope to control what impression we make? Can we regulate others' reactions to our behavior?

Our experience of privacy is also likely to vary widely. For some of us, it is the ability to live a life unobserved, or to have a zone where we can develop intimate relations, blow off steam, relax and be ourselves in a way that is impossible in public. For others, it is to have a room or a life of their own, where they are freed from interference, judgment, and social pressure to pursue their interests, develop their talents, and take the sorts of chances that can be risked only in private. For some, privacy is what gives them a chance to repair their psyches and accumulate the moral and psychic capital they rely on when they emerge into public. For some of us, privacy is experienced in anonymity, the pleasure of being unknown or unrecognized when we travel to another city or take a vacation. (Surely one of the most significant losses of privacy for the modern celebrity is the inability to go *anywhere* without being recognized.) For some of us, privacy simply allows us to live in the twilight of public and private where we can go out unshaven, change jobs, and even relationships without being subject to publicity. For others, privacy may simply mean not being walked in on by parents or siblings; or it may be the power to choose what they reveal about themselves to others.

Each of us will react differently to violations of our privacy; we not only have different standards, we also calibrate our responses depending on our closeness or relationships with others. But we all have our own ladders of privacy, beginning with our closest relations, moving downward in descending orders of intimacy. For some, the ladder might look like this:

spouse
[priest, minister, rabbi]
brothers and sisters
parents
children
friends
in-laws
coworkers
neighbors
marketers
employers
government
news media
ex-spouses
potential rivals/enemies

Our willingness to share information declines with each rung. Information we would share with a sister, we might be unwilling to share with a parent, much less an in-law or a neighbor. We might have no qualms about giving our neighbor information about our habits that we would be very reluctant to share with our employer; and though we might share details of our sex lives with a friend, we would be horrified to share it with a government agent or (God forbid) the media. Certainly, our greatest fear would be for an enemy to compile a detailed and damaging dossier on us.° Each

---

°One of the Founding Fathers, John Adams, captured this sensibility when he wrote: "Some Things which ought to be communicated to some of our Friends, that they may

person probably has a slightly different ladder, and different criteria for sharing information. But everyone has such limits and measures, because it is nearly impossible to live without them.

THE RISE AND FALL
OF PRIVACY

Until modern times, of course, people had remarkably little privacy; many of them led their whole lives without ever really being alone. Every detail of their lives was subject to the scrutiny of family members, members of the tribe, or community. Over the past two centuries, the rise of the modern has been the rise of the individual. The literature of the last 200 years is a chronicle of what it meant to discover the power and the freedom of being alone. Undoubtedly, other societies and ages have done without much privacy, but *we* cannot. Even so, a fair history of the state of privacy would not resemble anything like an even sweep either of rise or decline; there was no golden age from which we have fallen. Although we can chronicle the technologies that have enhanced the possibilities of privacy in our lives, every development and milestone has been shadowed by another taking us in quite a different direction.

The spread of prosperity, the single-family home, the automobile, the invention of television and computers have all made it possible for us to live private lives unimaginable to previous generations. We no longer live cheek by jowl with our neighbors, we can move about without crowding into buses or trains; our entertainment comes to us virtually one on one; we do not have to go to theaters or share our tastes with our neighbors. Once, our lives were hedged about by neighbors who would watch us nearly as closely as members of our own family; they would be silent—or not so silent—audience to our lives, acting sometimes as a support network, other times as a chorus of censure or unsolicited advice. They knew

---

improve them to our Profit and Honour or Pleasure, should be concealed from our Enemies, and from indiscreet friends, least they should be twined to our Loss, Disgrace or Mortification. I am under no moral or other obligation to publish to the World how much my Expenses or my incomes amount to yearly. There are Times when and Persons for Whom I am not obliged to tell what are my principles and Opinions in Politicks or Religion." Quoted in John H. F. Shattuck, *Rights of Privacy* (New York, National Textbook Company, 1976) pp. xiii–xiv.

how we dressed, how we shopped, whom we dated, and the meaning of the various noises and odors coming from our homes.

Today, we may not even know their names. Many of us can go through life with only a nodding acquaintance with the people who live around us and even work with us. As Janna Malamud Smith notes, an adult living in a modern suburb is unlikely to have more than a few people who know her across time in different settings.[1]

But this account runs parallel to another story: the same technologies that help separate us from the crowds also make it possible to monitor and record our behaviors. Although fewer people have intimate knowledge of our lives, many people—mostly unknown to us—know something about us. Here is the rub. The very technology that was supposed to free us from mass society and the conformity of mass media, has turned out to be as much a fishbowl as an information highway. In modern society, we have discovered that being free often means also being naked. The same society that allows us to live anonymously relies on surveillance to keep track of us because we are a society of strangers. We can close the blinds on our neighbors, but we have also opened doors to strangers who now know what we eat, what we wear, how we shop, who our doctor is, how much we earn, where we work, what drugs we take, and what we read.

Historical comparisons are useful, but also limited because the conditions of privacy in the modern technological world are, in fact, radically different from the challenges it faced in the past. Some critics dismiss concerns about massive commercial databases that track individual purchases and buying habits, by saying that such information was really no different from small-town gossip. But this misses the fundamental difference between being known by neighbors and friends, and being monitored by a faceless database. As intrusive as small-town gossip might have been, it was always shaded by some personal knowledge and connection. Being watched by a neighbor is not at all of the same magnitude as being watched by a bureaucracy, or tracked by a dataweb that misses little and forgets nothing.[2]

The second paradox of privacy is that even though most of us have far more physical privacy, many of us seem extraordinarily anxious to get rid of that privacy. A man can reasonably expect to be left alone in his home, safe from prying eyes. But that same man can turn on the television set on any given afternoon and find a window into the most graphic, embarrassing details of the lives of others.

WATCHING EYES

Perhaps the best way to understand privacy is to consider what life is like when we are stripped of a zone of privacy. Most of the time, we simply take our privacy for granted, especially in our relations with those closest to us. But imagine this scenario: You are in a public place, spending what you think is a private moment with your child. But imagine now that you are being watched and scrutinized. Imagine that your interaction is being recorded. Your reaction will probably be determined by *whose eyes* are doing the watching. Imagine that some are hostile, some amused, some disapproving. Imagine that this unguarded moment with your child will be publicized and used to illustrate your child-rearing abilities. Knowing this at the time, what are the chances your intimate moment will be the same as if you were not subject to such scrutiny? If you were alone?

Would you behave in exactly the same way? And would you be sure what would be for show? And what was for real? At what point is intimacy transformed into exhibitionism?

Take another example: What woman would behave the same with her lover in the presence of her parents as she would when the couple was alone? What is the chance that the couple will achieve any real intimacy if they are always within earshot of others? Or if she was being watched by a friend? A stranger? A coworker? What suitor shares his hopes and fears in front of a newspaper reporter?

How do you feel when you go into a pharmacy to buy an item of personal hygiene? A condom? Viagra? Imagine now that your in-laws know this information. How about your coworkers? Your employer?

When it comes to privacy, context also matters. Imagine, for example, that an adversary or rival came into your office one day and handed you a dossier that included detailed information about your home, business, and family. It lists your Social Security number, your home phone, your driver's license number, the value of the property you own, the record of your recent purchases or travels, perhaps a printout of recent phone numbers you have called. Imagine that the dossier also included similar information about your spouse or your children, including photographs of them going to and from work or school, and pictures of your home. Taken individually, each piece of information is probably harmless. But in context, they become something else. Even if your adversary did not say a word, you would recognize the dossier as a *threat*. He had trespassed on your life; broken into and burglarized your privacy.

Again, imagine that when you shopped, spies wrote down what you bought, how you paid for your purchases, and even what you might have looked at. (In many ways this describes shopping today on the Internet). Or imagine that your likes and loves were chronicled daily in the pages of the local newspaper, complete with speculations from gossipy neighbors about your character and your sexual preferences and practices. What might that mean for your relationships with others?

How would the spotlight affect the genuineness of your interaction with friends, lovers, and family? How long would it take before intimacy became display, personality mere show, and life flat, false, and furtive?

Think now about the most painful episodes of your life: the time you were fired, got divorced, when your child failed at school or ran afoul of the law, or when you wrestled with what seemed unsolvable dilemmas about the medical care of an aged parent. Now imagine that any of those events had been played out on the public stage or that they had been the subject of gossip columns, exposés, or the fodder for talk shows. Imagine that your divorce, your failure at work, the tribulations of raising your children were read about and commented on by your coworkers, your neighbors, people you have never met nor ever will meet; that your children's friends read about you as well. Imagine how it would feel to have your life stripped down, summarized in a few paragraphs, and your reputation fixed immovably in the amber of modern publicity, as undoubtedly was done to someone in the paper you read this morning at breakfast.

Taking our thought experiment a step further, consider what happens when privacy is utterly extinguished. Imagine a society where the personal is always the political and the distance between comrades is dissolved. We can imagine a society (George Orwell has done it for us) where we are constantly at the mercy of snoops; either informers, or surveillance devices that watch us, keep track of where we go, what we read, whom we see, what we believe, whom we love. We can easily picture a society (our century has also done this for us), in which the police have the right to burst into any home, or any room, at any time; in other words, a society in which there was no place that is off-limits, no place where we are safe and where we could hide. Or a society that restricted personal choices, regulating whom you can marry, how you can raise your children, or what you can read in the privacy of your own home. What we cannot imagine is such a society that is also *free*.

Both the prison and the concentration camp deprive inmates of freedom, but the tearing away of every shred of privacy is what deprives them of dignity and causes them to surrender their hold of the sense of self. The mark of a totalitarian society is precisely its lack of respect for persons and the subjection of every part of life to scrutiny, surveillance, and monitoring. A state that invades the privacy of its citizens shrinks them. Concentration camps strip humans of their dignity by stripping them of any tiny corner of privacy, where they can be undisturbed or unobserved. At Auschwitz, wrote Primo Levi, "solitude in a Camp is more precious and rare than bread."[3] In the totalitarian society, everything is public, open for examination, even the most trivial aspects of life. Even lesser violations can be devastating. A successful professional woman, who was subjected to a strip search by police, describes being stripped of her defenses and dignity. Within minutes, a lifetime of accomplishment and esteem was "totally dismantled."[4]

I have a friend who discovered recently that her neighbors were watching her house, taking note of who came and went and reporting this information to others, including members of the news media, who made it subject of widespread gossip. Although no publication ensued, she felt completely violated. Her house had always been her sanctuary, a place where she could step back from the rigors of a difficult profession, where she could take pleasure in simple domesticity. The discovery that she was under surveillance by her neighbors destroyed whatever pleasure she had in being in and around the one place she had always regarded as safe.

To a lesser extent, patients in hospitals (where the gowns are designed specifically for their immodesty) or other institutional settings experience the same loss of identity and dignity.

The question is not necessarily whether you have anything to hide; it is whether you should have some control over who knows—or who has access to—the details of your life. Privacy is not the same thing as secrecy, although the two are often confused. There are many aspects of our lives that we expect to keep to ourselves that are not necessarily secrets. They might include our relationship with our spouses, our children, or with God. A phone tap that overheard me ordering fried chicken would not reveal any dark secret, but it still invades my privacy.[5] Our political opinions, the charities we support, the books we read, and movies we watch are seldom secrets, but we might wish to keep them private. A private matter becomes a secret only when snooping eyes forces us to hide or conceal things that are no one else's business.

Not surprisingly, when someone's privacy has been violated, they often use the language of rape to describe their feelings of violation. Something has been taken away from them that defines their humanity and is central to their sense of their individuality and their personhood. Privacy is not simply a matter of being protected *from* invasions, it is also a means *for* defining oneself, and entering into relationships that provide us the security to become vulnerable. In fact, it is the decision to share such confidences that defines our most intimate relationships. We don't share indiscriminately, but unveil ourselves bit by bit as we establish trust, commitment, and affection. It is in these relationships that we open ourselves and make ourselves vulnerable. We let others see us in a way that we would be ashamed to let others see us. A person with no secrets has no power to decide what he shall reveal about himself and to whom; he is denied the chance to be intimate with anyone because intimacy involves the voluntary opening of oneself. If there is nothing to open, if all secrets have been stripped out, this becomes impossible. We become a society with no place to hide.

"Just because you know some details about a person's life doesn't mean you know the person," says the actress playing Jacqueline Kennedy Onassis in the Broadway play, *Jackie: An American Life.*[6]

Many people know details of our lives. Those details are laid out in reams of data about our habits, our loves, likes, tastes. They can be scanned, merged, collated, sold, examined. Our lives are on file—or, at least, the details of those lives, which is not the same thing at all. This may sound like an abstract point, but we can recognize it instinctively. A single event of our lives or even a series of things—conversations, purchases, comments—can be made to seem like a portrait of our lives, but they are not, because they cannot be understood isolated from their context. And that context can be understood only by those who know us well, those with whom we have chosen to share varying levels of insight into our characters, likes and dislikes. Even if we stumble across one of our own letters or keepsakes from decades ago, we may momentarily be unable to associate it with the affections and emotions that once animated it and gave it meaning. Without that dimension, it is simply a dry artifact, a meaningless clue, rather than a living part of our lives. The same is true of almost all of our relationships. Take the intimate relations between a man and a woman; strip away the privacy of the sex act and it becomes not intimacy, but exhibitionism. Drain it of affection and intimate attachment, and it becomes pornography.

Indeed, some experiences seem to be meant only for privacy, and change their character fundamentally if they are made public. In moments of great grief or trauma, why do we seek out solitude, or the company of loved ones? Why do our most profound moments occur away from the limelight? Part of the answer is instinctual: We are still the creatures who blush. But our reticence also has to do with a sense of propriety. Love exposed to public attention inevitably becomes mere show, while acts of "conspicuous goodness," confession, contrition, and emotionalism run the risk of devolving into preening and self-indulgence. Dietrich Bonhoeffer, who died in terrifying circumstances at the hands of the Nazis, cautioned even against discussing feelings such as terror in public, because such sharing "involved a near inescapable element of exhibitionism."[7]

We frequently justify such random acts of self-exposure are as evidence of our "sincerity." But public sincerity is sincerity in search of an *edge*.

Emotions once reserved for privacy become tools for political advantage, to create or burnish an image, or perhaps to evade responsibility. The false note creeps into every display of public emotionalism. Celebrations of grief become pleas for sympathy or advertisements for our sensitivity; acts of penitence are turned into ruses to evade punishment. Public weeping and confession—a la televangelist Jimmy Swaggart—seem fake and cynical precisely because they are emotions played to an audience. Swaggart and others might well have heeded the New Testament's warning against parading one's piety and Christ's admonition that the loudest prayers are often declarations of moral superiority and sanctimoniousness rather than acts of humility or piety.

PUBLIC AND PRIVATE

Lost in much of the debate over what should be made public and what should be kept private is the role of the private life in making our public life possible. We can easily understand the importance of shielding our private lives from the glare of publicity. But it is equally important for the future of the public realm of our lives to preserve a sacred zone of privacy, walled off from the tumult of politics, publicity, and debate. Hannah Arendt argues that privacy guarantees the depth of life because it contains "a great many things which cannot withstand the implacable light of the constant presence of others on the public scene."[8] But she also warns against tearing down the walls that guarded the sacred privacies of life, because these same walls also made public life itself possible. The personal could not be the political because by definition, she wrote, there could be no public life without the wall between public and private. "Without it, a public realm could no more exist than a piece of property without a fence to hedge it in; the one harbored and inclosed political life and the other sheltered and protected the biological life process of the family."[9] Her metaphor was not merely rhetorical, because privacy and private property really represented one and the same thing.

The link between democracy and privacy is not at all accidental; without a private zone, public life is impossible. That perhaps helps explain why our era's constant assault on the privileges of private life has also meant the trivialization and erosion of public life. "Any man who was the same in both public and intimate life would be a monster," remarks Milan Kundera. "He would be without spontaneity in his private life and without responsibility in his public life."[10]

■

PART 2

The Surveillance Society

3

■

Trapped in the Dataweb,
or,
What Have You Got to Hide?

"In a few hours, sitting at my computer," writes Carole A. Lane, "beginning with no more than your name and address, I can find what you do for a living, the names and ages of your spouse and children, what kind of car you drive, the value of your house, and how much you pay in taxes on it. From what I learn about your job, your house, and the demographics of your neighborhood, I can make a good guess at your income. I can uncover that forgotten drug bust in college . . ." If anything, Ms. Lane is being modest. For a small fee, she can uncover far more about you: your Social Security number, your bank balance, any stock, bonds, and mutual funds you own, your telephone records, your credit history, even your medical history.[1]

For two months in 1997 the Social Security Administration put the detailed income history of millions of Americans on the Internet, where it could easily be accessed with a few pieces of information and keystrokes. It backed off only after a public outcry over potential invasions of privacy.[2] But there are no legal restrictions on the distribution of Social Security numbers by private companies or individuals. Such information is still readily available from a number of private sources.

Even strict rules protecting "confidentiality" of information in government files do not prevent leaks and abuses. A federal audit found that hundreds of IRS employees continue to snoop illegally through confidential taxpayer files. The computerized medical records of tens of millions of patients are especially vulnerable to abuse because there are few controls on the highly confidential medical information that is being widely shared among providers, government agencies, employers, and marketers. In Maryland, state workers sold the names and Social Security numbers of Medicaid recipients to HMO recruiters. Other states keep detailed data banks identifying every patient who stays in a hospital, is injured on the job, gets a flu shot, has a sexually transmitted disease, has ever been treated for drug use, or is considered likely to deliver a baby prematurely.

Private investigators can find even more, tapping into commercial databases, government records, and even law-enforcement files that, theoretically, should be inaccessible to civilians. It is remarkably easy and inexpensive. With less than $50, a writer for the on-line publication CNET found that a complete stranger (or disgruntled employee, or ex-lover) could obtain a wealth of personal data with only a fax machine and connection to the Net. Within minutes he found his "target's" phone number and home address; with minimal effort he found her e-mail address, where she worked, where she went to school, memberships in organizations, and newsgroup postings. For only $30, he was able to find her Social Security number; for another $16, he found her credit report. Using a faked signature (actually signed by the willing "target"), the reporter was granted entry to her complete credit history, including the numbers of all her credit cards. For another $200, he could have accessed her bank balance.[3] Even the superrich are vulnerable. CNET also easily found the Social Security numbers of such business moguls as Time Warner Vice Chairman Ted Turner, and Microsoft cofounder Paul Allen.[4] And that was only the start of what could have been discovered.

Professional (and even amateur) investigators are faced with an embarrassment of virtual riches as they snoop into your life because modern life is crisscrossed and bound by a web of data that continues to grow in scope and tighten its grip on privacy. In less than three minutes, subscribers to a service provided by DBT-Online can get the Social Security number, date of birth, and telephone number of any person. Subscribers to the service, known as "Faces of the Nation," reportedly include journalists, as well as bill collectors, insurance companies, and private eyes.[5] Another information broker, CBD Infotek, advertises that it has 1,600 databases covering more than three and a half billion public records.

One detective agency, known as "The Cat," advertises, as one of its services, background checks of potential employees or business partners, but also of someone "you're dating or engaged to," and "nuisance neighbors." The detectives will search for voter, marriage, driving and court records, as well as search for probate and real estate sources. They claim:

> We use advancing state-of-the-art technology, strategies and resources to help you discover "Just the Facts" about your subject's background. We can discover marriages, divorces, former addresses, current and previous employment verification, references and developed reference checks, credit reports (for permissible purposes only), bankruptcies, check nationwide for outstanding criminal warrants, and the list goes on and on! . . . Unusual requests . . . Please Inquire.[6]

Among the techniques the agency suggests to someone interested in probing someone's background are surprising the person at home during an "unexpected time like the evening or on the weekend. This will definitely give an idea how this person 'really' lives." The agency also suggests checking out the glove compartment of their cars, hitting the redial buttons on a person's phones, and checking out their monthly bank statement or credit-card bill—"This is most interesting reading around or shortly after a holiday (St. Valentine's Day?)."

It is also easy enough to track when and where some people travel. Blending data provided by the government with information on the Internet, snoops can easily track the comings and going of the 10,000 or so privately owned airplanes—anywhere in the country. For a small fee, subscribers to on-line services such as The Trip.com and Dimensions International can quickly find out where any corporate plane is located, where it is going, and when it is scheduled to arrive. Though such information has been in the public domain for several years, it became available on the Internet only in 1997, when the Federal Aviation Administration approved the release of the information on the net, thus enabling the plane's owners—along with anyone else so inclined—to track their airplanes.[7]

Given the ubiquity of the dataweb, the only way to avoid being included in the databases is to not be born. Government records follow us literally from cradle to grave, and much of that information is not only public record, but actually marketed by cash-hungry governments to private brokers.[8]*

Few Americans have anything but the vaguest idea how much of their lives is recorded in such data. As Ashley Dunn has noted, for most of us, the erosion of privacy does not seem alarming since "the core of our private lives remains in the physical world." The scattered bits of data in the electronic universe can seem to be "nothing more than the odds and ends of our lives—data lint that only the perverse would bother collecting." What makes the current attacks on privacy so insidious is the fact that few of us have any idea how those bits of lint are being gathered into a lint ball of truly remarkable dimensions. "I see this material as junk," Dunn notes, "no closer to a representation of my true soul than the Vatican trash can is of Catholicism. But the point is not whether it is true or not. What matters is that those who collect and use the information accept this gangling ball of lint as truth. *In these computers, we are what the data says we are.*"[9]

Not only do we not know how much of this information is out there, or who has it, but we also have only a very slim chance of being able to assure

---

*Just a partial list of resources for a determined sleuth includes: CD-ROM and on-line databases, Internet search engines, professional licenses, motor vehicle records, FAA records, consumer-credit records, earnings histories, Workers Compensation histories, OSHA records, medical records, tenant screening databases, court records, stock ownership records, campaign contribution records, phone records, mailing lists, foundation and grants databases, biographical books, directories, the FamilyFinder Index, company staff directories, magazine subscriptions, warranty registration cards, criminal records, the Advance Passenger Information System, Automated Fingerprint Identification System, the Consolidated Asset Tracking System, Consolidated DNA Identification System, Counterdrug Information Indices System, Crime Information Network, the INS Automated Fingerprint ID System, INS Passenger Accelerated Service System, Integrated Automated Fingerprint Identification System; the National Crime Information Center; the National Incident Based Reporting System, National Drug Pointer Index System; drivers license data; driving records; vehicle registrations; vessel registers, death records, CDB Infotek's CompuTrace; Public Records Vendors, franchise tax records, property tax records, income tax records within Public Records, Medical Registries, Medical Insurance Databases, business articles of incorporation, bankruptcy files, criminal records, divorce files, mechanics liens, probate records, SEC reports, sales and use tax permits, Uniform Commercial Code (UCC) Indices, business credit records, professional license records, fish and game licenses, the US Postal Service's National Change of Address forms, utility company records, voter registration records, and watercraft ownership records.

that it is accurate and almost no control over who might have access to it, including insurance companies, creditors, employers, journalists, government investigators, or ex-spouses. What might be included? Everything from your brushes with the law, your school records, bankruptcies, marital problems, whether you have ever had a sexually transmitted disease, or an abortion, your student loan status, your political and religious affiliations, salary, whether you are taking Prozac or Viagra, and your taste in Web sites are potential bits of recoverable data.

Every piece of information has a price: Using 1997 prices, your salary and consumer credit report can be obtained from an information broker for $75; your stock, bond, and mutual-fund records for $200. For $450, brokers can obtain your credit-card number; for $80 to $200 they can put their hands on your telephone records. Your personal medical history for the last ten years is for sale for $400. Not all of this information can be obtained ethically, or even legally. But it *can* be obtained from what *New York Times* reporter Nina Bernstein called the "thriving gray-black market in purloined privacy."[10] There is nothing new about private eyes or snooping, of course, but technology has transformed both the capabilities and the threats. Ever-more-powerful computers and the proliferation of government and private databases make it infinitely easier to access all of this information. Records that had once sat in the backrooms of remote courthouses are now available at the touch of a button. More important, however, the new technologies make possible extraordinary links and mergers of information that can be used to compile detailed dossiers. As Carole Lane remarks, "once information is entered into a database, it takes on a strange new life of its own. . . ."

All signs indicate that the information pool will continue to grow. Governments are making tens of millions of dollars selling public records to junk mailers and other businesses. What efforts have been made to curtail the flow of personal information have been halfhearted, at best. In 1994, after actress Rebecca Schaeffer was murdered by a stalker in 1989 who had obtained her home address through California's driver-license registry, Congress passed a law forbidding states from releasing such personal information as addresses and Social Security numbers. But the law left gaping loopholes: It exempted government agencies, tow-truck operators, junk mailers, and private detectives.[11] In effect, the ban on releasing information applied only to private citizens. In an irony that escaped lawmakers, the new law would not have protected Miss Schaeffer, since her killer had obtained her address from a private detective—who is still entitled to obtain such data under the law.[12]

Among the richest sources of personal information are the handful of super credit bureaus, including TRW, Equifax, and Trans Union, which reportedly maintain files on 90 percent of all American adults.[13] Although they claim to be zealous guardians of the information in those files, the bureaus routinely sell information to employers, landlords, insurance companies, and any business offering credit. Several years ago, *Business Week* tested the bureaus, obtaining detailed credit reports on magazine employees for a mere $20 apiece. For a $500 initial fee, the magazine's writers were able to access the bureaus' databases from their home computers. They were not only to able to check colleagues for $15 a shot, but were able to snoop into the credit files of several well-known individuals, including then–Vice President Dan Quayle.[14]*

All of this is purely theoretical, until it hits home. Even if you understand the scope and breadth and ease with which your life can be dissected, the reality can still come as a considerable shock. The reality of violation is quite different from the *idea* of violation; it is the difference between reading a newspaper article about crime and coming home to find your house trashed by burglars.

One day after I had been working on this book for more than a year, and had written much of the preceding chapter, an investigative reporter for a local newspaper dropped off a sealed manila envelope. Inside were the results of a quick background check into . . . me. On the front page of the packet was my Social Security number, my date of birth, my home phone number, my driver's license number, the assessed value of my house, how much I paid for it, along with every address I had lived in for the past decade.

But it did not stop there.

---

*In a classic case of reverse spin, one of the most voracious pursuers and compilers of personal informal information, Equifax, reportedly has a bronze plaque in its headquarters: "Every person has the right to personal privacy consistent with the demands and requests he or she makes of business. Every person is entitled to have his or her privacy safeguarded through the secure storage and careful transmission of information."

By running a single check, the reporter had found both my wife's and my daughter's Social Security numbers and drivers' license numbers. There was also my college-age daughter's address at college and her home phone number. The dossier listed my father's Social Security number and the month and year of his death. The service to which the reporter subscribed offered other information as well: It cast a web that captured almost everyone around me. The names, addresses, and phone numbers of every one of my neighbors was listed. There was the Social Security number of the people who bought my old house, along with every address they had had in the past decade. I also now have the Social Security numbers of the couple from whom I purchased my current house. I know everywhere *they* have lived for the past three decades.

But there was more.

Because the scan had also picked up my workplace, the dataweb snared nearly two dozen of my coworkers, printing out the dates of birth, Social Security numbers, home addresses, and past addresses of people with whom I had the merest nodding acquaintance. Intriguingly, some of the company's management—and their spouses—fell into the dragnet. I confess I more than half-enjoyed walking into their offices and reading off their information—including addresses they had long forgotten, watching for their reactions. Information is power. It is also profoundly unsettling.

The public got a taste of the brave new world of datawebs in 1996, when Lexis-Nexis, one of the country's best-known research companies, announced that it would provide a new tracking service with access to hundreds of millions of Social Security numbers. The company boasted that its product, known as P-TRAK Personal Locator, "puts 300 million names right at your fingertips." With a few keystrokes, the system would provide "a quick, convenient search [that] provides up to three addresses, as well as aliases, maiden names, and Social Security numbers." The announcement highlighted the fact that while the government was limited in the ways its could use Social Security numbers, there were no restrictions on their use by private companies, like Lexis-Nexis. Specifically, Lexis-Nexis was targeting lawyers, corporations, investigators, law-enforcement officials, librarians, and journalists who might subscribe to the service. Almost immediately, privacy concerns were raised about the new service, including fears that the service left individuals vulnerable to fraud or even the theft of their identities by someone with access to their Social Security numbers. Initially, Lexis-Nexis brushed off such concerns, saying it was not responsible for what happened to the information it would send out. "Our company's policy has been, and continues to be, that this product is to be used in a legal manner and that's one thing that we try to stress with our customers," an executive said. "If something did happen, we wouldn't deal with it because we are a third party."[15]

Such insouciance did little to calm critics, and after an onslaught of criticism and complaints—much of it generated through the Internet— the company dropped the service after only ten days.[16] Although the case has been widely cited as a victory of privacy advocates, the fact is that the information offered by P-TRAK is still readily available on the Net and through information brokers. Privacy advocates had won another Pyrrhic victory in the early 1990s, after the Lotus Corporation unveiled a new marketing product known as "Marketplace: Households," a CD-ROM with data on the buying practices and incomes of 120 million Americans. Faced with public outcry, the CD-ROM was withdrawn, but again, the victory was only partial. As David Brin notes, "[I]ronically, Marketplace would only have provided the same access for small business that big companies already enjoy."*

The trend seems to be accelerating, driven not only by technology and the private market in information, but also by rather dramatic expansions of government databases. Perhaps the most extraordinary is the National Directory of New Hires, and workers' database, which were created as part of immigration and welfare-reform legislation. Ostensibly designed to facilitate the enforcement of child-support orders, the New Hires directory is a massive computerized tracking system that will include every person hired by every employer in the country. Beginning October 1, 1997, private employers are required by law to tell the government the names,

---

*In 1997, American Online was also forced to back off a plan to sell lists of customer's phone numbers to direct marketing firms, including telemarketers. Once again, the victory was only partial: AOL continued to sell lists of its subscribers' names and addresses. Such information sharing is a huge business. AOL's marketing agreement with telemarketer CUC International Inc. is said to be worth $50 million, while its marketing deal with a discount long-distance phone company, Tel-Save, Inc. was worth $100 million. ("American Online Backs Off Plan to Give Out Phone Numbers," *New York Times,* July 25, 1997)

addresses, Social Security numbers, and wages of every new employee, creating one of the most extensive "data dragnets" in history.[17]

Reflecting the apparently inexhaustible appetite of federal agencies for personal information, in 1998 the nation's banking regulators proposed new rules that would, in effect, require banks and savings and loans to spy on their customers. Dubbed the "Know Your Customer Rule," the proposal by the Federal Deposit Insurance Corporation (FDIC) and other agencies* would have required banks "develop a program designed to determine the identity of its customers, determine its customer's sources of funds; determine the normal and expected transactions of its customers; monitor account activity for transactions that are inconsistent with those normal and expected transactions; and report any transactions of its customers that are determined to be suspicious."

News of the proposal generated widespread outrage and opposition from some bankers' groups. "We think the regulation is by its very nature, at odds with attempts to protect customer privacy," said Paul Stock of the North Carolina Bankers Association. Ostensibly, the rule was intended to "reduce the likelihood that [banks] will become unwitting participants in illicit activities" such as money laundering and drug trafficking by flagging out-of-the-ordinary withdrawal or deposits. But the rule did not apply simply to customers who were under suspicion—it applied to *every* customer at *every* bank. Defending the proposal, the FDIC insisted that any such system should "should respect the private nature of the relationship that customers have with their financial institutions." But the entire point of the regulation is that the relationship is NOT private. On the contrary, it effectively deputized the nation's banks to act as agents of federal law-enforcement agencies, by requiring them to maintain detailed dossiers and profiles on their own customers. Banks would not only have to learn where each customer's money came from, but would have to keep surreptitious watch on every deposit and withdrawal and blow the whistle to the feds whenever a customer deviated from the norm. By dramatically extending the reach of federal agents into our bank accounts, the proposed rule

---

*The rule was also backed by Board of Governors of the Federal Reserve System, the Office of the Comptroller of the Currency, and Office of Thrift Supervision. Faced with overwhelming opposition, it was dropped in early 1999.

marked yet another step toward the criminalization of society, in which average citizens are now subject to the kind of scrutiny and surveillance—from fingerprinting to video monitoring—once reserved for criminal suspects. Indeed, no society has ever been watched as carefully as ours.

THE SURVEILLANCE SOCIETY

None of this is science fiction:

Parabolic microphones can listen in on a conversation from more than a mile away and a new German laser version can pick up conversations even through closed windows within the line of sight. So-called Kindercams, linked to high-speed telephone lines, enable moms to watch their child in day care over the Net, a technology that poses countless possibilities now that video cameras can be stored or hidden in objects the size of a sugar cube. Even if we can't watch someone, we can follow them more easily than ever. Newly marketed personal transponders allow individuals to be located electronically; so far, such devices have been implanted into livestock and pets, but they are now being marketed for children who might wander off.[18] Technology that was originally designed to help us "reach out and touch someone," is quickly becoming technology that helps others reach and *track* someone. Global-position satellites can compile detailed information about your movements, especially if you use a cell phone. (A parallel technology allows cell-phone users to be located by triangulation—measuring the arrival time of signals received by network antennas at different locations.)[19] In late 1998, the Federal Communications Commission gave preliminary approval to new rules that will require cell-phone operators to make it easy for law-enforcement officials to quickly pinpoint the exact location of any mobile-telephone caller—in effect, turning the average cell phone into a high-tech locating device.[20] Using so-called "Van Eck Monitoring," snoops can read information from someone's computer by capturing the electromagnetic radiation from the monitor, processor, and other attached devices. The FBI reportedly used such technology to nab convicted spy Aldrich Ames.[21]

But the revolution in surveillance is not merely technical—it is also political in nature, an ironic product of the end of the Cold War. As recently as the 1960s, even the most totalitarian regimes were limited to low-tech, labor-intensive methods of watching their citizens. Surveillance relied on informants, perhaps an occasional breaking and entry. But it was slow, tedious, and highly inefficient. It might take as many as six full-time agents to follow a suspect around the clock. Before the Berlin Wall came down, the legendary East German Stasi employed as many as 500,000 informers and 10,000 agents just to listen in on their comrades' phone calls. Now both the technology and the enemy have changed. Even as the technology of snooping became ever more sophisticated, the end of the Cold War has meant two dramatic changes.

First, defense and intelligence agencies have shifted both their funding and their intelligence from military matters to combating drugs and terrorism.

Second, as military and black-budget (secret intelligence) spending declined, many of the high-tech companies that had developed and sold spook technology to the government have had to turn to new markets, at home and abroad. That has meant that some of the technology originally designed for military purposes is being used by local law-enforcement and social bureaucracies here and abroad, where they have proven to be especially useful in developing new means of surveillance, identification, and networking. It is also being used to sell us stuff.

As privacy advocate David Banisar notes, the new technologies "facilitate mass and routine surveillance of large segments of the population without the need for warrants and formal investigations. What the East German secret police could only dream of is rapidly becoming a reality in the free world."[22]

AND NOW FOR THE REALLY SCARY STUFF . . .

Intelligent Transportation Systems (ITS), which include automated toll-collection devices and other traffic management technologies, give authorities—and others—the power to keep track of anyone who moves.* Several states already use automated toll collections, but law enforcement is already deploying such technology to create round-the-clock tracking

---

*"The possibilities grow more alarming if ITS information is linked with law enforcement, medical, insurance, lifestyle, or credit data. Linking travel data with other personal information will sharpen any profiles developed, making them that much more precise, and that much more valuable to governments, direct marketers and others." (Ann Cavoukian and Don Tapscott, *Who Knows,* New York: McGraw-Hill, 1997, p. 165.)

systems. Britain has deployed the new Talon system, which used a neural-network technology to recognize license-plate numbers. The system, which can watch cars both night and day, was incorporated into the "ring of steel" around London and is able to record which cars enter or leave the cordon on any given day.

Although designed for traffic control, such technologies have less benign applications, as the Chinese have demonstrated. A report to the European Parliament, for example, noted that the cameras used in Tiananmen Square were originally sold not as instruments of state security, but as "advanced traffic-control systems" by Siemens Plessey. Nevertheless, they proved particularly useful after the 1989 massacre, when authorities began a massive roundup of subversives. As the European Parliament report noted, "The Scoot surveillance system with USA-made Pelco cameras were used to faithfully record the protests, the images were repeatedly broadcast over Chinese television offering a reward for information, with the result that nearly all the transgressors were identified." Having proved efficacious in stamping out the democracy movement, Chinese officials are reportedly buying elaborate new "traffic-control systems" for export to Lhasa in Tibet. As the report noted wryly, "Lhasa does not as yet have any traffic-control problems."[23]

Technology already exists to record the mileage and average speed of cars and trucks. No less an authority than Bill Gates foresees proposals in the future to outfit every car with digital recorders and transmitters that can locate cars and record their whereabouts at any given time. "After all," he notes, "airplanes have 'black box' recorders today, and once the costs drops, there is no reason they shouldn't be in our cars." Stolen cars could be located immediately; police investigating a hit-and-run could identify every car within a two-block area during the time of the accident. "The black box could record your speed and location," writes Gates, "which would allow for the perfect enforcement of speeding laws. I would vote against that."[24] Others might not.

Other government agencies have found the "smart card" to be an extraordinarily efficient way to keep track of citizens. For several years, the federal government has considered using such "smart cards" for recipients of Medicaid, welfare, food stamps, and other benefits. As the Office of Technology Assessment notes, such cards could be used to link public databases to private ones. "Medical information supplied by doctors and hospitals could then become part of that database," notes one critic. "Insurers would be part of the communication link in order to certify that Medicaid clients had exhausted their private coverage. Food stores could also be part of such a national database, providing information on buying habits of millions of Americans. Changes of this nature could increase the surveillance capabilities of the national database."

A step up on the technological ladder is Forward Looking InfraRed (FLIR), which detects even the tiniest difference in temperatures and enables its user to detect what is happening inside buildings, by more or less looking through the walls themselves. Developed originally to help the Air Force locate enemy aircraft, FLIR is already being widely used by law-enforcement agents hunting for fugitives, drug dealers, and other miscreants. So far the courts have disagreed about whether FLIR violates Fourth Amendment prohibitions against illegal search and seizure. Some federal courts have ruled that government agents should be able to scan suspects without a warrant because all that is detected is "waste heat." The Tenth Circuit, however, has raised questions about the new technologies, including FLIR. The Court threw out a drug case in which agents had used FLIR to locate marijuana by detecting the heat of artificial lamps used to grow the plants:

> To hold otherwise would leave the privacy of the home at the mercy of the government's ability to exploit technological advances: the government could always argue that an individual's failure (or inability) to ward off the incursions of the latest scientific innovation forfeits the protection of the Fourth Amendment. . . . [T]he government would allow the privacy of the home to hinge upon the outcome of a technological measure/counter-measure between the average citizen and the government, a race, we expect, that the people will surely lose.[25]

In an article titled "Techno Prisoners," Rick Crawford describes another technology that can turn random bits of seemingly innocuous data into an extraordinarily detailed portrait of our activities. Law-enforcement agencies have the ability to use a largely unknown technology known as Realtime Residential Power Line Surveillance (RRPLS) which uses special meters to monitor how much electricity is being used and what appliances are turned on and off at a specific home at any given time. Crawford offers this scenario to illustrate how powerful and useful such surveillance technology might be if combined with other transactional data:

> Contrary to a household's normal pattern, one of its occupants, a 43-year-old married male (according to his driver's license data) arises early one Saturday morning, showers, shaves with his electric razor, and irons some clothes. He buys gas in town, then that night pays for two dinners and two tickets to a show (all on his credit card). After returning home, the stereo is turned on (a rare event according to his RRPLS file). The data from the waterbed indicates an unusual night—every time the sheets are thrown back, the RRPLS detected the waterbed heating cycling. The next morning, data indicates an unusually long shower, followed by two uses of the hair dryer. The second use is much longer than normal for the male occupant, indicating he probably shared the shower with a longhaired person.
>
> During this time, commercial transaction records indicate the occupant's wife is halfway around the globe on a business trip paid for by her employer. RRPLS data from her hotel room also indicate an overnight visitor. Within days, the couple is inundated with direct-mail solicitations from divorce lawyers.[26]

Other new devices allow security agents to conduct body searches through a target's clothes, in effect an electronic strip-search. Massive millimeter wave detectors, using a form of radar to scan under a person's clothes, reportedly are able to detect the presence of drugs from 12 feet or more away. The body scanners would also be able to reveal artificial limbs, penile implants, or catheter tubes, and evidence of other medical conditions and procedures that would normally be considered highly intimate and personal facts. Remarked a spokesman for the ACLU: "If there is ever a place where a person has a reasonable expectation of privacy, it is under their clothing."[27]

Increasingly sophisticated biometric systems such as retinal scans, facial thermography (which measures heat patterns from individual faces) "hand geometry" identification systems, and the federal government's Automated Fingerpoint Identification System can be matched and merged with other technologies to boost the science of surveillance and identification into the next century.[28] (California already requires thumbprints on all drivers' licenses.)

Often sold as a weapon to fight terrorism, crime, and fraud, such high-tech surveillance has also proven useful for tracking Ivy Leaguers. At Yale and Princeton, the comings and goings of students are monitored and recorded through around-the-clock electric key systems. Every time a Princeton student uses one of the cards, known as "proximity cards," to gain access to his or her dormitory, an electronic record of the entry is transmitted to campus police, where it is kept on record for several weeks. Although a majority of Princeton's students object to the system—on grounds of convenience as well as privacy—it is strongly supported by many female students, who like the security it provides. A spokeswoman for Yale acknowledged to the *New York Times* that, like Princeton, "We do have the capability of tracking individuals and their comings and goings from the residential college . . ." but insisted the school had not received any complaints about the privacy implications of such a system. But Deborah Hurley, the director of the Harvard Information Infrastructure Project, noted that the surveillance systems raised questions about who controlled the information and whether the personal data collected was proportional to the risk that students otherwise faced. "I think the answer is no," Hurley said. "It's not only an individual's privacy—it's freedom of movement and freedom of association. In this case, Princeton is gathering reams of data about all of its students, and the students are the appropriate ones to have control and ownership of that data." Objecting to the electronic entry/monitoring system, one Princeton senior gibed, "It seems as if you're living in a prison."[29]

THE WATCHERS

Then, of course, there are the cameras: the ones that watch us on city streets, that take our picture when we use an ATM, or enter an apartment building—the ubiquitous eyes of a society of strangers. We don't know each other, so we use the cameras—the ones that record you every time you enter a convenience store or cash a check, that stand on guard at parking lots, shopping areas, highways, school buses and school buildings, apartment buildings, sidewalks, intersections, hotels, airports, banks, and parks. Even workplaces are increasingly watched by unblinking security cameras. The more advanced cameras can read a newspaper from 100 yards away, even in low light.

In Tempe, Arizona, officials installed a rotating surveillance camera on top of its municipal building, where it tracked citizens in the area. Known as "sneaky peak," the camera's images were broadcast on the Internet, where it became the most popular hit on the Tempe municipal Web page. Although surveillance cameras seldom live up to their billing as law-enforcement tools,[30] they can be linked with other high-tech technology that dramatically expands their powers, such as the Danish Jai stroboscopic camera, which can take hundreds of pictures in mere seconds, thus providing a photograph of every person who walks on a particular street or participants in a demonstration or march.* New "face-recognition" technology can scan millions of digitized pictures a second, matching them with the faces captured by surveillance cameras. Immigration officials are reportedly already testing using the cameras and databases to identify illegal aliens, terrorists, and drug traffickers. The private sector is not far behind. A large midwestern retail chain was forced to admit that it had required its salesmen to wear tiny hidden cameras and secretly record transactions with customers without their permission.[31] One of the largest market rating companies has patented a face-recognition system that could be used to identify shoppers and track their buying habits. This could become especially easy as states begin selling driver's-license photographs to marketing firms.[32]

Overhead, on any given day, at least five billion-dollar spy satellites are orbiting the earth at the speech of Mach 25. Some of them—known as "Keyhole class" satellites—can distinguish an object as small as five or six inches large on the ground. Others, which use radar-imaging technology— can distinguish objects three feet long or larger. As one report noted: "While satellites cannot read license plates, they can tell if a car has one. While they cannot tell a mullah by the length of his beard, they can help

---

*A number of cities that previously used video cameras—for example, Miami Beach, Fla., Newark, N.J., White Plains, N.Y., and Fredericksburg, Va.—have abandoned them, concluding that they were not worth the expense. Surveillance cameras that had been mounted for twenty-two months in New York City's Times Square led to only ten arrests before they were dismantled, prompting the *New York Times* to dub them, "one of the greatest flops along the Great White Way." (Nadine Strossen, "Everyone is Watching You, *Intellectual Capital,* May 28, 1998.)

analysts figure out how many people are chanting along with him at a street demonstration. And while they cannot hover over an area and provide real-time images, other assets, such as unmanned aerial vehicles, also known as drones, can do that."[33]

There are obvious attractions to video surveillance, including the sense of safety they sometimes afford in an otherwise-deserted area. But even if we no longer take much notice of them, they still can raise the tiniest bit of hair on the back of our necks. In an essay in the *New York Times*, Peter H. Lewis evoked the new routine of contemporary surveillance. He describes how cameras "followed the attractive young blond woman through the lobby of the midtown Manhattan hotel, kept a glassy eye on her as she rode the elevator up to the twenty-third floor and peered discreetly down the hall as she knocked at the door to my room:

> I have not seen the videotapes, but I can imagine the digital readout superimposed on the scenes, noting the exact time of the encounter. That would come in handy if someone were to question later why this woman, who is not my wife, was visiting my hotel room during a recent business trip. The cameras later saw us heading off to dinner and to the theater—a middle-aged, married man from Texas with his arm around a pretty East Village woman young enough to be his daughter. As a matter of fact, she *is* my daughter. But still . . . I wonder sometimes what the security guards think as they monitor their guests through the window of a video display, just as my former landlady in a small Kansas town kept tabs on her neighbors through the parted veil of her living-room curtains.[34]

If they can't watch, they can listen. Using a cell phone these days is pretty much like carrying on a conversation in a room crowded with listeners. But phones that use landlines are also vulnerable. New communications technology makes it possible, for example, to design a system in which agents have the power to take phones "off the hook" and listen into conversations taking place near the phone, without homeowners ever knowing they are being monitored and without anything like an old-fashioned bug being planted. In contrast, the technology that captured Monica Lewinsky's conversations with Linda Tripp was relatively mundane. On December 21, 1996, top Republican members of Congress, including Speaker Newt Gingrich, were recorded during a telephone conference call by a Florida couple using a scanner.[35] Even this is very much last year's technology. Today, a laptop computer can tune into all of the cell phones in a given area simply by running a cursor down to their number. Computers can also search for targeted numbers to see if they are active.

NIGHTMARE SCENARIO

Is all of this merely hypothetical? Are such speculations unduly paranoid? Unfortunately not. Already, the dataweb has become a political weapon with chilling implications. Fringe groups have already discovered the ease with which dossiers can be assembled and published on the Internet, where they can be accessed from every computer in the world including those owned by unstable individuals.

The so-called "Nuremberg Files," for example, was an Internet site featuring dossiers on doctors who work in abortion clinics. The site included photos, names, Social Security numbers, home addresses and phone numbers, and descriptions of the cars and license-plate numbers not only of the doctors themselves but also of members of their family, *including their spouses and their children.* Its authors claimed that the purpose of the site is to collect detailed evidence that might someday be used during "war crime" trials of the doctors, but others see it as a more ominous threat.*

The site also targeted nurses, security guards, police officers, judges, and politicians, all of whom face the prospect of being the subject of a data profile on the site. The operators of the site actively solicited information for the dossiers, including:

"1. Photos or videotapes of the abortionist, his car, his house, friends, and anything else of interest (as many and as recent as possible); (sic)

---

*Doctors who sued the site on the grounds that it violated a 1994 federal law protecting abortion providers against threats of violence won a multimillion-dollar jury verdict in early 1999. The plaintiffs had sought to have the court ban the site and award $200 million in damages to the plaintiffs. It is unclear, however, what will happen on appeal and, despite a move to shut down the site by the Internet provider, so-called "mirror" sites—based abroad and thus beyond the reach of the United States law—quickly appeared, providing the same information.

2. Current and past personal data including date and place of birth, home and business addresses and phone numbers, Social Security numbers, automobile plate numbers, names and birthdates of spouse(s), children, and friends;

3. Criminal records, including driving record, mug shots, and finger-print card;

4. Civil suit records, including informative depositions and divorce file (if any);

5. Affidavits of former employees, former patients, former spouses;

6. Newspaper clippings, news videos;

7. Statements of factual interest from investigators or pro-lifers who have had regular dealings with the abortionist;

8. Contemporaneous notes, journals, or diaries by surveillance work-ers, sidewalk counselors, or picketers; and

9. Anything else you believe will help identify and convict the abor-tionist in a future court of law."

As dozens of medical professionals and their families have discovered, much of that information is readily available and accessible. An on-line dossier of one doctor in the Midwest (framed by computer simulations of dripping blood) featured what appears to be a mug shot of the doctor. It listed his date of birth, Social Security number, a physical description, his home address, and a detailed description of his medical career. As with the other dossiers, the site also targeted his family. It reported the make of car his wife drives, her license-plate and driver's-license numbers, and the val-uation of the couple's home. With a single click, any visitor to the site could see photographs of the doctor's house, apparently taken from across the street. With another click, viewers could examine surveillance photos of the doctor's car in a parking lot, the doctor getting into the car, and pho-tographs of the doctor walking from the car to a building wearing surgical scrubs. The site accompanied this information with charges that the doctor has committed "genocide," "mass murder," "torture," and "crimes against humanity."

If the threat is not explicit—there are no direct calls for violence against the doctors—it is nevertheless clear and unmistakable. The "Nuremberg Files" depicted doctors who have been killed with a single black line drawn through their names. The names of doctors who have been wounded were shaded in gray. Understandably, doctors who have found themselves on the list have expressed fear for their lives, some going so far as to begin wearing bulletproof vests and changing the routes they take to work. Others are fearful of even going to dinner in the same car with members of their family. "Suddenly," says one doctor on the list, "I feel real visible to individuals who might not be quite balanced."[36]

Although such tactics are not yet widespread, it is not inconceivable to imagine such on-line dossiers being used in other political contexts by animal-rights activists targeting research scientists; by industry targeting environmental activists; by labor unions targeting scabs; by litigants targeting lawyers or one another; or ideological combatants pursuing the politics of personal destruction: the list can go on ad infinitum.

ABUSES

The potential for the abuse of centralized government databases has been controversial since at least the 1960s, when the Johnson administration proposed creating a National Data Center that would merge the data about individual Americans collected by twenty different federal agencies into a single computer database. Although the administration claimed that the centralized computer system would be more efficient, the idea of a massive, unified dossier—including school records, military service, income histories, credit ratings, and "personality traits," was doomed by public outcry. At the time, the prospect of the new technology and the radically expanded scope of government alarmed critics.

In 1972, the National Academy of Sciences turned to mythology to explain the new power of the data era. In the years after World War II, a NAS report declared:

> It seemed as though the role of the Three Fates might be reappearing in modern dress. The life thread of each man was now spun in the formal records that gatekeeper organizations began to keep about him at birth. He was measured at each step of his growth according to the information woven into these proliferating files. And when critical decisions affecting his adult life were made by managers of the government agencies, commercial enterprises, and private institutions which controlled the destiny of individuals in industrial civilization, the individual's personal record was perhaps the most important single re-

source to make those judgments. The Three Sisters with shuttle and shears had been replaced by the record-weaving looms of larger organizations.[37]

And this was even before the explosion of electronic data processing.

By 1971, privacy expert Arthur Miller would look back on the Johnson administration's proposal for the mega-dossier and quip: "In retrospect, that suggestion has proven innocuous compared to the reality of some of the systems already functioning in the executive branch of the government."[38]

Describing what he called the "Surveillance Society," Miller cited three developments that threatened even the most basic notions of privacy. First: "Americans are scrutinized measured, watched, counted and interrogated by more government agencies, law enforcement officials, social scientists, and poll takers than at any time in our history." Second: "Probably in no nation on earth is as much information collected, recorded, and disseminated as in the United States." Finally: "The information gathering and surveillance activities of the federal government have expanded to such an extent that they are becoming a threat to several basic rights of every American— privacy, speech, assembly, association, and petition of the government."[39]*

---

*In the early 1970s, civil libertarians were outraged by the number of databases that seemed to be forms of government "blacklists," including the army's worldwide Automated Military Police Operations and Information System, the Department of Housing and Urban Development's Debarred Bidders List; the FCC's Checklist; SEC's Name and Relationship System; the State Department's Passport Lookout File; DOT's Deterrence of Air Piracy System and its National Driver Register. The Department of Justice kept seven blacklists, including the Internal Security Division's file on "Civil Disobedience," the Organized Crime Intelligence System; the FBI's National Crime Information Center Wanted Persons filed; the FBI Known Professional Check Passers files; and three LEAA funded filed on Wanted Persons, Organized Crime and Civil Disorders. The Treasury Department maintained nine blacklists filed, including four IRS Intelligence files; IRS Special Service Staff files; Customs Service files, and Secret Service files. Even the Small Business Administration kept Investigative Records of "character checks."

In 1967, the FBI created the National Crime Information Center (NCIC), which was charged with creating a computerized database of every citizen's criminal records. The NCIC today interacts with more than 19,000 state and local government computer networks, and contains records of perhaps as many as 19 million people—anyone who

But government was not alone: Increasingly, credit agencies, employ-ers, and insurance companies were creating their own data dragnets, using polygraphs and investigators to dig into the backgrounds of employees and applicants. Credit dossiers came to include not only one's jobs and salary, and history of debt, but also such information as your boss's opinion of your job performance, even your IQ from a high-school test twenty years ago. Increasingly, the bureaus were supplementing hard financial data with "soft data," that often sounded a good deal like gossip. Consumer advo-cates like Ralph Nader accused the bureaus of imposing quotas on inspec-tors. He charged that they were expected to come back with negative recommendations on somewhere between 8 and 10 percent of the appli-cants. "If he has not met his 'quota,'" Nader observed in the early 1970s, "the temptation to use any rumor, without confirmation, may be over-whelming."

One faculty member at an Ivy League school had her car insurance canceled after a credit bureau gave her a bad credit report, because she had been living in the same house with a man "without the benefit of wed-lock."[40] A report that described someone as a "hippie type" might also cost someone his or her coverage.[41]

The result of government and commercial intrusions was, in effect, the democratization of the violation of privacy. "Invasion of privacy used to carry an almost luxurious connotation," Nader noted, "a concept reserved

---

has ever in any way run afoul of the law. The computerization of criminal records is, of course, an invaluable, perhaps even indispensable tool for fighting crime, but employ-ers also use such records for other purposes, including background checks. One study found that nearly 90 percent of criminal histories were available to public and private employers. This poses a new set of problems, especially given the questions raised pe-riodically about the reliability of the NCIC. A 1982 study by Congress's Office of Tech-nology Assessment found that one-third of the state crime records failed to say whether arrests had resulted in a conviction, an acquittal, or a dismissal. "Therefore," the OTA warned, "an arrest in one state, which may have resulted in a dismissal or an acquittal, could in another state influence the decision to withhold bail or to prosecute the de-fendant as a 'career criminal.'" That study found that—at best—less than half of the criminal histories were "complete, correct, and unambiguous." Such errors or lapses have profound implications for an individual's protection against unlawful searches and seizures, since the information that he has been previously arrested could be used as a pretext for detentions and searches. Given the use of such data by employers, it theo-retically could also affect the employment prospects of millions of individuals.

for special public figures whose private lives were invaded by scandal-mongers or seekers of vicarious thrills. It is no longer an elitist term."

Concern over government abuse and invasions of privacy led to an early flurry of laws. In 1967, Congress approved the Freedom of Information Act, which gave citizens the right to obtain certain files. In 1968, it passed an antiwiretapping law; in 1971, the Fair Credit Reporting Act regulated credit bureaus and allowed consumers access to information about them, as well as the right to challenge and correct any errors. In 1974, Congress passed the Privacy Act, which limited the federal government's authority to collect and disseminate information. This act gave citizens the right to know what information the government had collected about them, how it was used, and gave them the right to examine and correct such data. The same year, Congress also passed the Family Educational Rights and Privacy Act, which limited the types of information schools could gather and disseminate about students. Once again, it provided citizens with both access and recourse; parents and students were given the right to examine their school files. In 1976, Congress passed legislation restricting the ability of the IRS to disclose information about tax returns.

Although the momentum seemed to be behind greater privacy protections, it soon waned. Congress created a Privacy Protection Commission to further examine the issue. But by the time the commission, which was headed by University of Illinois professor David Linowes, issued its recommendations in 1977, the tide had shifted. The commission recommended eleven bills to expand the privacy protections to the private sector. Some, such as restricting employers' ability to use lie detectors, became law. But most of the commission's proposals were ignored, including its recommendations for tighter controls on how credit and insurance companies gathered and disseminated information, protections of medical privacy, and proposals for voluntary employer privacy policies.

As time went on, it also became clear that the original privacy bills did not always live up to their billing. The Privacy Act extended only to the federal government, not to the private sector, and is considered weak and full of loopholes. In the early 1980s, Congress further weakened its protections by allowing the disclosure of information to credit bureaus about those who owe money to the government and permitted the IRS to divulge mailing addresses to locate federal debtors.[42] This opened a significant hole in the privacy protections of many Americans. Indeed, a congressional investigating committee found that foreign spies had found the information held by private credit bureaus to be a particularly rich source of information about individuals in sensitive positions who might be having financial problems. The House Armed Service Subcommittee on Investigations reported that Defense Department officials "advised that one way in which hostile intelligence agents select potential targets [for espionage] is by obtaining personal information through nationwide credit data systems."[43]

Similar problems crippled other legislation. One critique calls the Fair Credit Reporting Act of 1971 "more loophole than law"—the act, for example, did not apply to banks and still allowed the credit bureaus to sell credit reports to businesses with a "credit, insurance, employment, or other business need" without getting the subject's permission. Even with the new legislation, the next two decades saw the consolidation of the credit bureau industry under three major bureaus—Experian Information Systems, Inc., Equifax, and Trans Union Corp.—who were able to deploy some of the most advanced technologies to gather and analyze financial information.[44]*

The Right to Financial Privacy Act limited federal access to bank records, but permitted exceptions for law-enforcement officials. The 1968 antiwiretapping law specifically exempted switchboards or other equipment on the premises of a business, so companies could continue to listen in on employees. In 1986, the Electronic Communications Privacy Act extended protections to e-mail and other new technology, but continued to allow companies to eavesdrop on their employees' electronic communications, including e-mails. When Congress passed the Drivers' Privacy Protection Act, it was advertised as a measure to restrict access to Department

---

*In the early 1990s, one of the largest of the credit unions, Trans Union Corporation, was caught distributing and selling targeted-marketing lists based on consumer credit data. Federal law bars the credit unions from selling anyone their credit data except for "consumer reports" for a client's use, or with the consumer's permission. Trans Union insisted that its sale of lists for marketing purposes fell under that loophole, but in 1998, an administrative judge rejected that argument. Among the information peddled by Trans Union were lists of persons with auto loans and with open bank cards; information about mortgages, and its "income estimator," which calculates a person's estimated income based on its credit data. ("FTC Charges Against Trans Union Upheld," Office of Public Affairs, Federal Trade Commission, August 26, 1998.)

of Motor Vehicle records, but the Act included exemptions for nearly everyone except the general public and the media. Similarly, the Consumer Credit Reporting Act made credit agencies correct erroneous information more quickly and required them to get a customer's permission before furnishing it to employers. But it included a loophole that allows a company to share credit reports and insurance applications with other companies within the same conglomerate. In addition, the law allowed credit bureaus to sell sensitive information from the "credit header," which contains your mother's maiden name, phone number, and recent address, and other key identifying information, to anyone who wants it—information that now can be easily downloaded from the Internet.[45]

Congress did act to pass tough protections for video-rental records—the so-called "Bork" bill—but it repeatedly has killed measures to protect medical privacy, workplace privacy, and to regulate the dissemination of personal information in the private market. Indeed, the legislative momentum has largely been in the opposite direction. In the early 1990s, Congress killed legislation that would have regulated clandestine video-taping and wiretapping of workers on the job. In 1996, after lobbying by the direct-marking industry, Congress killed a bill that would have restricted companies gathering information about children without their parents' consent. Congress also killed legislation that would have restricted insurance companies' release of information about policyholder claims; as well as legislation that would have barred Internet providers and on-line services from releasing or selling information about customers without their permission.

Our own laissez-faire policies contrast with the European Union, which has issued a directive that requires all of the countries in the union to follow a common set of privacy protection standards. The European rules give citizens the right of access to their data, the right to fix erroneous data, recourse for violations, and the right to keep their information from being used for any marketing purpose without their permission. Unlike American laws, the Europeans guidelines apply not only to government, but to the private sector as well. Moreover, the European directive bars the dissemination of personal information about its own citizens to any other country with looser privacy protections. As a foretaste of what that might mean, Sweden insisted that American Airlines delete all the health and medical information they had gathered on Swedish passengers unless the airline obtained the "explicit consent" of those passenger. The order led to a lengthy and protracted legal challenge, merely a hint of the kinds of problems the European privacy rules might cause American businesses—especially those in the banking, travel, and electronic commerce. The directive raised the possibility, Simon Davies warned, that "the US may soon find itself unable to access personal data relating to almost half the developed world." In Europe, the cost of compliance was estimated to run as high at $20 billion.[46]

THE NEW DATABASES

In contrast to the European trend toward privacy, in recent years the tide here has seemed to run in quite the opposite direction. Despite the skepticism that has greeted other massive computer-surveillance systems, the Directory of New Hires passed with little public notice, and warnings from privacy advocates were largely ignored. The new law gave the IRS, the Justice Department, and the Social Security Administration access to the new directory, as well as state welfare officials. In 1995, a coalition of civil liberties and privacy groups called the proposal "the single greatest move toward an Orwellian national ID system in recent years," and predicted that the New Hires directory and a new worker's directory mandated as part of "immigration reform" would accelerate the creation of a de facto national ID system by requiring the inclusion of the SSN on nearly every government document or application for a government license. "The use of the SSN as a means of tracking every encounter between an individual and government will expand the treasure trove of information accessible to the unscrupulous individual who has gotten hold of another's SSN," the report noted. "The use of the SSN as the mandatory national identifier will facilitate linkage between various systems of governmental and private sector records further eroding individual privacy and heightening surveillance of each American's life."[47]

But the national directory was only the tip of the privacy-limiting iceberg. State governments were authorized to create their own databases, which would amount to "data dragnets," gathering information from a startlingly wide array of agencies. Applications for hunting licenses, as well as fishing, boating, and snowmobiling licenses were now shared with agencies searching for deadbeat dads. By one estimate, the child-support enforcement database in the State of Wisconsin—known as KIDS—included data matches with no fewer than seventeen different agencies. Such data matches are nothing new for state governments. In Wisconsin, for example, one study identified more than 140 individual computer matching programs. Not even sensitive medical information shared with state agencies is exempt. More than thirty state agencies were authorized to collect, process, and share health information.[48]

The "dragnet" matched and merged information from the IRS, the Social Security Administration, the US Postal Service, the major credit bureaus, the state Department of Revenue, the Department of Natural Resources, the Department of Transportation, the Department of Corrections with child-support files.

The power—and the danger—of such database merging is that it uses information gathered by government agencies for purposes utterly unrelated to the original reason that it was gathered. In the case of the KIDS database, the government used its power to compel information for one reason, but then used that data to create a system of surveillance that inspects every citizen of the state. Surveillance is matched by enforcement, and the information is compiled by state agencies that have every intent of using it against the individuals caught in the dragnet.

Under the new system for tracking down deadbeat dads, state officials could enter into agreements with financial institutions ranging from money-market funds to banks and under the law those institutions could be forced to turn over an individual's assets without a court order. State officials were also given new powers to confiscate personal property and place liens on a person's assets without a court order. They were also given extraordinary powers to cut off professional, recreational, and driver's licenses to enforce child-support payments. And, lest any corner be left unmonitored, officials were given access to records of utilities and cable companies—both usually confidential—to help them locate deadbeat parents quickly.[49]

Besides the more obvious privacy concerns, the new enthusiasm for databases raised a host of questions. The first is how long will it be before governments expand the number of people who have access to such information and how long before the information is used for other enforcement efforts. This is what is known as "function creep," of which the most notable example is the Social Security number. Originally designed specifically for the use of the Social Security system itself, the Social Security number has become virtually a national identifier. In 1943, President Roosevelt issued an executive order authorizing any federal agency to use the Social Security number for any new data systems requiring permanent account numbers. For many years, it was not widely used. But in 1961, the IRS decided to designate the SSN as the universal taxpayer ID number, and other government agencies quickly got into line. Social Security numbers became the military personnel service number, the number to which Veterans Administration hospital records were keyed, and the number required for the purchase of Treasury bonds. Within years the Social Security number was required for old-age-assistance benefits accounts, for state and federal civil-service records, and Indian Health Service patient records. In 1976, Congress explicitly allowed states to use the Social Security number for motor vehicle registration and drivers licenses, as well as for the administration of local and state tax laws and welfare. After 1984, anyone with a bank account was required to provide their Social Security numbers to their banks so that it would be easier for the IRS's computers to monitor our finances. The ubiquity of the Social Security number in the public sector has spread into the private sector as well. Many universities have adopted the number as their student ID, and it is now routine for stores and businesses to ask consumers for their Social Security numbers.

More recently, the Department of Transportation has proposed rules that would require states to encode the Social Security number onto every driver's license, ostensibly as another weapon against illegal immigrants. Under such proposals, the newly minted licenses would be the only form of identification that government agencies would be permitted to recognize.[50] Such a move, of course, would effectively turn the driver's license into a national ID card. As critics have noted, the driver's-license proposal is a backdoor approach to a system of control and monitoring that has repeatedly been rejected in the past as an unacceptable diminishment of privacy and freedom alike.[51] The specter of officials demanding that American citizens "show their papers" has lead Congress again and again to reject proposals to explicitly declare the Social Security number the national ID.

What's wrong with a national ID?

In a society based on information and knowledge, the ID becomes the ultimate key. A single number makes it vastly easier to access, compare, and match all of the information gathered about any individual, making it easier "to trace any individual from cradle to grave and thus encloses each person ever more tightly in a 'record prison.'"[52] As the ACLU notes, a national ID—by definition—presupposes the existence of a national government database, which would blend almost imperceptibly into private databases as well. "The linkage of government databases with corporate databases," the group warns, "increases the likelihood that intimate personal information—credit histories, spending habits, unlisted telephone numbers, voting, medical and employment histories—could easily be accessed without a person's knowledge."[53]

Another difficulty facing the new databases is the chronic problem of error. Many of the child-enforcement dragnets are already plagued by inaccurate or out-of-date information. But the problem is a larger one. The new matching and merging of information among unrelated agencies and businesses vastly multiplies the potential effects of mistakes, all the more so since the unwitting victims will know neither who has the inaccurate information nor to what use they may put it. Few of the agencies that receive the data in such matches bother to check with the original sources to ensure its accuracy. Reliable data is somewhat difficult to find, but some studies have put the rate of serious errors in credit-bureau files at 29 percent or higher.

Even so, the Clinton administration was especially enamored of databases, proposing no fewer than five. In addition to a database for immigration enforcement, and the New Hires database for child support, the administration also proposed a national database of sex offenders, a national medical database, linking every patient with a health identifier number, and a potentially huge database to track every actual and potential air traveler.[54]

Reacting to security anxieties raised by the bombing at the 1996 Atlanta Olympics and the explosion of TWA Flight 800, the administration endorsed a host of antiterrorism measures aimed at beefing up airport security. One of those measures was a plan to screen passengers by matching them against certain "profiles" developed by law-enforcement agencies. Overriding civil liberties and privacy concerns, an administration commission headed by Vice President Al Gore endorsed the practice of "profiling" air passengers to see whether they posed any security risk. Any traveler fitting the "profile" would be subject to heightened security measures and searches by law enforcement. The system requires the creation of a huge new database containing information about individual travelers, which is accessible to both airline and law-enforcement personnel. "The risks to privacy are enormous," a coalition of civil-liberties and privacy groups warned, "and run not only to those who 'fit the profile.'" By definition, they pointed out, the usefulness of the system depended on it applying to *every* person who took a flight—literally *everybody*. The development of the new database—which would match FBI and CIA information with airline databases—would require the creation of specific individual dossiers on every passenger. Such information might include pictures, descriptions, fingerprints, addresses, and whether or not the passenger had a criminal record. The "profile" inevitably would also include information about the individual's behavior and patterns of travel, how they paid their bills, and other details of their lifestyles.[55] Much of this information was already in government hands. As one report to the president recommended: "[P]ro-filing can leverage an investment in technology and trained people. *Based on information that is already in computer databases,* passengers could be separated into a very large majority who present little or no risk, and a small minority who merit additional attention."[56] But in order to keep such profiles up to date, the government will have to continually monitor other databases and track individuals every time they fly. David Sobel, a lawyer for the Electronic Privacy Information Center called the Gore Commis-sion's "profiling" plan "a realization of Big Brother concerns people have about computer technology . . . There are going to be massive databases that will track our actions and activities. If you think of increased capabili-ties to collect information, it's even scarier."[57]

One of the early "catches" of the profiling regime was Charles Si-monyi, the chief architect of Microsoft, who found himself unexpectedly flagged when he tried to board a flight to Los Angeles in 1997. Simonyi was asked to open his carry-on luggage, which was unpacked and handsearched by security agents. The following day, Simonyi found a note in his ticket envelope. "Why was I chosen?" it asked helpfully. The note explained: "Passengers are selected both randomly and through an objective system-atic approach based on direction from the FAA." Could he avoid this in the future? Sorry, no. "Please understand that Federal Regulations prohibit FAA personnel [and airline employees] from sharing specific information regarding this program with the public."

A self-described "shaggy-looking guy with a foreign accent," Simonyi accompanied his account of his "profiling" in *Slate* magazine with a picture captioned, "Do I look like a terrorist?" Only if you are a mild-mannered computer geek.

Although other travelers might have regarded the heightened scrutiny as a minor irritant and perhaps even as a reasonable tradeoff for increased security, Simonyi found the experience decidedly disturbing. He wrote later:

> I suddenly felt as if in the grip of a giant vise, a terrible feeling I had last experienced as a teenager before fleeing Communist Hungary . . . The communism I had fled was hardly traumatic or violent. One aspect of the horrible vice was the constant minor humiliations . . . such as the interaction with the block warden, the party overlord of a block of houses, who had to give his assent to all matters tiny or grand including travel. On this Friday in the United States, I was being singled out for an unusual and humiliating search.[58]

BIG NANNY

The attraction of comprehensive databases—and snooping—appears to be irresistible to bureaucracies of all sorts. In early 1997 administrators of the Fairfax, Virginia schools proposed creating an $11 million computer file that would compile electronic profiles on students that could include thousands of pieces of information about their academic performance, personalities, and families. The student database, The *Washington Post* reported, was intended "to track students from pre-kindergarten through high school and could include information such as medical and dental histories, records of behavioral problems, family income and learning disabilities," a mandate so sweeping that it led some school-board members to call the plan "Orwellian."[59]

Indeed, as public schools increasingly take on the role of surrogate parents, they have grown ever more aggressive in probing into what were once regarded as the privacies of family life. A "Human Interaction" course in one California school district, for example, asks children about their parents' income, whether "a close relative" has ever been an alcoholic or suffered from a mental illness, and whether the students "feel OK about crying" and "allow" themselves to do so. Students are asked about their parents' political leanings, what form of transportation family members use, and are actively encouraged to "share" intimate details of their lives with their peers. When questioned about the intrusiveness of some of the curriculum, an assistant superintendent told a reporter that it was "pretty generally believed" that parents did not do a good job of communicating with their children, so the schools needed to intervene to get communication going again. One way the school went about opening those lines of communication was a worksheet on "Family Systems" which described "open" families as "pure democracy," whereas "closed" families were labeled "hierarchical," an assignment that undoubtedly *did* inspire a number of interesting discussions at home.

But even this pales in comparison with what one observer called the "hybrid mélange of watered-down child psychology, mental health, tests and measurements, and non-practical clinical psychology" that has become commonplace in classrooms across the country.* One of the great growth industries of our century has been the professionalization of activities once done by families, individuals, and communities. Whatever their theories or styles of operation, the "helpers" share the conviction that they know better, often leading them to behave like an army of moms rummaging under your bed, but without the cookies afterward.

In the upscale Illinois community of Wilmette, for instance, seventh graders were asked to fill out a detailed questionnaire about their family lives. Among the questions the students were asked to answer were:

"How much time does your family spend together at work and play?"

"Do you actively practice your religion? How does it affect your daily life and community?"

"What are your monthly household expenses for Food: Clothing: Household goods: Luxury items: School: Other:"

---

*Writing about schools of education in the early 1960s, critic James Koerner was struck by what he called the "distressing lack of respect in these courses for the rights of privacy of both parents and student. Too much time is spent in fruitless and questionable attempts at the psychological analysis of student behavior, as well as impudent speculations about parents and home life."

"What is your family's energy consumption and cost? Electricity: water:"

"How much waste do you generate: and how does your family dispose of its waste?"

"What is each family member's most values possession? Why?"

"What decorative or heirloom objects do you own? What types of objects are decorative or heirloom?"

"What types of sacred objects are around the house?"

"Describe the kinds of clothing each family member owns?"

"Alcohol, tobacco and firearms: Are they available and what family members use them?"

"Does your family rent or own your house?"

"How much does it cost/month?"

"Is it government subsidized?"

"How much did it cost to buy? How did you do it?"

"What type of health care do you receive?"

"Do you lock your door at night?"

"Do you do anything to protect yourselves?"

"Does your family take vacations? When and where?"

Beyond the merely intrusive questions ("How much time does your family spend together?"), the questionnaire occasionally reads like "A Burglar's Guide to Wilmette." Families were assured that the "information and results will be kept confidential. . . . They will not be shared in any way, shape or form in class or with any other person or persons."

Having been offered such reassurance, parents were also told that the information would be used to "build perspectives" and that a final research project on the "material world" would focus on the findings the students reached during the study. The teachers did not explain how the answers to the question could be kept confidential, while at the same time they were also being used in the research report, which presumably, would not be confidential.

Understandably, some parents were uncomfortable with the survey. But others defended it on the ground that it encouraged more "openness" and "dialogue" between parents and students. But it is possible that some parents might not have wanted quite so much "dialogue" with their adolescent?

Might some of them have thought that not only was such information none of the school's business, but also none of their own children's business? This, of course, raises the question of how much privacy members of a family can expect from other family members. The Wilmette schools assumed that students had a right to know the details of their parents' finances. Did they also assume that parents had the right to withhold such information?

And if the parents had no right to tell their children to buzz off, what privacy rights could the preteens expect for themselves? After all, the virtues of "openness" and "dialogue" tend to run both ways. Given the emotional explosiveness of that question—privacy concerns tend to be one of the flash points in every adolescent rebellion—it seems both risky and unwise for the public schools to assume that all families would react to the question of privacy in the same way.

4

■

Big Brother at the Mall

In the mid-1970s, the U.S. Supreme Court upheld the Bank Secrecy Act's requirement that banks keep customer records for up to six years and give authorities virtually unlimited access. Justice William O. Douglas wrote in dissent:

> In a sense a person is defined by the checks he writes. By examining them the agents get to know his doctors, lawyers, creditors, political allies, social connections, religious affiliations, educational interests, the papers and magazine he reads, and so on ad infinitum. These are all tied to one's Social Security number; and now that we have the data banks, these other items will enrich that storehouse and make it possible for a bureaucrat—by pushing one button—to get in an instant the names of the 190 million Americans who are subversives or potential and likely candidates.[1]

Indeed, Douglas wrote, "It would be highly useful to governmental espionage to have like reports from all our bookstores, all our hardware and retail stores, all our drugstores. These records too might be 'useful' in criminal investigations." Two years later, the Court ruled 5 to 3 that individuals had no constitutional rights to privacy in their bank records, reasoning that customers surrender privacy when they open a bank account because they turn over the record keeping to a third party.[2] Douglas's calculated exaggeration is no longer an exaggeration. But such information is not simply of interest to the cops, it has also proven to be of considerable value to marketers.

In fact, the growth in government databases and tracking devices has been closely paralleled in the private sector, not a surprising development given the almost collegial relationship between many of the companies that are developing commercial "profiling" systems and government agencies who have pioneered such surveillance technologies. One of the ironic consequences of the end of the Cold War and cuts in military and intelligence budgets has been the transfer of much of the surveillance know-how of the nation's intelligence agencies to private companies, including those in the business of tracking the likes and dislikes of consumers. Technologies such as artificial intelligence, biometrics, and intelligent transportation systems have the potential to be powerful tools both for marketers and for law enforcement.[3] In recent years, the Department of Defense has handed out tens of millions of dollars to companies who might want to turn military surveillance technology to commercial purposes.

The result is a symbiotic relationship between the databases in the public and private sectors. Government technology and public records form the backbone of the direct-marketing programs. In turn, the resources of the private market vastly expand the capabilities of the government agencies themselves. In some ways, the new datawebs have turned privacy protections on their head. If anyone ever proposed permitting government agents to track our purchases, monitor our phones, read our medical files, or keep us under video surveillance, the suggestion would have been rejected out of hand and with extreme prejudice. But, increasingly, government agencies no longer need such powers because we are already being watched by others who do not have the limitations put on the government by the Fourth Amendment. Even though much of the information is gathered by private entities, they have, in effect become surrogates for government agencies that want to keep track of us. All the agencies have to do is buy the information like anyone else. According to privacy expert David Banisar, the FBI, DEA, and IRS have all secretly purchased direct-marketing lists to add to their own investigative databases. Banisar notes that the DEA went so far as to have the Tennessee Valley Authority purchase such lists on its behalf.[4]

Before public outrage forced them to reverse their decision, officials in several states, including Florida and South Carolina, sold millions of driver's license pictures to a New Hampshire firm compiling a new database of personal information and photographs. Ostensibly, the new database was supposed to help retailers prevent "identity theft"; but once the digital images are sold, there are few restrictions on how they might be used. In time, marketers—and others—could have access to the world's largest collection of mug shots, matched and merged with a wealth of other personal data.[5] Again illustrating the tangled relations between private and public snooping, it turned out that the U.S. Secret Service had quietly provided nearly $1.5 million in cash and technical assistance to the company that had purchased the driver's-license photos and was in the process of creating the national photo database. Although the company had stressed the value of the database to combat bogus checks and credit-card fraud, the government was interested in extending the same technology to combating terrorism and enforcing various immigration laws.[6] Once again, the episode illustrated how personal data flows from individuals to government agencies, from the agencies to private vendors, and back again to government monitors.

At their worst, the new technologies threaten to create "a seamless web of surveillance from cradle to grave, from bankbook to bedroom." But they also carry obvious attractions for businesses, marketers, and even consumers. In theory, the technologies carry the promise that businesses can interact one-on-one with their consumers, thus making it easier for them to anticipate and meet their needs, target their advertising, and build customer loyalty. Few Americans, however, have any idea how closely their behavior is watched, recorded, and traded among different companies.

Almost any transaction in the electronic world generates data about you that is recorded: Every time you fill a prescription, shop at a supermarket using a discount card, order from a catalog, surf the Internet, or fill out a warranty card, someone is recording your action, filing it away, adding to your profile. A billion-dollar industry revolves around the sale and exchange of this information, which may be bartered, matched, and merged with other databases that may also have been watching you.

But a multibillion-dollar industry also depends on assuring consumers that their privacy will be respected and protected. Concern over privacy is perhaps the single greatest barrier the Net must overcome before it can achieve its growth potential. A 1998 Georgia Tech survey found that Internet users rated privacy as the most important issue facing the future of the Net—replacing censorship as the top concern.[7] Another major survey in 1998 by Louis Harris & Associates, and Dr. Alan F. Westin, sponsored by

Privacy & American Business and Price Waterhouse LLP, found that 81 percent of Net users in general and 79 percent of Net users who buy products and services on the Net are concerned about threats to their personal privacy and strongly support calls for businesses to post notices on their privacy policies. Another Harris survey found that 41 percent of all respondents said that they felt that their privacy had been invaded by a business; 82 percent said that consumers had lost control over how their personal information was used.[8]

A *Business Week*/Harris survey found that 78 percent of Web users would use the Web even more if their privacy were guaranteed. Anxiety over the security of the information they provide on-line is by far the most important reason Net users give for not using electronic commerce more often. Sixty-five percent were "very" concerned and another 15 percent "somewhat" concerned with using a credit card to make an on-line purchase.[9]

This finding would seem to suggest that companies that succeed in establishing their identity and credibility as privacy-friendly could reap huge dividends, as customers who have refrained from buying their products on the Net could come forward.

The only problem with this scenario is that many on-line services rely heavily (or entirely) on advertising revenue, so their survival depends on finding a way to make their ads effective. "Advertisers and publishers want a better eyeball," says one Net ad salesman, "and a better eyeball is a more targeted eyeball." Especially one that is watching you. The appeal of the new technology to marketers is the promise that it can get inside your head, to figure out how you reason and make choices. The new programs are touted as tools to sell a wide range of products. But what they are really selling is *you*.

Admittedly, this may not amount to all that much for most people, except for the occasional catalog or junk mailing. But there are occasions when a chink in the system provides an unsettling perspective. A Ohio woman named Beverly Dennis received an obscene letter from a stranger, who made it clear that he knew where she lived, all about her divorce and her personal habits, including the brand of soap she used when she showered. In page after page, the writer interwove details of his sexual fantasies with intimate details of her life.[10] As Nina Bernstein of the *New York Times* reported, Ms. Dennis's experience placed her at the heart of the debate over privacy in American society. As it turned out, the letter writer was an inmate in a Texas state prison who had been entrusted with entering the personal data of millions of consumers into a database for Metromail, one of the nation's largest marketing companies. By the truckload, Metromail shipped the results of data to the Texas prison system where inmates entered the information into Metromail's database, which reportedly includes information on more than 90 percent of the nation's households. Many of the prisoners entrusted with the data were sex offenders; it was only after Ms. Dennis's case was publicized that the Texas legislature barred the use of convicted sex offenders from data-processing jobs. "We lost some damn good programmers—pedophiles," the director of the state prison complained afterward. "Some of our best computer operatives were sex offenders."[11]

The scope of the information they handled was nightmarishly detailed. When Beverly Dennis sued Metromail she learned that the company's dossier on her ran to twenty-five single-spaced pages of information—including more than 900 separate pieces of information about her habits going back to 1987. Metromail knew—and was prepared to sell—information about her dental care, what antacids she preferred, whether she used room deodorizers and even her choice of sleeping aids and hemorrhoid ointments. A native of Ohio's coal country, Beverly Dennis felt, Bernstein wrote, "as though her privacy had been strip mined by the dark side of the information economy."[12] But aside from the letter from the inmate, there was nothing unusual about Ms. Dennis's dossier. Along with millions of other consumers, she had filled out questionnaires she received in the mail on the promise that she would receive free coupons or samples. That information is then widely marketed to other companies or individuals who may have very different reasons for wanting to know your tastes and habits. In a macabre demonstration of the ease with which such information can be obtained, a reporter for the *Los Angeles Times* actually obtained detailed information about 5,000 children from Metromail, which readily sold the data, even though the reporter bought it using the name Richard Allen Davis—the man convicted of murdering twelve-year-old Polly Klaas.[13] (It is also less than comforting to know that at least twenty-seven other states besides Texas also use convicted criminals to enter records. Inmates of federal prisons do work for the IRS, and prisons in several states contract with private information brokers to process commercial data.)

Ironically, faced with the loss of revenue from data processing, Texas prison officials moved quickly to sign contracts for prisoners to work on new technologies that pose even greater potential threats for privacy. Prisoners from the Ferguson State Prison in Midway were put to work creating maps, using an extraordinarily powerful new technology known as Geographic Information Systems (GIS). The technology puts together high-resolution aerial photographs, maps, and demographic information in computerized forms. One application permits city planners to create detailed plat records, showing the locations of utility meters and the location of every house on every lot. More ambitious applications allow users to access not only tax information about every home, but also photographs of residents and profiles of their consumer behavior generated by matching and merging various databases. GIS technology has disturbing implications for the growing use of video monitoring of public areas, including parking lots. By combining the vast array of available data with car licenses, for example, GIS technology can access an individual's name, income, driving record, and shopping behaviors gleaned from the sorts of datanets that had snared Beverly Dennis.[14]

While much of the information about Ms. Dennis resulted from surveys she had filled out herself, not all of the dossiers require consumers to take any direct action at all, because the information is gathered passively, without the customer's ever being told. Every call to a customer-support number, every point-of-sale transaction generates more information for the datanet. Lifestyle data is compiled through surveys attached to manufacturers warranty materials. There are, in fact, more than 10,000 publicly traded databases on the market. Many of them are extraordinarily detailed, listing right-handed mechanics, or practicing doctors selected by type of medicine, or airplane owners by the type of aircraft they own.

In North Carolina, for example, a woman who is newly diagnosed with diabetes might open her mail to find an informational package telling her about preventing eye disease, along with a coupon for an examination. A parent of a toddler might get a postcard reminding her that it is time for her child's next immunization. The notes are not from the patients' doctors: they are generated by Blue Cross and Blue Shield of North Carolina's state-of-the-art database, a sort of Big Nurse, which watches over their thousands of clients.[15]

Companies like AT&T spend millions of dollars on systems that enable them to compile vast storehouses of personal information on more than 100 million customers and prospects. AT&T uses the database to identify customers who are known as "spinners"—those who flip-flop between long-distance carriers more than three times in order to cash in on the end-less round of come-ons, bonuses, and incentives. As a case study by the company's data manager notes, "The company can now suppress such un-profitable individuals from future acquisition efforts . . . ," which seems to mean that at least some customers can eat their dinners in peace, without being interrupted by telemarketers from AT&T.[16] Competitor MCI is equally aggressive, creating *warehouseMCI*, a vast data-collection project that will record "usage history" from the company's 23 billion annual net-work transactions and combine that data with financial and demographic information, which is then overlaid with "psychographic" information from other databases. The result is a detailed portrait of the behavior, incomes, and histories of 140 million customers and prospects.[17]

Even *Playboy* has shed its inhibitions, saying that it was thinking about sharing information about its catalog customers with marketers. Under the company's plan, it would not only be the models who found themselves exposed. In late 1998, *Playboy* said it would contract with First Data Solu-tions to track the buying habits of its customers. Along with its new part-ner, *Playboy* would combine that information with other available personal information—such as age and income—to create a database that would be used both by *Playboy* and other marketers who might want to gain access to *Playboy*'s customers. The database would, for example, make it possible to identify and target individuals who buy videos about sex toys and also own high-priced stereo equipment or luxury cars.[18] This might prove in-teresting to a number of people, including some with whom the customer might not have intended to share his tastes when he entered into the orig-inal transaction.

Indeed, the sale of personal data by banks themselves has become so widespread that the Comptroller of the Currency, John Hake, Jr., warned banks in mid-1999 that they should either put an end to abuses or face congressional action. "Unfortunately," he declared, "there's mounting evi-dence of an increase in banking practices that are at least seamy, if not down-right unfair and deceptive—practices that virtually cry out for government scrutiny." The day after Hawke's remarks, the attorney general of Minnesota filed suit against U.S. Bank, accusing the bank of selling confidential customer information to a telemarketing company. The suit alleged the bank violated the Fair Credit Reporting Act and state consumer laws by sharing with telemarketers the names, addresses, and telephone numbers of their customers, as well as checking account numbers, credit card numbers, Social Security numbers, account status, homeowner status, occupation, as well as such information as their average account balances, year-to-date finance charges for credit card accounts, credit insurance status, and recent credit card purchases.[19]

Gathering together every conceivable bit of information about you, from coupon redemptions to scanner data to surveys, is called "data warehousing." The art and science of turning all of this data into a portrait of who you are and how you behave is know as "data mining." As authors Michael J. Berry and Gordon Linoff write, "Nothing can replace the creative intuition of the sole proprietor who recognizes customers by name, face, and voice and remembers their habits and preferences. But through the clever application of information technology, even the largest enterprise can come surprisingly close."

THE NEW SPOOKS

How close? The most enthusiastic proponents of the latest technologies believe they can create monitoring programs that will watch you so closely that they will know you better than some of your closest friends; know you so well they will be able to predict your choices even before you make them. The next wave of technology is the application of artificial intelligence (AI) to the collection of information about consumers, using so-called "neural networks" to detect relationships and patterns. The neural nets are designed to act like the human brain, with its ability to make connections, draw inferences, and learn from the information it gathers on you. No longer science fiction, the technology is already being used in law enforcement. One of the larger government databases to use modern intelligent technologies is the Treasury Department's Financial Crimes Enforcement Network, which links together hundreds of government databases as it watches for suspicious patterns and transactions. The FBI uses similar systems employing artificial intelligence to link relationships, phone usage, and associates of suspects in terrorism, drug, and organized-crime investigations.

But similar technology is being deployed against consumers.

Imagine that every time you go shopping, you are watched by a camera, which records every product you look at, follows you from department to department and store to store, taking note of what interests you and what you ignore. Imagine that it watches what you read and how you read, not just the books or magazines, but the actual articles. Imagine that the camera is programmed to recognize you whenever you return and to compare your habits to your last visit, adding to its growing record of your every move. Imagine that it watches you, learns about you, and remembers you. And offers this information for sale.

Does that sound unduly paranoid?

Compare our hypothetical surveillance system with Aptex Software's description of how its new customer-monitoring engine, SelectCast, works on the Internet. The company brags that the program "acts as virtual salesperson, unobtrusively observing each client. . . ."[20]

Like a live salesperson, the company explains, "SelectCast observes a client's interests and behaviors" to determine what products might interest a specific customer.

> By observing customers' interests from the moment they enter the virtual door of your on-line shopping site, SelectCast profiles and remembers each person's unique interests. The observation is accomplished without any explicit judgments—no client preference forms are involved. Clients leave clues about their interests based on the pages they view, the advertisements they click on, the terms they search with and the products they purchase.
>
> Using observed interests coupled with behavior, SelectCast can up-sell, cross-sell, provide insights about groups of customers and predict future purchase behavior.

It does this by watching how an on-line user behaves, what she reads, how she surfs, and then builds a "psychographic profile" of her behavior. Using this information, the system serves up advertising "banners" that are matched to the interests of the customer. For example, someone who is observed reading articles about sports, or travel to Mexico, might be offered ads for sports gear and information about vacation packages to Puerto Vallarta. Such personalized profiles are stored and updated with the help of the system's "tracing cookie," quietly left behind in the user's computer after every visit. The company explains: "Unobtrusively establishing a customized profile for each user enables SelectCast to present information visitors are more likely to be interested in first."

Aptex itself provides some examples of its surveillance of customers. A fictitious woman named Jane logs onto an on-line store in late October. SelectCast recognizes her. It has been monitoring her for months. It knows that she has been browsing "home-related Christmas items" while ignoring other products. It also knows that last year she bought a Twelve Days of Christmas sixty-piece decorative set. Using this information, the on-line merchant offers her a series of holiday-related products, including "Diana, Princess of Wales—A Tribute."

Aptex also offers systems for tracking editorial content by, in effect, looking over customers' shoulders every time they read an article on-line. The program, the company says, is so sophisticated that it profiles customers in "real time." In other words, it is learning about customers at the very moment they are browsing. Aptex not only can figure out what you are interested in, it can also "infer demographic characteristics such as gender and age, based on user behavior."[21]

By watching you, they believe, they can *know* you.

"We can predict that you're straight or gay, whether you like sports, and a hundred other things," says Aptex's CEO, Michael Thiemann. "Basically, your presence on any given site gives us a lot of information that allows us to begin profiling you immediately."[22]

The technology can do this because it is able to learn from examples, can analyze words, symbols, and behavior, and then make assumptions about relationships. Using what Aptex calls "the world's most advanced context-sensitive information-system retrieval system," SelectCast converts words and ideas into geometric patterns, comparing, for example, concepts like "Iran-contra" and "aid to the contras" (closely related) with "insider trading" (not closely related) to "make precise behavioral predictions."

If this all sounds a bit spooky, it is because, traditionally, the biggest customers for such "neural networks" were agencies of the federal government. Indeed, SelectCast was created under a government contract.[23] An article in *Wired* magazine describes Michael Thiemann, the CEO of Aptex, as being "nonchalant" about Aptex's relationship with spy agencies. In fact, Aptex was spun off from a company called HNC, which had close ties to certain agencies in the federal government, acting as a longtime contractor for many of the most advanced analysis and surveillance systems. "Call it government intelligence agencies," *Wired* quotes Thiemann as saying, discussing the company's "traditional customer base." HNC was selected early in the 1990s to develop the latest generation of research technology for some of those black-budget agencies. Thiemann brags, "HNC has probably received more money for advanced analysis research than any other company around." The company was also a leader in shifting its focus from national security to the private sector. "In 1995," Thiemann told *Wired*, "we were shipping our most advanced systems to the U.S. government and the Internet was taking off. We at HNC were saying, 'This was working so well at government operations—why not apply it another high-information stream environment: the Internet?' "[24]

Big Brother has simply set up shop at the nearest mall. The evidence suggests that he is doing a brisk business. Although surveys continue to show that users of the Internet are deeply concerned about privacy, technology and economics continually change the rules of the game. Many of the biggest commercial Web sites have already entered into agreements to pool information about their customers into a massive new system that now tracks the behavior of tens of millions of users. The system known as Engage, designed and run by CMG Information Services, gathers together information from dozens of sites into a central database, providing extraordinary dossiers on everything from your taste in magazines to your sporting enthusiasms. Engage works by planting an identifying number on the computer hard drive of every person who visits one of the sites in the system. By mid–1998, Engage reportedly had already created anonymous profiles of 15 million Net surfers.[25] The ID number then allows participating businesses to learn everything that other businesses have also learned about you. "If someone comes to your bookstore for the first time," explains David S. Wetherell, CEO of CMG, "you can find out if they are interested in mountain climbing, organic gardening and tennis; you can present them books related to their interests immediately."[26]

Referring to such technologies, Tara Lemmey suggests this analogy: "Consider how this would play out with a restaurant analogy. If you order food in one restaurant and pay by credit card, you do not assume another restaurant will know when you walk in what you ordered in the last and start making it for you. Nor do they have a copy of your card on file, or seat you next to other patrons you may have something in common with because a waiter overheard your conversation and felt you might have an affinity for these folks. On the Net, this happens now without an alert."

"There is a fine line," Lemmey notes, "between good service and stalking."

There is also a fine line between marketing and snooping, especially when sensitive personal information is being gathered. In this brave new world, would red flags go up if a user began accessing information about ovarian cancer? Or impotence? Might insurance companies be interested if a client began contacting suicide support groups, or began researching AZT? Who might be interested to know that a middle-aged man is observed downloading sites specializing in gay sexuality? Or that a surfer—married, with children—begins to log onto singles Web sites, then buys airline tickets for distant locations, while downloading data about child custody and divorce litigation?

Acknowledging the potentially profound implications of privacy, the operators of Engage say they will not record names, street addresses, credit-card numbers, or e-mail addresses of customers caught in their profiling net. In addition, recognizing the intimacy of the information that consumers might reveal, Engage will not track behavior relating to sexual or health-related topics. Though this may be superficially encouraging, it is important to note that Engage's restraint is not binding on any of its competitors, since no law restricts either the gathering of such information on the Net or the sale of such data to others.

Although Engage will not collect names, it will keep records of every user's age, gender, income, zip code, and number of children, along with every customer's unique identification number, certainly raising the possibility that such information, combined with an intimate dossier, could be linked to individual identities.

Moreover, assurances that a user's privacy will be respected may be rendered moot by new developments in electronic marketing. In early 1999, the Intel Corporation announced plans to embed electronic serial numbers in their new Pentium III microprocessors that would make it possible to identify individual computers whenever they were used to access the Internet. The new identifier chip was hailed as a boon for E-commerce, but to critics, Intel's announcement sounded a death knell for privacy on the Net, because it would enable Web sites to instantly verify the identity of any visitor and make it vastly easier to track their behavior. Comparing the new chip with the "cookies" planted on hard drives to allow marketers to track users, privacy advocate David Banisar called the new identifier chip a "super cookie, a nuclear cookie." Unlike traditional "cookies," which usually differ from one site to another, the chip's new serial number would stay the same and would not be easily changed or deleted. In practical terms, the identifier made it vastly easier to blend and merge the records of many different companies and sites together to create a comprehensive data dossier, without the user's ever knowing what was happening. Although there are already other identifiers in cyberspace, Intel's announcement was especially alarming because of the company's dominance of the microprocessor market; few of the other identifiers enjoy such widespread use. "It makes you wonder," Banisar remarked, "if maybe Intel should change their logo from 'Intel Inside' to 'Big Brother Inside.'"[27]

Faced with the outcry, Intel quickly announced that it would modify the chip so that it could be disabled unless users turned on the feature, a move that did little to mollify privacy advocates. Intel's decision left it up to the computer manufacturers to decide whether to turn off the new identifier, and privacy advocates worried that third parties, including hackers, might be able to turn the identifier back on without a user's knowledge.[28] Even with the ability to turn off the identifier, nothing would stop Web sites from banning any user who chose such a privacy option.

Perhaps the most troubling issue of all was raised by the Electronic Privacy Information Center, which asked whether Intel had developed the tracking number at the behest of federal agencies, which have long sought to plant listening, decoding, and tracking devices into the nation's telecommunications infrastructure. (See Chapter 9, "The Government's War on Privacy.") The FBI in particular has made no secret of its interest in being able to intercept and de-encrypt phone calls more easily and has waged a decades-long fight to limit the use of encryption in electronic communications. A year before Intel's announcement, FBI director Louis Freeh told a Senate subcommittee that it would "be beneficial for Internet service providers to capture and retain caller ID data on persons accessing ISP lines" to assist law enforcement in child-pornography cases. For privacy advocates, this sounded very much like what Intel had ostensibly done on its own—claiming that it was intended for private and corporate use.[29]

CLOSING THE CIRCLE

Beyond the world of E-commerce itself, the next logical step in creating a seamless dataweb is for the information gleaned from monitoring people on-line to be combined with the detailed dossiers kept on those same people by companies like Metromail—thus completing the data circle. Under a system developed by the California-based company, Adforce, Inc., every time a user would begin surfing a Web site, the provider would give Adforce his or her name and address. In turn, the company would match the person with the dossier—complete with its detailed demographic and behavioral profile—compiled by its partner, Metromail. In effect, the system would attach the vast non-Net databases to the Net's systems of customer surveillance, thus providing a dramatically more detailed portrait of their visitors and potential customers.[30] Adforce insists that it wouldn't give the individual names to advertisers and will not use the information it gathers about behavior on the Web, but privacy advocates nonetheless tend to expect the worst, especially as the stakes rise and the market becomes more competitive. The only guarantee of discretion is the goodwill and ethics of the various surveillance systems. Experience suggests reasons for skepticism.

One of the major participants in the new system is "GeoCities," a collection of more than two million personal Web sites that attracts tens of millions of visitors. In August 1998, the Federal Trade Commission charged that GeoCities had lied to its more than two million subscribers when it had promised to protect their privacy. The FTC found that GeoCities had gathered information about children who played games on the site and then sold that information. (As a result, GeoCities reached a settlement with the FTC and stopped gathering such information.)[31]

Despite the insistence by the marketing industry that it can regulate itself, the evidence suggests otherwise. A Federal Trade Commission survey of 1,400 Web sites found that more than 85 percent of the sites collected personal information from users, but only 14 percent of them told consumers how that information was used and a tiny 2 percent provided a comprehensive privacy policy. Even those policies left much to be desired.[32] "When you read these so-called privacy policies closely you see most of them should really be called no-privacy policies," according to Russ Smith, director of Consumer.Net.

The scope and breadth of the information gathered was vast. The FTC found a medical clinic's on-line service which invited consumers to "submit their name, postal address, e-mail address, insurance company, any comments concerning their medical problems, and to indicate whether they wish to receive information on any of a number of topics, including urinary incontinence, hypertension, cholesterol, prostate cancer, and diabetes." The on-line application specifically asked consumers for their name, address, phone numbers, date of birth, marital status, gender, insurance company, and the date and location of their last hospitalization. As the FTC noted, "The clinic's Web site says nothing about how the information consumers provide will be used or whether it will be made available to third parties." The FTC also found a Web site for an auto dealer, who offered consumers a chance to fix their credit ratings, asking them to provide their names, addresses, and Social Security numbers—but, again, said nothing about how such information would be used.[33]

Sites aimed at children were especially egregious violators. Fully 89 percent of children's web sites collected personal information *from children.* The FTC found that while a little more than half provided some form for disclosure about how they handled the information, few sites took steps to ensure that parents would have any sort of involvement in the transactions involving their children. Fewer than one in ten made any provision for parental control over the collection or the use of information from their children.

Some of the sites asked for very detailed information from the children who visited. One asked children about their personal finances, including whether he or she has received gifts in the form of stock, cash, savings bonds, mutual funds, or certificates of deposit; who gave such gifts; whether a child puts their gifts into mutual funds, stocks, or bonds; and whether the child's parents own mutual funds. This particular Web site did not ask children to tell their parents about the information they were providing or to seek permission before putting the information on-line.[34] Although other privacy protections continued to languish in Congress, the FTC report made it likely that some sort of legislation would eventually pass restricting the on-line collection of information from children.[35]

A survey by the Electronic Privacy Information Center was similarly critical of the industry's self-restraint. EPIC found that of the net's 100 most popular sites, about half collected some sort of personal information from users, but only seventeen sites even mentioned the issue of privacy—and only a handful made anything like reasonable disclosure of what would happen with the information it was collecting. Not one of the sites, EPIC declared, "met basic standards for privacy protection." EPIC also found widespread use of "cookies"—nuggets of information left behind on a consumer's hard drive when they visit a Web site. Of the 100 top sites surveyed, EPIC found that twenty-three left cookies in users' PCs, usually without the user ever knowing about it. None of the sites told visitors about the gratuitous gift of the cookie.[36] Noted EPIC's Marc Rotenberg, "Some people who think they are surfing the Net are actually swimming in a fishbowl."[37]*

Unlike the European Union, which heavily controls the dissemination of personal information by the private sector, there are few legal limits on marketers or the operators of databases. But as concern for privacy rises, so does public support for privacy legislation that would protect them from business, as well as from government. In one major survey, 93 percent of the respondents said that companies that sold information should be required to ask permission before making their personal information available.

Anxious to head off this sort of government regulation, industry groups continue to insist they can be trusted to regulate themselves. In 1997, more than a dozen major companies that traffic in personal information announced "voluntary" limits on their dissemination of sensitive data. Joining the pledge were such giant info-merchants as Lexis-Nexis, the major credit unions, Metromail, Acxiom Corporation, DCS Information Systems, the National Fraud Center, and the Professional Electronic Network. Together, they account for nearly 90 percent of current market in personal information in the United States. Under the agreement, the companies pledged to restrict the public's access to sensitive information such as So-

---

*A year later, EPIC surveyed the privacy policies of 76 members of the Direct Marketing Association, the industry group that was a leading proponent of self-regulation. EPIC found that 40 of the 76 new members had Web sites that collected some sort of personal information from consumers. Despite the Marketing Association's elaborate privacy policies, EPIC found that only 8 of the 40 sites had "any semblance of a privacy notice."

cial Security numbers, dates of birth, mother's maiden names, and unlisted phone numbers.

But the bold promise of a new era of database privacy—or at least restraint—was a good deal less than met the eye.

For starters, consumers could have privacy *but they would have to ask for it first.* Under the agreement, consumer privacy required individuals to "opt out," by contacting each of the fourteen companies to request that their names be removed from the public lists. Even as the companies announced the new policies, they admitted they had not figured out exactly how people would go about opting out. As a practical matter, this meant that the vast majority of people whose data resided in their dataweb would remain there, because most consumers still have only the vaguest idea of who knows what about them, much less how they could access such information.

Second, the proposed privacy barriers were porous. The fourteen data-merchants proposed only "somewhat restricted" (but not fully restricted) access for "commercial users"—such as marketers, banks, lawyers and journalists—to such information as unlisted addresses, unlisted phone numbers, Social Security numbers, date of birth and information about children. Corporate security agents, private investigators, and law enforcement would have absolutely unrestricted access to all of that information, plus your mother's maiden name, your credit history, financial records, and medical records.[38]

Those loopholes made the voluntary privacy guidelines a kind of Potemkin Village of privacy—an elaborate series of impressive-looking fronts, meant to conceal business as usual. When all was said and done, the general public was barred from seeing much of the information, but consumers gained little or no protections because would-be snoops could still simply hire a search firm to do their investigations.

LOOPHOLES IN CYBERSPACE

Timothy McVeigh thought he had found a place in cyberspace where his privacy would be respected. He was wrong.

McVeigh—no relation to the convicted bomber of the Oklahoma City federal building—would find himself pitted against both the nation's premier on-line service and the United States Navy. In the end, even though he eventually emerged triumphant, his case would demonstrate:

- The fragility of many of the protections that supposedly protect private information
- The porous quality of the walls between the private and public sectors
- The ambiguity of the laws protecting private information
- And finally, the glaring loopholes that remain in such protections.

For McVeigh, the stakes of maintaining his privacy were high: nothing less than his career—a seventeen-year record of service in the U.S. Navy—was on the line. In his most recent performance evaluations, Senior Chief Petty Office McVeigh was described by his superiors as "an outstanding role model" and "the embodiment of Navy core values." McVeigh's private life had never interfered with his duties, and it is unlikely the two zones of his life would ever have collided were it not for his involvement in a Christmas toy drive for the children of members of his crew aboard the U.S.S. *Chicago,* the nuclear-powered sub where he served as crew chief.

In September 1997, McVeigh sent a seemingly innocuous e-mail message to a fellow crewman's wife about the toy drive. What caught her eye, though, was McVeigh's return address—"Boysrch." Concerned that the screen name apparently was a contraction of "boysearch," the woman logged onto AOL's biographical profile for the user, who was identified as "Tim," listed his home as Honolulu, and his interests as "driving, boy watching, collecting pictures of other young studs." Tim's marital status was listed as "gay."[39]

This information was passed on to Navy's investigators, one of whom, Squadron Legalman LN1 Joseph Kaiser placed a telephone call to AOL. Without telling the customer representative that he was an investigator for the U.S. Navy, Kaiser was able to find out that the AOL subscriber who used the screen name "Boysrch," was, in fact, Senior Chief Petty Officer Timothy R. McVeigh.[40] The Navy acted quickly. When the U.S.S. *Chicago* pulled into port, McVeigh was ordered to immediately present himself to the squadron's legal officer, who confronted him with the AOL information. The same day he was relieved of his duties, and the Navy proceeded to dishonorably discharge McVeigh.

The discharge of McVeigh brought to the surface the latent and unresolved contradictions of the military's "don't ask, don't tell" policy. The Navy insisted that by posting his biography on-line, McVeigh had waived his own privacy. In effect, they said, he had "told" the world of his sexual orientation. But what the Navy insisted was public was considered private by critics. McVeigh's case, insisted David Sobel of the Electronic Privacy Information Center, "cuts to the heart of the issue of on-line privacy." "What this case highlights," said Barry Steinhardt, of the Electronic Frontier Foundation, "is how easily information becomes public and how easily it can be misused."[41]

Gay activists were especially appalled. Like many users of the Web, McVeigh was taking advantage of the anonymity of cyberspace either to invent or reveal a personality that was impossible to expose while he was serving in the Navy. The reality was that AOL had become a popular meeting place for gays, a private zone for those who dared not reveal their identities in the real world. It was especially popular among servicemen and women who faced extraordinary pressures to keep their identities private.

"These service members have so few options to be their authentic selves," remarked Tom Reilly, an executive of an on-line gay meeting place and news service. "According to military policy, they have to lie if they want to serve in the military. Going to the last frontier of their privacy is truly disturbing."[42]

But McVeigh did not want his case to center on the issue of gay rights. McVeigh repeatedly declined to say whether he was a homosexual, arguing that his sexual preference was not relevant. Instead, he saw it as strictly a privacy issue. The heart of McVeigh's case was his contention that the Navy had violated the Electronic Communications Privacy Act (ECPA), which barred the government from obtaining private information from on-line providers such as AOL without a warrant, a court order, or the consent of the subscriber. The law had been passed specifically to assure the privacy of on-line communications, but it was not at all clear how that law would be applied.

American Online, which was faced with its own furor over the leak of information, charged the Navy with deception, but also admitted that its own customer representative had violated the company's own rules on confidentiality. "This is a case of human error under very unusual circumstances," a spokesman insisted.[43] But the "human error" highlighted one of the nagging difficulties of securing personal privacy. AOL's own contractual "Terms of Service" clearly barred the company from giving out any personal information to any third party "unless required to do so by law or legal process." But as it turned out, neither federal law nor AOL's own contract with subscribers protected Timothy McVeigh's privacy. The most elaborate privacy protections fell victim to a single "human error" and a few keystrokes.

In January 1998, Federal Judge Stanley Sporkin handed McVeigh a clear, if preliminary, victory by ruling that the naval investigators had "likely" violated the federal law when it contacted AOL. Sporkin ruled that "the government knew, or should have known, that by turning over the information without a warrant, AOL was breaking the law. Yet the Navy, in this case, directly solicited the information anyway." Sporkin declined to cut either the Navy or AOL any slack:

"In these days of Big Brother, where through technology and otherwise, the privacy interests of individuals from all walks of life are being ignored or marginalized, it is imperative that statutes explicitly protecting these rights to be strictly observed." His decision was applauded by groups like EPIC, which noted that "with literally the entire world on the World Wide Web, enforcement of the ECPA is of great concern to those who bare the most personal information about their lives in private accounts through the Internet."[44]

Even so, the victory for privacy was less than complete. In fact, Sporkin's ruling ran directly contrary to a ruling from a higher federal court, which had looked at the enforcement of the same law. In that case, local police wanted to look at the telephone subscriber records of a suspect, even though they did not have a warrant or a court order. The defendant charged that the police had clearly violated ECPA and cited the identical section of the law as lawyers for McVeigh. But in 1996, the U.S. Court of Appeals for the Fourth Circuit upheld the government's action, ruling that the federal law only allows the victim to sue the service provider for disclosing his personal data, but had no remedy against the government which had accessed that data.[45] If the same principle had applied to McVeigh's case, he would have been able to sue AOL, which had been duped by the Navy—but the Navy would have been home free.

As it turned out, both the Navy and AOL settled McVeigh's case out of court. In one of the case's many ironies, McVeigh had been promoted to the Navy's highest enlisted rank. Just months after Sporkin's ruling and under his agreement with the Navy, McVeigh was allowed to retire as Master Chief Petty Officer with full benefits as well as money for his legal fees.

AOL also agreed to pay McVeigh undisclosed damages and apologized. In addition, the on-line service announced improvements in its employee training to avoid a repeat of the McVeigh fiasco.[46]

For McVeigh, the settlement was both a legal and personal victory. But was it also a vindication for on-line privacy rights? Unfortunately not. Like virtually all of the federal laws dealing with privacy, ECPA also had a yawning loophole: The law provides *no protection at all* to violations by the private sector. Like the federal Privacy Act, the law applies only to actions by the government, and would not apply to private employers who behaved as the Navy did. If you work for a private company, no federal law prohibits your boss from calling up an on-line service to obtain information about your identity and activities. McVeigh's attorney, Christopher Wolf, noted that the law that protected his client against the Navy "does not govern the same disclosure of information to non-governmental entities or persons. You or I can call up an on-line service and get information about a subscriber, including e-mail, and there is no federal law prohibiting that conduct."[47]

That doesn't mean though that there are no remedies for such violations. If an on-line service had promised confidentiality in its user agreements, a victim could, in theory, sue the provider for breach of contract. But some user agreements require that any disputes be subject to private arbitration, which bars redress to the courts. Even those suits that are allowed might well end up in state rather than federal courts, where users could face a patchwork of inconsistent and conflicting laws and rulings.

5

■

Losing Ground:

The Courts and Privacy

Unfortunately, despite its lengthy philosophical and political pedigree, privacy has a decidedly mixed record in the courts, both as a constitutional question and as a cause of private legal action. In both cases, it is not going too far to say that the state of the law is a mess, a patchwork of false starts, inconsistent applications, and muddled and contradictory rulings. In constitutional law, the courts have lagged far behind the developments in technology in applying the Fourth Amendment to intrusive new methods of surveillance. In late 1998, the U.S. Supreme Court ruled that Fourth Amendment privacy protections did not extend to visitors to a private home. By a vote of 5 to 4, the justices said that Americans could have no "legitimate expectation of privacy" while visiting a home other than their own and therefore could not invoke constitutional protections against unreasonable searches by police. (Under other court rulings, however, overnight guests still may be able to have somewhat higher expectations of privacy.)[1]

Today, for the most part, the legal remedies for private-sector invasions of privacy are practically nonexistent. The record of court judgments is a roll call of futility:

- A woman who was publicly identified by the *Des Moines Register* as having been subjected to forced sterilization lost when she sued for invasion of privacy.[2]

- The courts also sided with a Georgia newspaper that ran a picture of the partially decomposed, chained body of a murdered fourteen-year-old girl. Even though the paper went so far as to offer for sale grisly photographs of the girl's body, the parents' claim that their privacy was violated was rejected on the grounds the pictures were "newsworthy."[3]

- In New York, the state's highest court rejected an invasion of privacy suit by a female patient at a private psychiatric clinic whose picture was taken and published by the *New York Post*. Although the woman was not a public figure, she had the misfortune to be walking one day next to fellow patient Hedda Nussbaum, who was the center of a highly publicized murder case. The New York Court unanimously ruled that the photo was justified by public interest in the story.[4]

- Courts have also been willing to embrace more elastic definitions of newsworthiness to justify invasions of privacy. In one case, CBS photojournalists filmed two construction workers in Manhattan holding hands. Although the man explained that he was married and his friend was engaged to another man, and demanded that the film be destroyed, CBS aired the footage twice in a feature on "Couples in love in New York." In rejecting the privacy suit the court ruled that even the subject matter of "romance" was of sufficient public interest to override the couple's expectations of privacy.[5]

- In 1982, a court in Florida sided with a newspaper that published a picture of a woman who had been kidnapped and stripped naked, as she was rescued and rushed to safety by police, covered only by a dish towel. Terrorized by her assailant, she was further humiliated by the publication of the photograph in the next day's edition of her local paper. Although she won her suit for invasion of privacy at the trial-court level, she lost on appeal. In a remarkable ruling, the judges seemed to argue that the very sordidness of the event justified the invasion of the woman's privacy, describing her abduction and terror as "a typical, exciting, emotion-packed drama to which newspeople and others, are attracted."[6]

- Television cameramen entered a private home and later broadcast footage of a man dying of a heart attack while his stricken family watched helplessly. The cameramen had been riding along with paramedics, and family members later said that they did not even notice the cameras until they saw the horrifying images on television. Although the case seemed to present a clear instance of invasion of privacy, courts ruled that the only person who could sue for invasion was the dead man. Even so, the family sued, arguing that the broadcast of the pictures had been an invasion, and also sued on grounds of intrusion. A trial court threw out all counts. On appeal, the higher court rejected the suit for invasion of privacy based on the broadcast, but allowed the action for intrusion to go ahead. Eventually, the case was settled out of court. Other cases involving media "ride-alongs" have resulted in victories for the plaintiffs. In one case, the court upheld a claim against a New York television station for entering a woman's home with an investigator for the Humane Society. Another judge also allowed a suit against CBS to go to trial for invasion, after reporters entered an apartment with U.S. Secret Service agents. Even though the suspect was not present, the CBS crew recorded pictures of the man's wife and family, as well as the contents of shelves and drawers in the home. Said the judge: "CBS had no greater right than a thief to be in the home."[7]*

THE CONSTITUTIONAL RIGHT
OF PRIVACY

The word "privacy" does not appear in the U.S. Constitution, an omission that has led some conservative critics to question whether there is any constitutional right to privacy. Even as the Court explicitly recognized the right of privacy in the 1960s, prominent jurists insisted that the court was simply manufacturing the right out of whole legal cloth. "I like my privacy as well as the next one," wrote Justice Hugo Black, "but I am nevertheless compelled to admit that the government has a right to invade it unless prohibited by some specific constitutional provision." Similarly, Justice Potter Stewart insisted, "I can find no such general right of privacy in the Bill of Rights, in any other part of the Constitution, or in any case before decided by this Court."[8]

---

*In 1999, the Supreme Court sharply limited the practice of media ride-alongs, by allowing similar suits for invasion of privacy.

Despite the skeptics, however, there is no way to gainsay the pedigree of privacy rights both in English law and the experience of the American colonies. One of the catalyzing issues of the Revolution was the government's sweeping claims of the right to search houses for antigovernment literature, contraband, or to enforce tax laws. The use of the so-called "general warrant" led directly to the Fourth Amendment, with its prohibition of illegal searches and seizures. The Founders recognized a powerful connection between private property and political freedom and were animated by the conviction that the reach of the government should cease at the door of a man's home. As William Pitt the Elder, the Earl of Chatham, put it famously: "The poorest man may in his cottage bid defiance to the Crown. It may be frail—its roof may shake—the wind may enter—the rain may enter—but the King of England cannot enter—all his force dares not cross the threshold of the ruined tenement!"[9]

Such claims were vindicated by English courts in several celebrated cases, including the prosecution of John Wilkes, the publisher of an anonymous antigovernment pamphlet, known as the "North Briton." Wilkes was arrested after the secretary of state, Lord Halifax, issued a "general warrant" commanding the arrest of anyone involved in putting out the subversive sheet. At his trial, Wilkes denounced what he called "ridiculous warrants against the whole English nation," and won a landmark victory in the Court of Common Pleas. Declared Chief Justice Pratt, "to enter a man's house by virtue of a nameless warrant, in order to procure evidence, is worse than the Spanish Inquisition. . . ."

Similarly, in a case involving a clerk named John Entick at an antigovernment newspaper, the British Court invoked the right of property to denounce the seizure of papers and books under the Government's warrant:

> The great end for which men entered into society was to secure their property . . . By the laws of England, every invasion of private property, be it ever so minute, is a trespass. No man can set his foot upon my ground without my license. . . .
>
> Papers are the owner's goods and chattels; they are his dearest property . . . where private papers are removed and carried away the secret nature of those goods will be an aggravation to the trespass, and demand more considerable damages in that respect.

American colonists were outraged by what were known as "writs of assistance" used by the officers of the crown to enforce searches of private homes. In 1761, James Otis passionately argued against the renewal of the writs, which had expired on the death of King George II. In language that would echo in the Declaration of Independence and later in the Bill of Rights, Otis declared the writs:

> the worst instrument of arbitrary power, the most destructive of English liberty and the fundamental principals of law that ever was found in an English lawbook. . . . It is a power that places the liberty of every man in the hands of every petty officer. . . .
>
> Now, one of the most essential branches of English liberty is the freedom of one's house. A man's house is his castle, and whilst he is quiet, he is as well guarded as a prince in his castle. This writ, if it should be declared legal, would totally annihilate his privilege.

As the constitutional law developed, the connections between property and privacy strengthened, but privacy also came to be associated with other liberty interests as well. In *Pierce* v. *Society of Sisters*, for example, the Court struck down laws requiring all students to attend public schools. Citing what could be construed as a right of privacy, the Court said that the Constitution "excludes any general power of the state to standardize its children by forcing them to accept instruction from public teachers only. The child is not the mere creature of the state; those who nurture him and direct his destiny have the right, coupled with the high duty, to recognize and prepare for him additional obligations."[10] In *Meyer* v. *Nebraska,* the Court overturned a law barring the teaching of a language other than English—again on the ground that it violated personal autonomy. In 1942, the Court struck down an Oklahoma law that provided for the mandatory sterilization of recidivists. Writing for the majority, Justice William O. Douglas said that the sterilization law "involves one of the basic civil rights of man. Marriage and procreation are fundamental to the very existence and survival of the race."

The courts also recognized privacy as an essential element in preserving political freedom, including the right of disputants to maintain their anonymity. "From the very beginning of the Republic," noted Burt Neuborne, "we have recognized that a sense of anonymity vis a vis the government was a practical precondition to the proper functioning of a political democracy." Both supporters and opponents of the ratification of the Constitution, for example, carried on their debates under pseudonyms. Over the years, at least six presidents, fifteen cabinet members, and thirty-four congressmen published anonymous political tracts. Recognizing an explicit right to privacy in political associations, in 1958 the U.S. Supreme Court struck down Alabama's attempt to compel the NAACP to disclose its membership lists. Ruling that "the right of the members to pursue their lawful private interest privately and to associate with others" might be chilled by the state's attempts to compel the organization's membership lists, the Court declared: "This Court has recognized the vital relationship between freedom to associate and privacy in one's associations. . . . Inviolability of privacy in group associations may in many circumstances be indispensable to preservation of freedom of association . . . "[11] Two years later, in 1960, the Court overturned a law banning anonymous pamphlets.[12]

As the Court elaborated its understanding of privacy, several themes emerged. Privacy involved not only restricting access to one's person and the individual's right to associate with others, but also restricting information about oneself and, most controversially, the right to make decisions about matters that went to the heart of one's sense of identity. Covered under the umbrella of privacy were the individual's choice of a marriage partner, decisions about procreation, about how one raised children, and what one read.

In other cases, though, the Court was slow to apply constitutional principles to changing technology, most notably in its 1928 *Olmstead* ruling that Fourth Amendment protections did not extend to wiretapping.[13] Even so, the famous dissent by Justice Brandeis in that case laid the foundation for the later development of privacy rights in general. *Olmstead* was finally overturned in the 1960s, when the justices recognized that the right to privacy included not only tangible property but also "an individual's communications, personality, politics, and thoughts."

It was not until 1965, in *Griswold* v. *Connecticut*, a case involving the distribution of contraceptives, that the Supreme Court formally recognized a right of privacy in the Constitution.[14] For conservative critics like Judge Robert Bork, the discovery (he would say the invention) of a constitutional right to privacy by the Supreme Court was an egregious example of the imperial judiciary writing its own preconceptions into law. It was also the means by which the Court had "adopted an extreme individualistic phi-losophy" of moral relativism. Indeed, privacy's constitutional nativity was notably inauspicious. Writing for the majority in *Griswold*, Justice William O. Douglas sought to cast the Court's decision as a defense of traditional values, especially the sanctity of marriage.

But where was it in the Constitution? Here Douglas stumbled, fa-mously and fatuously. In language that has become notorious for its pre-tentiousness, Douglas argued that "specific guarantees in the Bill of Rights have penumbras, formed by emanations from those guarantees that give them life and substance." Unfortunately for privacy, it has never quite been able to shake free of the shadow of those "emanations" and "penum-bras," or from the suspicion that they were simply covers for what Bork called "the privatization of morality." From *Griswold* to *Roe* v. *Wade,* the right to privacy would be entangled in the politics of sexuality, contracep-tion, and abortion. Inevitably, it was implicated in the cultural divisions in American society. For Bork, the Court's creation of a right to privacy "has little to do with privacy but a great deal to do with the freedom of the in-dividual from moral regulation."[15]

Leaving aside the complex emotional politics surrounding abortion, was the right of privacy merely an invention of an activist Court? Unfortu-nately, Justice Douglas's vaporings about "penumbras" and "emanations" clouded the issue. Critics like Bork argued that there could be no right of privacy because none is specified in the Constitution. Douglas took a very different tack, arguing that there are rights that are so fundamental that they predate the Constitution. "We deal with a right of privacy older than the Bill of Rights—older than our political parties, older than our schools system," Douglas declared. Even though Douglas's argument was occa-sionally sloppy, he seemed to be appealing to the tradition of natural law, an approach that ought not be rejected out of hand by conservatives.

Under that tradition, the Constitution is not seen as conferring our rights upon us. Instead, those fundamental rights derive from God or from nature. Indeed, many conservatives view the Constitution as a document that *limits* the scope of government, enumerating the few powers granted to it and the many actions denied to it. It is not the fount of our rights. We would still have the right to worship God freely even if it were not granted to us in the First Amendment. We do not have a right to property merely because the government cedes it to us, but because it is a fundamental, preexisting right. Our freedom does not proceed from a conditional grant from the Constitution, but rather the other way around. Free men establish the Constitution to protect their freedoms, which derive from God.

Bork gives relatively short shrift in his own writings to the "natural law," but his disdain for the idea of natural rights seems to lead him toward a positivistic approach to the law. Unless a right is granted in print, it does not exist, or is at least not enforceable in the constitutional system. Indeed, Bork seems unable to find constitutional protection for the right to procreate because it is not specified in the document. Although Bork takes a strict view of the Constitution itself, he seems to suggest a rather expansive view of what government is permitted to do. He seems to hold that majorities acting through the democratic process have the right to pass any measure reflecting their values and use the force of law to impose them on individuals, unless a right specifically enumerated in the Constitution is violated. But the Constitution was not designed to exhaustively define the rights of its citizens. In particular, the Ninth Amendment states: "The enumeration in the Constitution of certain rights shall not be construed to deny or disparage others retained by the people." That certainly can be read as a reference to the rights conferred on free men by natural law. It was, moreover, written by men with a keen sense of the inviolability of their homes, families, and personal affairs by the government. They understood the need to draw a strong wall between the public and private realms because they understood the sacred links between private property and freedom and between privacy and citizenship.

PRIVACY'S HIGH WATERMARK

The Court's ruling in *Griswold* was followed in short order by a series of cases that continued to expand the zone of constitutionally protected privacy. In *Loving* v. *Virginia*,[16] the Court overturned bans on interracial marriage; in *Stanley* v. *Georgia,* the Court held that individuals could not be arrested for possessing obscene materials in their home. "If the First Amendment means anything," wrote Justice Thurgood Marshall, "it means that a State cannot tell a man, sitting alone in his house, what books he may read or what films he may watch."[17]

In *Griswold,* the Court had affirmed the right of married *couples* to purchase contraceptives, but the Court quickly shifted its emphasis in the *Eisenstadt* case, which overturned laws against the sale of contraceptives to single people as well. The *Griswold* Court had emphasized the importance of privacy in support of traditional marriage and the family. But in *Eisenstadt*, the Court broke the link between marriage and the right of privacy, instead vesting it in the autonomous individual. Clearly laying the ground for the expansion of the "zone of privacy" in what would become *Roe* v. *Wade*, Justice William Brennan declared, "If the right of privacy means anything, it is the right of the individual, married or single, to be free from unwarranted governmental intrusion into matters so fundamentally affecting a person as the decision whether to bear or beget a child."[18]

In *Roe* v. *Wade*, the Ninth Circuit Court of Appeals overturned Texas' abortion laws, citing the Ninth Amendment's reservation of rights as the locus of the constitutional right to privacy.[19] Taking a somewhat different tack, the Supreme Court ruled that the right of privacy involved in abortions was found in the Fourteenth Amendment's concept of personal liberty and restrictions on state action. The majority argued that the Court had long recognized a right of personal privacy, but that only those personal rights that were "fundamental" or "implicit in the concept of ordered liberty" were included in the guarantee of privacy. Citing cases that had extended this definition to activities related to marriage, procreation, contraception, family relationship, child rearing and education, the Court concluded that the right was broad enough to cover a woman's decision to terminate a pregnancy.

In his dissent, Justice William Rehnquist challenged both the majority's interpretation of the right of privacy and its finding that abortion involved a private decision. Noting that the Texas law had banned abortions by licensed physicians, Rehnquist argued, "A transaction resulting in an operation such as this is not 'private' in the ordinary usage of that word. Nor is the 'privacy' that the Court finds here even a distant relative of the freedom from searches or seizures protected by the Fourth Amendment to the Constitution, which the court has referred to as embodying a right to privacy. . . . " Setting the stage for decades of debate over the parameters of the right of privacy, Rehnquist rejected the Court's development of privacy as a "fundamental" personal right. He was also suggesting that the relationship between a physician and patient should not be considered "private." Indeed, the Court has never explicitly recognized the confidentiality of patient-doctor relations, an omission that seems even more puzzling in light of the underlying finding of the *Roe* Court.

Rehnquist also highlighted one of the striking weaknesses of the *Roe* decision: the attempt to locate the right of privacy in the Fourteenth Amendment's liberty clause. Rather than articulating the historical, legal, and philosophical rationale for privacy as a specific and distinct constitutional value, the Court played into the hands of critics who saw its declaration of "privacy" as a legal confusion for liberty in general. Indeed, the Court's conflation of liberty and privacy merely fed suspicions that it was inventing the right from whole cloth. Unfortunately, the Court's failure to make a compelling and principled case for privacy would shadow the debate for years to come.

ROLLING BACK PRIVACY

In 1977, in *Moore* v. *City of East Cleveland,* the Court extended privacy rights to family composition and living arrangements.[20] But, unfortunately, privacy had already reached its high-water mark. In a series of rulings, the justices seemed to back away from the implications of their earlier privacy rulings. In 1976, for example, the Court ruled 5 to 3 that the Constitution did not give individuals a right to privacy in their bank records. The next year, the Court similarly ruled that individuals could not expect privacy in their long-distance phone bills, and a decade later ruled that Americans did not have a constitutional right of privacy in their garbage.[21]

Reflecting growing skepticism even about the individual's right of privacy in intimate relations, the Court upheld a Georgia law making the act of sodomy a crime, even between consenting adults. The case involved more than a clash of cultural values: It marked sharply diverging attitudes toward the way that privacy should be understood and applied to intimate personal decisions. Pursuing an unrelated case, police found a man named Michael Hardwick performing a sexual act on another male in his bedroom. Georgia's law made it a crime any time a person "performs or submits to any sexual act involving the sexual organs of one persona and the mouth or anus of another." Citing the Court's privacy rulings, Hardwick appealed his conviction all the way to the Supreme Court.[22]

Writing for the Court, Justice Byron White said: "The issue presented is whether the Federal Constitution confers a fundamental right upon homosexuals to engage in sodomy and hence invalidates the laws of the many States that still make such conduct illegal and have done so for a very long time."

But the majority seems to have misconstrued the real issue. In fact, the Georgia statute did not make any distinction at all between homosexual and heterosexual behavior or between married and unmarried couples. Trying to distinguish the case from its previous rulings, the Court argued that no connection between family, marriage, or procreation on the one hand and homosexual conduct on the other had been demonstrated. But the *Eisenstadt* case had already held that the right to use contraception was not limited to married couples or "families." In its *Bowers* ruling, the Court seemed to be saying that it was willing to protect various forms of intimacy and interpersonal relationships—but not "nontraditional consensual intimate sexuality." The distinction was not persuasive to the minority, who cited the Court's earlier rulings involving privacy and pornography: "Only the most willful blindness could obscure the fact that sexual intimacy is a 'sensitive, key relationship of human experience, central to family life, community welfare, and the development of human personality.' "

Conservative critics, including Judge Robert Bork, have been especially critical of the dissenters in *Bowers* for insisting "that a person belongs to himself and not others nor to society as a whole." But one does not have to accept a radically individualistic posture to recognize that the rightful issue before the court was (to paraphrase one notable critic of the decision) not what Michael Hardwick was doing, but what the police were doing in his bedroom in the first place!

In his decision in *Roe* v. *Wade,* Justice Harry Blackmun had failed to flesh out a compelling case for a constitutional right of privacy. Perhaps learning from that lapse, his dissent in *Bowers* relied more heavily on the Fourth Amendment's protection of the sanctity of the private home. "Just as the right to privacy is more than the mere aggregation of a number of entitlements to engage in specific behavior," he wrote in dissent, "so too, protecting the physical integrity of the home is more than merely a means of protecting specific activities that often take place there." Drawing a connection between privacy and private property, Blackmun quoted Justice Brandeis's admonition that the essence of a Fourth Amendment violation is not the 'breaking of [a person's] doors, and the rummaging of his drawers,' but rather is 'the invasion of his indefeasible right of personal security, personal liberty and private property.'" Citing the Fourth Amendment's protection of the right of the people to be secure in their homes as "perhaps the most 'textual' of the various constitutional provisions that inform our understanding of the right to privacy," Blackmun insisted that "the right of an individual to conduct intimate relationships in the intimacy of his or her own home seems to me to be at the heart of the Constitution's protection of privacy."

This is not to suggest, of course, that society has no rights whatsoever to regulate private behavior. Recognizing the right to engage in intimate relations does not invalidate laws against abuse, bigamy, or incest, for example, because those acts can be measured against the public harms that result. Setting out a definition of the state's right to legislate behavior, John Stuart Mill declared "that the only purpose for which power can be rightfully exercised over any member of a civilized community, against his will, is to prevent harm to others. His own good, either physical or moral, is not a sufficient warrant." In an interesting twist in the law of privacy, twelve years after *Bowers,* the Georgia Supreme Court would strike down the same antisodomy statute, on the grounds that it violated the state constitution's guarantee of a right to privacy. Writing for the state's high court in 1998, Chief Justice Robert Benham noted that Georgia's high court had recognized a constitutionally protected right to privacy sixty years before the U.S. Supreme Court recognized the right in *Griswold.* Writing in 1998, the justices declared: "We cannot think of any other activity that reasonable persons would rank as more private and more deserving of protection from governmental interference than consensual, private, adult sexual activity." The justices ruled that "such activity is at the heart of the Georgia Constitution's protection of the right of privacy."[23]

THE RIGHT TO BE LET ALONE

The right of privacy is not merely a constitutional right; it also exists in the law of torts. As a cause of civil action, the right to privacy is only a little over a century old and can be traced to a single, extraordinarily influential law-review article by Samuel Warren and Louis D. Brandeis. Citing "recent inventions and business methods," Warren and Brandeis set out to create what they recognized was a wholly new right, but one they saw as a natural evolution of existing common law and legal principles.[24] Although their project was largely unsuccessful in the long run, Brandeis and Warren shaped the development of the law for decades, even if they did not actually invent the idea that privacy meant the "right to be let alone." That honor goes to Judge Thomas M. Cooley, whose treatise on torts insisted that "the right to one's person may be said to be a right of complete immunity to be let alone. . . ."[25]

Although the constitutional right to privacy grew out of outrage against tyrannical overreaching government, the development of tort law was a reaction to the outrages of an increasingly active and prying press, especially the urban newspapers that grew up in the decades after the Civil War. "Instantaneous photographs and newspaper enterprise have invaded the sacred precincts of private and domestic life," they complained, "and numerous mechanical devices threaten to make good the prediction that 'what is whispered in the closet shall be proclaimed from the house-tops.' "

Warren and Brandeis recognized the limits of constitutional protections. Prohibitions of illegal searches and intrusions by the state meant little if private citizens had no recourse against any of the modern threats to the integrity of their personal life. "The common law has always recognized a man's house is his castle, impregnable, often, even to its own officers engaged in the execution of its commands. Shall the courts thus close the front entrance to constituted authority, and open wide the back door to idle or prurient curiosity?"

With a passion that has led some commentators to suspect a personal grievance, Warren and Brandeis described a contemporary press that "is overstepping in every direction the obvious bounds of propriety and of decency. Gossip is no longer the resource of the idle and the vicious, but has become a trade, which is pursued with industry as well as effrontery. . . . In this, as in other branches of commerce, the supply creates the demand. Each crop of unseemly gossip, thus harvested, becomes the seed of more, and, in direct proportion to its circulation, results in a lowering of social standards and of morality."

Warren and Brandeis argued that "political, social, and economic changes entail the recognition of new rights," and that "the common law . . . grows to meet the demands of society." The right to life had gradually evolved to "mean the right to enjoy life—the right to be let alone; the right to liberty secures the exercise of extensive civil privileges; and the term 'property' has grown to comprise every form of possession—intangible as well as tangible." As the law had come to recognize the value of "sensations" and emotions, the legal protections against actual bodily injury were also extended, from actual injury to the threats of injury. Much later came protections against "noises, odor, against dust and smoke. . . . the law of nuisance was developed. So regard for human emotions soon extended the scope of personal immunity beyond the body of the individual. His reputation, the standing among his fellow-men, was considered, and the law of slander and libel arose . . . "

For Warren and Brandeis, this gradual adaptation and growth pointed inevitably toward legal protections designed to protect other nonphysical values, including the "intense intellectual and emotional life" of modern civilization. Although they noted that their right of privacy had a superficial resemblance to libel and slander in that it protected a person's reputation, they insisted that the damages in cases of libel were of material nature—the damage they sought to protect through privacy were "feelings." They insisted that the law should protect "the privacy of private life" by giving individuals control over whether, how, and to what extent their thoughts, sentiments, and likenesses would be disseminated to the public. Unlike libel or slander cases, they envisioned invasion-of-privacy suits in which neither the truth of the matter published nor the absence of malice would be defenses. "It is not for injury to the individual's character that redress or prevention is sought," they explained, "but for the injury to the right of privacy."

Because personal facts included in personal letters or manuscripts were of no monetary value at all, they also sought to distinguish the new right from traditional property rights. It was not the intellectual property that was being protected in such letters, they argued, but the "domestic occurrence." Setting out their new legal standard, Warren and Brandeis wrote: "The principle which protects personal writings and all other personal productions, not against theft and physical appropriation, but against publication in any form, is in reality, not the principle of private property, but that of *an inviolate personality.*" Such protection was not limited to any specific medium. The same protections applied to any expression, whether it was a manuscript, a song, a sonata, or a pantomime. The right of privacy protected the peace of mind and relief that a person enjoyed from the knowledge that he had the right to prevent the publication of such works. "If, then, the decisions indicate a general right to privacy for thoughts, emotions, and sensations, these should receive the same protection, whether expressed in writing, or in conduct, in conversation, in attitudes, or in facial expression." These were not rights arising from contracts or breaches of trust, but were "rights as against the world."

"The principle which protects personal writings and any other products of the intellect or of the emotion is the right of privacy."

"In general," they wrote, the law should allow the repression of matters concerning "the private life, habits, acts, and relations of an individual, and have no legitimate connection with his fitness for a public office which he seeks or for which he is suggested, or for any public or quasi public position which he seeks or for which he is suggested and have no legitimate relation to or bearing upon any act done by him in a public or quasi public capacity."

But the exemption for public office seekers was not absolute. Even public figures, they insisted, deserved some degree of privacy. "Some things all men alike are entitled to be kept from popular curiosity whether in public life or not, while others are only private because the persons concerned have not assumed a position which makes their doings legitimate matters of public investigation."

In retrospect, several factors proved to be almost insuperable barriers to Warren's and Brandeis's proposal. The first was perhaps the most obvious: by definition a lawsuit over an invasion of privacy requires the victim to place himself or herself before a public court. As a practical matter, those individuals most concerned to protect their privacy would be least likely to endure the exposure and rigors of litigation. A man who files a lawsuit claiming that his private life was invaded is likely to make matters even worse, attracting even more publicity to issues that, by definition, he regards as being especially sensitive. But the second problem was more fundamental.

Warren and Brandeis sought to use the weapon of the law to protect "spiritual" values. "It now appears that this project was ill-fated from the start," Rochelle Gurstein remarked, "because of the untranslatability of the one language into the other."[26] Litigation is an adversarial process that sets up the judiciary as an arbiter of a clash of rights. Inevitably, this both narrowed and distorted protections designed to protect and shield the "inviolate personality." This became clear in the early cases involving the tort of privacy invasion.

One of the cases involved a woman named Roberson whose picture was used without her permission by a milling company in its advertisements. The New York courts flatly rejected Warren's and Brandeis's theory that she should be compensated for her humiliation. In reaction, New

York's legislature passed its first privacy measure, a law that prohibited the use of the name or likeness of any person for "advertising purposes or for the purposes of trade." As it turned out, though, the legislation was a disaster for privacy law. Not only was it exceptionally narrow but, as Arthur Miller has noted, the "courts have read the statute as castrating their freedom to remedy privacy invasions in other situations."[27]

The new right of privacy fared better in Georgia, where a 1904 case known as *Pavesich v. New England Mutual Life Insurance Co.* provided the basis for what was to become the leading case establishing the right that Warren and Brandeis had envisioned. The case centered on an advertisement for New England Mutual Life, featuring a picture of a man named Paolo Pavesich. In the ad, Pavesich was depicted as a happy and healthy man who undoubtedly owed his fine fettle to the fact that he had purchased a policy from New England Mutual Life. Next to Pavesich's picture was a sickly, sloppily dressed figure, illustrative of the sort of man who would pass up the company's coverage. Pavesich not only had never purchased a policy from the company, but he had also never given the company permission to use his picture. In ruling for Pavesich, Judge Cobb found precedents for a constitutional right of privacy in the Fourth and Fourteenth amendments, and inferred privacy protections from constitutional guarantees of the protection of life, liberty, and happiness. "The right of privacy is embraced within the absolute rights of personal security and personal liberty," Cobb wrote in his decision.

> Liberty includes the right to live as one will, so long as that will does not interfere with the rights of another or of the public. One may desire to live a life of seclusion; another may live a life of publicity; still another may wish a life of privacy as to certain matters and of publicity to others. The right of one to exhibit himself to the public, and in a proper manner is embraced within the right of personal liberty. . . . Each is entitled to liberty of choice as to his manner of life, and neither an individual nor the public has a right to arbitrarily take away his liberty.[28]

Judge Cobb did not ground privacy rights in property rights. Instead, he cited other laws that stamped "the unbreakable seal of privacy" upon communications between husband and wife and attorney and client, as precedents not only for the right of privacy, but of the principle that "for the public good, some matters of private concern are not to be made public even with the consent of those involved." Despite such a ringing victory, the right of privacy never developed as Warren and Brandeis had hoped. This is not to say that the invasion of privacy is not recognized as a legitimate cause of action. To the contrary, many states have explicit privacy laws, and the vast majority have secured the right of persons to file suits for invasions of privacy. Indeed, four separate causes of privacy action are recognized:

1. Appropriation of another person's name or likeness for personal advantage;
2. Intrusion upon a person's seclusion, or solitude, or into private affairs;
3. Public disclosure of embarrassing personal facts;
4. Publicity that places a person in a false light.[29]

But, as Arthur Miller noted some years ago, the law of privacy has been "so fluid that a judge once compared privacy doctrines to a 'haystack in a hurricane.'"[30] Though the courts have been willing to uphold claims of actual intrusion, they have been decidedly reluctant to sanction the media for publishing or picturing private facts, or even for using a person's likeness without his or her consent. (Legal protections have proven so ineffectual that radio talk maven Dr. Laura Schlessinger was unable to use privacy laws to stop nude pictures of herself from being broadcast on the Internet.)[31]

Some notable invasion of privacy cases have actually resulted in significant rollbacks in the right of privacy. In North Carolina the Supreme Court rejected the private facts tort in the state in a case involving a story revealing an adoption. The U.S. Supreme Court has never decided whether truthful publication was always constitutionally protected, but the trend of the decisions has been to give the press ever greater latitude. The North Carolina high court went further, flatly declaring that "at the very best," lawsuits based on the publication of *truthful* private facts were "constitutionally suspect."[32]

Although the earliest privacy cases had centered on the improper appropriation of a person's image or likeness, even that tort has had a shaky track record. When a picture of a black professional named Clarence Arrington was used on the cover of the *New York Times Magazine* to illustrate a story on the black middle class, Arrington sued the paper, citing the state's laws barring the use of a private individual's image for commercial purposes. His case was rejected by an appeals court, which took the occasion to opine: "An inability to vindicate a person's predilection for greater privacy may be part of the price every person must be prepared to pay for a society in which information and opinion flow freely."[33] In an ironic twist however, the court said that though Arrington could not sue the newspaper, the actual photographer and agent might be liable for legal action—a ruling that resulted in the New York legislature further weakening the state's privacy law, by exempting photographers and their agents.

What went wrong?

Inevitably, the push for privacy rights also clashed with free-press rights; there was no way to enforce the kind of repressions that Warren and Brandeis advocated without significantly violating established rights of speech and of the press. Privacy rights also became entangled in both the legal and cultural ambivalence over how to balance privacy with matters of public interest. "We are loath to believe," one nineteenth-century court ruled, "that the man who makes himself useful to mankind surrenders any right of privacy thereby."[34] The rest of society was not so sure.

6

■

Medical Privacy

What I may see or hear in the course of the treatment or even outside of the treatment in regard to the life of men, which on no account one must spread abroad, I will keep to myself holding such things shameful to be spoken about.

——Hippocratic Oath: Fifth century B.C.E.

A physician should respect confidences and protect the patient's secrets. In protecting a patient's secrets, he must be more insistent than the patient himself.

——Hal Abbas (Ahwazi), advice to a physician, 10th century C.E.

I will respect the secrets which are confided in me, even after the patient has died.

——Geneva Declaration, World Medical Association, 1940

If there is one area of life where most Americans expect privacy, it is in their relationship with their doctors. A 1993 Louis Harris poll found that 96 percent of Americans thought that federal legislation should designate personal medical information as "sensitive" and impose penalties for its unauthorized disclosure. An equally overwhelming 96 percent said that it was important that individuals have the legal right to obtain a copy of their own medical records.[1] In addition:

- 85 percent said that protecting the confidentiality of medical records was "absolutely essential" or "very important" in any health-care reform.

- 75 percent said they were worried that medical information from a computerized national health information system would be used for many nonhealth purposes. More than one-third (38 percent) were "very concerned."
- 60 percent believed that it was not acceptable for their medical data to be given to direct marketers by their pharmacists without their permission.
- 64 percent objected to medical researchers using their records for studies, unless they first got a patient's consent.
- 56 percent endorsed comprehensive legislation protecting the privacy of medical records "as opposed to continuing with existing state and federal laws and professional standards."*

The findings were consistent with a 1994 ACLU poll that found more than two-thirds of Americans (69 percent) thought that it was none of the employer's business whether they have ever seen a psychiatrist or a counselor. Three-quarters of the respondents in that survey said they were concerned either a "great deal" or a "fair amount" about insurance companies putting their medical records into a computer database.[2]

Although most patients believe that their relationship with their physician is confidential—analogous to their relationship with a priest or a lawyer—the reality is very different. No federal law protects the confidentiality of medical information or prevents its transfer, or even sale. In fact, no federal law even gives patients the right to see their *own* medical file. (Thirty-four states do have law covering the confidentiality of medical records, but only twenty-eight give patients the right to review and correct their own files.)[3]

In several highly publicized cases, celebrities and politicians ranging

---

*Other findings of the poll: 41 percent expressed concern that medical claims submitted under an employer health plan may be seen by their employer and used to affect their job opportunities; 86 percent favored creating a "national medical privacy board" to "hold hearings, issue regulations, and enforce standards" for protecting medical information privacy; 25 percent report that they or a member of their family have personally paid for a medical test, treatment, or counseling rather than submit a bill or claim under a health-care plan or program. (Source: Harris Equifax, "Health Information Privacy Survey," 1993.)

from tennis star Arthur Ashe and heavyweight boxer Tommy Morrison to members of Congress have had intimate details of their medical records leaked. They are hardly alone.

- When one Florida woman complained to a state consumer agency that she had been overcharged by her gynecologist, the doctor mailed state officials a complete summary of her medical history, which included revelations of her three abortions and genital herpes. When she sued for the invasion of her privacy, the courts ruled that the law provided no sanction against the doctor's conduct.[4]
- In Maryland, a local banker who also sat on the state's public health commission cross-checked his list of bank loans with the records of people who had cancer—and then canceled the loans of the cancer patients.[5]
- In Maryland, state workers sold the names and Social Security numbers of Medicaid recipients to HMO recruiters. A few years ago, the medical records of two million New England residents, including every senior citizen from the region's six states, were turned over to a private consultant working on a study for a government agency.
- When a Nevada woman booted up the used PC she had purchased for $159 at an Internet computer auction, she was stunned to find 2,000 patient records from a pharmacy in Tempe, Arizona. Stored on the computer's hard disk were not only the names of patients, but also their home addresses, Social Security numbers, and the list of every medicine they had purchased from the pharmacy. There, scrolling across the screen, were the records of patients who had prescriptions for AZT—used by patients with AIDS—as well as psychotropic and antidepressant drugs such as Prozac and Elavil, prescriptions for Antabuse, a drug for alcoholics, and narcotics such as Darvon and Darvocet. As it turned out, Arizona was one of the states that had no legal requirements that such data be destroyed before the computers could be resold. Later reports indicated that as many as thirty-four other computers that may also have carried similar medical information had also been sold. "I was alarmed at seeing the patient records," the woman said later. "I know a lot of people who would be devastated if they knew this kind of information was floating around." Even so, the incident might never have become known

if not for the fact that the woman who discovered it was especially sensitive to the issue of medical confidentiality, since she had herself once lost a job after her employer discovered she had multiple sclerosis.[6]

- A former employee of a Massachusetts health plan named Mark Hudson was similarly startled during a computer training class when he found that he could access the records of any subscriber. When he typed in his own name, he found himself looking at the complete record of his own psychiatric treatment including the type and dosage of the antidepressant drug he was taking. "I can tell you unequivocally," Hudson said, "that patient confidentiality is not eroding—it can't erode, because it's simply nonexistent."[7]

- A psychiatrist was appalled when he got a letter from a benefits-management company asking him specifically about the treatment of one of his patients, accompanied by a complete printout of his patient's prescription record. The benefits firm wanted to know why he had been prescribing his patient an antianxiety drug and whether such treatment would continue. The woman worked for one of the nation's largest drug chains, CVS, which was also the parent company of the benefits firm, PharmaCare. To the woman's doctor, it was chilling that CVS was looking through its prescription databases to monitor the medications being taken by its own employees. But CVS justified the practice by saying that it was simply trying to "improve the quality of care to our employees and to contain our benefit costs."[8]

- Explicit promises of confidentiality are often breached. Even though one woman's records of her stay at an alcoholism treatment center were clearly labeled "CONFIDENTIAL: DO NOT REPRODUCE," her doctor released the records when the woman's medical records were subpoenaed as part of an unrelated lawsuit.[9]

What had been a latent problem—society's casual approach to protecting medical privacy—has become an acute one, especially as those records are computerized and shared among linked databases across the country. New technology dramatically expands the potential for abuse. "Data is like a prostitute," says one advocate for the mentally ill. "Once it's on the street, everybody has access to it." Not all of the threats to privacy come from illegal leaks of information. Much of the information that is disseminated is systematic; simply part of the routine that passes your medical information from file to file, where it can be scanned by dozens—or perhaps scores—of people. This would become even easier if the federal government goes ahead with plans to assign every patient a "universal patient identifier" code that would enable a physician—or anyone else—to instantly access all of a patient's medical records.

The National Research Council has warned that the medical records of millions of Americans are vulnerable to abuse, noting that "today there are no strong incentives to safeguard patient information because patients, industry groups and government regulators aren't demanding protection."[10] But the threats are very real. As medical care is increasingly provided in nontraditional settings—outside of hospitals and doctors' offices—patients often have medical records scattered among a number of providers. Not only are records shared routinely among dozens of individuals, such sharing is largely unregulated and often occurs not only without the consent of the patient, but usually without his or her even knowing that it is happening.

How does medicine reconcile this invasion of privacy with the Hippocratic Oath?

"Hippocrates is 2,000 years old," says one executive of a managed-care company. "Medicine isn't one-on-one anymore. It's a team effort."

A short list of those who might have access to a medical file would include HMOs, insurance companies, private and public databases, pharmacists, hospital workers, and employers. Especially in managed care, confidential medical information is shared with a startlingly wide range of providers including insurers, pharmacists, state health organizations, researchers, employers, marketing firms, and pharmaceutical companies. The Medical Information Bureau in Boston maintains files on 15 million people who have applied for various kinds of insurance.

Even as the potential threat grows, the NRC panel found, there were few signs that anything will be done to protect medical privacy. Without a strong public outcry, there are few inducements either for politicians or medical providers to erect "firewalls" to prevent the wholesale leakage of medical data. Not only has privacy become collateral damage in the war against rising health costs, it is continually threatened by new technologies, government regulation, and professional acquiescence. Meanwhile science continues to race ahead of both law and medical ethics. There are some indications that anxieties over breaches of medical privacy may be creating a public-health crisis as patients avoid treatment for diseases and conditions for fear that such information might cost them jobs or insurance.

THE THERAPEUTIC PRIVILEGE

The erosion of privacy has already had dramatic effects in the fields of counseling, psychotherapy, and psychiatry. Here again, we come to another of the sharper paradoxes of modern privacy. Even as the Supreme Court was drawing a shield of privacy around the relationship between therapists and patients, the pressure of technology and economics was tearing it down.

In the 1996 case *Jaffee* v. *Redmond*, the Supreme Court went further toward protecting medical privacy than it had ever gone before, declaring that any communications between a psychotherapist and patient are confidential and could not be subpoenaed or revealed in any federal case. "Like the spousal and attorney-client privileges," Justice John Paul Stevens wrote for the Court, "the psychotherapist-patient privilege is rooted in the imperative need for confidence and trust." Patients who share their innermost secrets with a therapist or a social worker must be "willing to make a frank and complete disclosure of facts, emotions, memories and fears."[11]

The case grew out of a police shooting in 1991. The defendant in the case, Police Officer Mary Lu Redmond, shot and killed a man named Ricky Allen Sr., who allegedly was wielding a knife and threatening another man. Allen's family denied that he was armed and sued the officer, the city, and the police department, alleging that the officer had used deadly force that violated the dead man's civil rights. During the course of the trial, the judge ordered the defendants to turn over the notes of a licensed social worker Officer Redmond had visited for counseling sessions after the shooting. After the therapist refused to turn over the notes, claiming confidentiality, the judge instructed the jury to presume that the notes would have been unfavorable to Redmond's case. Jurors awarded Allen's family $450,000 in damages. The verdict was overturned by the Seventh Circuit Court of Appeals, which ruled that the value of the evidence needed to be weighed against a recognized therapist privilege.

But the Supreme Court went even further, rejecting the "balancing component" and declaring what seemed like blanket federal protection to conversations between therapist and patient. At the heart of its ruling was the Court's declaration that the privacy of conversations with therapists did not merely benefit private individuals, but served clear public ends "since the mental health of the Nation's citizenry, no less than its physical health, is a public good of transcendent importance."*

MAYBE I'LL BE MORE BRAVE...

But what the courts have given, the economics of health care is taking away. In managed care, many therapists are required to report details of their treatment. The more details they provide, the more likely their patients are to get coverage and the therapists to get paid. This means that therapists are asked to divulge extraordinarily sensitive information about the mental state of their patients to insurers: Are they depressed? Are they victims of incest? Do they have dangerous fantasies? In the case of a "utilization review," managed-care agents actually look at the specific files of individual patients, including charts and notes of patients who might be suicidal, wrestling with terrible guilt, bed wetters, or the victims or perpetrators of sexual abuse. Unless the psychiatrist wished to terminate his relationship with the managed-care company—and thus put his income at risk—those patients could not expect their secrets to be protected.

In one case described by the *Washington Post*, a psychiatrist was faced with the ethical dilemma of being asked to open his files to a managed-care provider, even though his patients included a wife beater, a closet homosexual, and "two women who were carrying on long-term extramarital affairs, one of them with a prominent Washington personage."[12] All of the

---

*Justice Anton Scalia dissented, rejecting the idea that the Court should recognize patient-therapist confidentiality:

"Ask the average citizen: would your mental health be more significantly impaired by preventing you from seeing a psychotherapist, or by preventing you from getting advice from your mom? I have little doubt what the answer would be. Yet there is no mother-child privilege.

"I see no reason why she should be enabled both not to admit it in criminal court and to get the benefits of psychotherapy. . . . It seems to me entirely fair to say that is she wishes the benefits of telling the truth, she must also accept the adverse consequences."

patients had signed a consent form, but "the psychiatrist says he was quite certain they wouldn't want to let a stranger rummage through their files and their lives with a fine-toothed comb." The psychiatrist faced a dilemma that pitted his ethics against his livelihood. "I was in a terrible bind," he told the *Post*. If he informed his patients what was happening, it would not only be upsetting to them, they might walk away from their therapy altogether. Even worse, they might threaten to sue him, "although any such attempt at recourse would probably only expose their private lives further."

On the other hand, reported the *Post*, "[I]f the psychiatrist concealed the audit from his patients, he would maintain tranquillity on the couch and protect his relationship with the managed-care company, which might otherwise drop him from the list of physicians it permits its members to consult." It was an awful decision. "Our whole relationship with the patients is supposed to be based on trust," the psychiatrist says. He agonized—and, in the end, chose the path of least resistance, with a guilty conscience. "I have children to put through college," he says. "When I retire, maybe I'll be more brave."

Others have made different, albeit also troubling decisions. Some therapists confess that they have found themselves almost unconsciously steering away from information in their sessions that might prove to be damaging if it made its way into the computerized databases of insurance companies. Others have backed away from patients who are in managed care. Many can recount stories of patients who have dropped out of treatment when they were told that their confidences might not be respected. Other patients have walked out when told that their therapist would have to label them with a mental disorder to justify continued coverage by the insurance company.[13] But medical economics almost demands that therapists violate their patient's privacy as deeply as possible. "The more specific you get," one Baltimore psychiatrist told the *Washington Post*, "the more dirty laundry you give them, the more approvals you get."[14]

The violation of patient privacy has taken a grim toll on both patients and doctors. As many as half of the patients who see therapists now avoid insurance altogether, choosing to pay themselves rather than risk exposure. That, in turn, has dried up the practices of many therapists. A 1997 survey in *Psychotherapy Finances*, a professional newsletter, found that one in five therapists was leaving the profession and that nearly three-quarters had seen their incomes drop.[15]

But what seems to be shocking when applied to the intimate secrets of therapy is routine when it comes to general medical care. Unlike the relationship between therapist and patient, the Supreme Court has never recognized a similar privilege for medical doctors and their patients.

IT'S NOT JUST THE GOWNS
THAT ARE OPEN

Many of the worst abuses of patient privacy occur within hospitals themselves. Hospital employees have been known to spy on one another's medical records, and there have been cases where employees have either leaked or sold medical information. Columbia University professor Paul Clayton estimates that some emergency-room employees make more money from passing information about patients to attorneys in search of clients than they do from their paychecks.

In 1993, an administrator of the University of Wisconsin Hospital became a patient at her own facility. Shortly after her admission, two hospital employees were caught snooping into her computerized medical records. The hospital subsequently toughened its security protocols and protections. But as the *New York Times* noted, the interest in security at the UW Hospital "derived from a fact of hospital life that few outsiders realize: hospital employees, up and down the ranks, are notorious for spying on each other's medical records. They are not necessarily more nosy than other people; they just have more opportunity."[16]

One study found that even within the relatively limited setting of a hospital, more than seventy-five people had legitimate grounds to see any individual patient's medical records.[17] Shortly before the 1992 election, someone leaked hospital records to the *New York Post* about an unsuccessful attempt at suicide by congressional candidate Nydia Velazquez. (She won the election anyway.) In another case, a former hospital employee who sued his former boss for discrimination claims that he walked away with logs describing blood samples taken from 2,000 patients—including those tested for pregnancy, drugs, or HIV. He claims that he kept the logs to document unsafe practices at the hospital, which denies his charges.[18]

Shortly after country-western singer Tammy Wynette checked into the University of Pittsburgh Medical Center in 1995, the *National Enquirer* reported details of her medical condition. The paper's source apparently was a hospital employee who had called up her medical records on the hospital's computer system.[19] In a case that dramatized the ease with which medical data could be misused, the thirteen-year-old daughter of a hospital clerk in Jacksonville, Florida printed out a list of people who had visited the hospital's emergency room and then began making crank calls to the patients—telling them that blood tests showed that they were pregnant or tested positive for AIDS.[20]

Despite the extraordinary sensitivity of a diagnosis that a patient was HIV-positive, the medical community has a sketchy record of protecting the confidentiality of AIDS patients. In 1995, a woman in Tampa, Florida opened a letter from Blue Cross and Blue Shield—to find that she had been sent fourteen pages of an AIDS patient's medical records. The next year, someone mailed a computer disk containing the names of thousands of AIDS patients to the *Tampa Tribune*. The incident set off panicked calls to AIDS support groups from patients fearful of losing reputations, insurance, and jobs. Although no names were ever published, the paper later quoted a computer security consultant, who noted: "It could have easily been posted to an Internet newsgroup. It could have been a worldwide disclosure."[21]

In Boston, a woman was promised confidentiality when she checked into a hospital with an AIDS-related illness. Her medical condition was so sensitive that the woman had spoken of it only with her doctors and close members of her family. But as *Investor's Business Daily* later reported, she was shocked when an acquaintance who worked at the hospital stopped by her room to express concern about her condition. The acquaintance was a secretary at the hospital and was able to read the woman's medical records on the computer system. The secretary told a neighbor, who also came to visit the woman. Shortly afterward, other neighbors also began to ask her about her "battle with AIDS." Even though they undoubtedly had the most compassionate motives, the woman was angered at the breach of her medical privacy. No longer feeling that she could trust her doctors, she cut back her visits and treatment. Although she could sue the hospital for violating her privacy, the loss cannot be repaired.[22]

In Pennsylvania, a pharmacy, which was paid by the transit authority to supply workers' drug benefits, provided the employer with information about workers who spent the most money. After examining the information, an executive determined that one transit worker was taking an AIDS drug and informed his supervisor. The courts rejected the worker's claim that his privacy had been violated, ruling that his employer's business interests outweighed his privacy rights.[23] One appeals court judge dissented from the decision: "I hope I am wrong," he wrote, "but I predict this case will make it easier for employers to disclose their employee's private medical information . . . and to escape constitutional liability."

The line between health care and marketing has also blurred the lines of confidentiality. Early in 1998, the giant pharmacy chain CVS admitted that it was selling information about patients to help drug companies market new medicines. Using its computerized records about the ailments of its customers, CVS provided profiles to direct-marketing firms, who would then target those customers with mailings about the new offerings of the pharmaceutical companies who had cut deals with CVS. The arrangement collapsed after the *Washington Post* reported on it. But such practices remain legal.[24] They also remain lucrative and tempting.

When Medco Containment Services—a large prescription-drug benefit company—merged with pharmaceutical giant Merck & Co., the companies set out to use medical information obtained by the benefit firm to steer doctors and patients toward Merck's products. As Minnesota's Attorney General later noted: "When health plan managers, who are assumed to be promoting cost-containment, can use confidential information to send prescriptions to themselves, you've got the fox guarding the chicken coop."*[25]

WHALEN V. ROE

Typical of the confusion that has dogged the development of privacy rights, the very case that established a constitutional right to informational pri-

---

*As part of a settlement with the attorneys general of seventeen states, Medco was also required to tell consumers "the extent to which confidential information in Medco's consumer files will remain confidential, including the fact that medical histories and prescription drug usage could be made available to the consumer's employers."

vacy was also a setback for the practical right to keep such information private. In terms of constitutional law, the case of *Whalen* v. *Roe* was a landmark: For the first time, the Supreme Court explicitly recognized two distinct types of constitutionally protected privacy rights. The first was the right to privacy established in cases like *Griswold* and later *Roe* v. *Wade,* which found constitutional protections for making intimate decisions about issues such as childbearing, contraception, and abortion. But, the *Whalen* Court ruled, the Constitution also protected "the individual interest in avoiding disclosure of personal matters. . . ."[26]

In that respect it continued the gradual expansion of constitutional protections for privacy. But in upholding New York's centralized drug database—which tracked patients by name—it also marked a broad retreat from the Court's willingness to apply privacy rights to specific cases.

In the mid–1970s, New York State passed a law requiring physicians to identify patients obtaining certain kinds of prescription drugs for inclusion in a statewide database run by the state's Department of Health. Specifically, the database would track prescriptions of so-called Schedule II drugs—narcotics that were legal but had a potential for abuse. The database would include the names of the doctors, as well as the patient's name, address, age, and drug dosage. Under New York's law, the records would be kept in strict confidence and destroyed after five years and public disclosure was limited to a small number of health-department employees and investigators.

Initially, a three-judge District Court blocked the system, ruling that the doctor-patient relation was one of the zones of privacy protected by the Constitution. The law's requirement that doctors report information about their patients to the state, the judges ruled, invaded that private zone with "a needlessly broad sweep." But when the U.S. Supreme Court considered the case, the justices were unanimous in upholding the legality of the medical database along with its reporting requirements.

Essentially, the high court ruled that a centralized database like New York's did indeed pose a threat to privacy, but that under the circumstances, New York's specific plan did not violate the Constitution. In a passage that can only be depressing to advocates of medical privacy, the Court based its ruling, in part, on the fact that New York's violation of medical privacy was really no worse than other ongoing, routine violations of medical privacy.

For years, privacy advocates have warned of the possibility that expectations of privacy would be defined downward as violations became more commonplace. In *Whalen,* they saw their fears confirmed. New York's reporting requirements, the justices wrote, "were not meaningfully distinguishable from a host of other unpleasant invasions of privacy that are associated with many facets of health care." Noting that "some individuals' concern for their own privacy may lead them to avoid or postpone needed medical attention," the Court concluded that nevertheless, "disclosures of private medical information to doctors, to hospital personnel, to insurance companies, and to public health agencies are *often an essential part of modern medical practice even when the disclosure may reflect unfavorably on the character of the patient."* (Emphasis added.)

That seemed to open the doors to a wide array of possible government tracking requirements and databases. But the Court also included a cautionary note:

> We are not unaware of the threat to privacy implicit in the accumulation of vast amounts of personal information in computerized databanks or other massive government files. The collection of taxes, the distribution of welfare and Social Security benefits, the supervision of public health, the direction of our Armed Forces, and the enforcement of the criminal laws all require the orderly preservation of great quantities of information, much of which is personal in character and potentially embarrassing or harmful if disclosed.

It noted that it was *not* deciding how it might rule if there were any "unwarranted disclosure" of the information in the data bank or how it would rule if it was not convinced that a system was not as safe and secure as New York's. Justice William Brennan went even further, noting that the "central storage and easy accessibility of computerized data vastly increase the potential for abuse of that information." He was not prepared, he wrote, to say "that future developments will not demonstrate the necessity of some curb on such technology."

But the Court has not done so, opening the door to the proliferation of state—and possibly federal—medical databases.

THE MEDICAL DATAWEB

In some states, government data banks monitor every time a patient is admitted to a hospital, is injured at work, gets a flu shot, has a sexually transmitted disease, or is considered at risk of delivering a baby prematurely.° Medicaid records are available for five years, and law-enforcement officials do not even need a court order to inspect them.

°State governments now routinely collect information about drug use and other behavioral information for worker's compensation and disability claims, research studies, protective placement, and registries that identify and track specific diseases. A study by the Data Privacy Project found that in Wisconsin, for example, no fewer than thirty separate entities collect and maintain personal health information that is either "identifiable or potentially identifiable." Moreover, such information was freely shared among a host of inside and outside agencies—released and rereleased, used and reused, passed among dozens of entities without patients ever being told or asked for their consent.

In Wisconsin a *partial* list of medical databases maintained by state agencies included the:
Breast and Cervical Cancer Screening Program
Carpal Tunnel Syndrome Program
Childhood Lead Surveillance System
Adult Blood Lead Level Evaluation and Surveillance
Immunization Program
Sexually Transmitted Diseases
AIDS Prevention and Control Program
AIDS Drug Reimbursement Program
AIDS Insurance program
HIV Partner Notification Program
Tuberculosis Prevention and Control Program
Children with Special Care Needs Program
Induced Abortion Reporting System
Live Birth Records and Death Records
Sensitive Death Records
Maternal and Child Health Reports and Data Analysis
Resident-based Nursing Home Survey Data System
Cancer Reporting System
Chronic Diseases Program (such as renal disease and hemophilia)
Wisconsin Care Program, which provides primary health-care services to low-income participants.

Data on confidential workers compensation and unemployment compensation claims, which may include information on illnesses, medical conditions and illnesses.
The state also keeps track of medical information maintained on adoptions, children in foster care, and other individuals under supervision of the Division of Children and

In April 1998, Wisconsin's governor signed into law a bill that will require doctors to report additional information about their patients to a new state data bank, despite warnings that such a move was not only an intrusion into doctor-patient relations, but also a gross violation of medical privacy. The State Medical Society fought hard against the measure, distributing fliers to patients reading: "ALERT: This visit with your doctor will be reported to state bureaucrats without your permission." The doctors warned: "The state should not have the right to know anything about your medical condition. It's your information about your health. Only you

---

Family Services; preadmission screening for the Bureau of Community Mental Health; ambulatory surgery data; inpatient discharge data; confidential medical information collected, reviewed, and analyzed as part of providing crime victim service; data on disabled sportsmen who qualify for reduced recreational fees; occupational health information collected for OSIER; and health-related information collected on children with handicaps for special education services.

The survey found that 40 percent of the data collectors subcontract all or part of their responsibilities to outside parties. The State's Department of Health and Family Services, for example, shares its health information with local hospitals, contract laboratories, researchers, and so-called "utilization review" committees. The survey also found that the department also has "an electronic matching program with Northern Wisconsin Central Credit Union." Other information is shared with University of Wisconsin researchers. Medicaid information is freely shared with the Department of Justice and other law-enforcement groups, while patient-identifiable data is shared with the federal centers for Disease Control, the National Center for Environmental Health, the Agency for Health-care Policy and Research, and the National Center for Environmental Health, the Agency for Health-care Policy and Research, and the National Institute for Health. Confidential vocational rehabilitation information is shared with a wide range of state agencies, including child-support collection agencies, as well as such federal agencies as the Veterans Administration and Social Security Administration.

Despite the rapid growth in the collection of data and the sophistication of the technology, few government agencies have kept pace, resulting in weak or lagging safeguards of the privacy of the information. Only one-third of the health-data systems were safeguarded with computer specifications tailored to their specific needs. The study found few restraints on mixing and matching, and merging this information among other governments or other state parties. Not only are there no extensive limitations on the reuse of patient data, the patients themselves are largely cut out of the process, because there are few chances for patients either to see their records or give their consent about the use of the information. (Carole M. Doeppers, "In the Balance: State Government and Medical Records Privacy," ACLU of Wisconsin Data Privacy Project, May 1998.)

should have a say in whether your sensitive health information is sent to the state."

But the reporting measure was backed both by labor and business, which argued that the data would help them monitor the "health-care marketplace." One prominent business advocate insisted that the bill would help consumers "make better decisions about health-care purchases." Supporters insisted that it would be impossible for anyone to actually identify an individual patient from the information in the new state database. But the state's medical society pointed out that it would not necessarily take a computer hacker to identify a patient's medical records because anyone could figure out the identity of a patient by looking at the information that is left on the insurance claim form. Because it is common practice for insurance companies to use Social Security numbers as their group number, it would take little effort to link the record to an individual patient.[27] As if that were not easy enough, a recently passed health-care bill provides for "universal patient identifiers," which would provide a nationwide link of all of a patient's files. With a universal identifier, all of the information from all of the data banks—both public and private—can be merged into a global dossier that traces every patient contact, every illness, and every drug, from birth until death.

But this is just the beginning.

Computers already have become part of virtually every facet of medicine: from research and the diagnosis of disease and monitoring of patients to managing benefits. They can help epidemiologists track diseases, help discover adverse reactions to drugs, provide physicians accurate clinical histories. An article in *American Medical News* enthusiastically predicts that "the Internet is showing signs that might profoundly change physicians' role in health care, and touts its role in "empowering patients" by putting all of their medical data on-line. One pioneer is the PCASSO program (which stands for Patient Centered Access to Secure Systems Online) at the University of California San Diego School of Medicine, which is testing the proposition that making their medical information available to patients on the Internet will "make them 'providers' of their own care."

What will PCASSO put on the Internet? Just about everything, from hospital admission, discharge, and transfer records to lab and radiology reports, operative reports, and consultation notes for both inpatients and outpatients. If the system's security measures pass muster, supporters argue that "PCASSO would establish the Internet as a safe and appropriate environment for medical records."[28]

It is not hard to see the attraction of many of the new technologies, from the perspective of both health-care providers and patients. Columbia University, for instance, is testing a program that could allow patients with chronic ailments such as asthma to see and add to their electronic medical records. Other doctors have found that their patients like the idea of communicating with them via e-mail at any time. Throughout the country, big health-care providers are downloading medical information into computers and putting those computers on-line. Some 80 percent of hospitals already use the Internet, but only 16 percent of them use it to give personal medical information directly to patients. That number is likely to rise dramatically. One California health-care plan, Kaiser Permante, plans to begin providing lab results over the Internet. Aetna U.S. Healthcare has also announced plans to use the Internet to disseminate information on benefits and the status of claims. Massachusetts-based Harvard Pilgrim Health Care has announced plans for a secure Web site that will allow members to obtain lab results, renew drug prescriptions, and schedule appointments with doctors over the Net.[29]

For some health-care providers, this is an exciting prospect. Supporters of the brave new world of medicine look forward to a time when doctors will be able to diagnose or treat a patient with unusual symptoms by tapping into a national databank, which will identify other patients with the same diseases or history, along with the record of their treatment histories. The alternative, says Dr. Christopher Chute, the head of medical information resources at the Mayo Foundation, is to "rely on folklore and anecdote" in providing treatments. Advocates insist that such systems enhance quality medical care by making medical information "accessible, timely, and accurate."

A possible version of the technological future can be found at the LDS Hospital in Salt Lake City, Utah where the Mormon overseers of the facility have linked together 5,000 microcomputers that monitor, collate, and analyze data from twenty-five clinical areas using sophisticated artificial intelligence systems. The computer system is so thoroughly integrated into every aspect of care that it will page nurses if it comes across lab results it thinks are anomalous. There are terminals beside every bed where physicians can check on X rays and lab tests. An enthusiastic report in the *New*

Republic chronicles how the new systems have helped individual patients by tracking drug reactions and cutting down on simple medical errors and misunderstandings. Of course, as the article noted, the LDS Hospital did not exactly serve a typical community, given that 70 percent of its patients are Mormons and come from a relatively homogenous cultural and economic background. But the LDS technology is genuinely state of the art, including, its architects insist, its protections of privacy. The hospital has built "firewalls" to protect the integrity of the data, using passwords and other keys to prevent unauthorized individuals from looking at the medical records. The system can also trace anyone who improperly accesses information. Hospital officials say that dozens of employees who have violated the stiff confidentiality rules have been "counseled" about their slips; a handful were fired.

Even so, hospital officials admit that for all its sophistication, confidentiality remains the system's Achilles' heel. That much is demonstrated in the otherwise-laudatory *New Republic* article, which noted that the week before the writer arrived at the hospital, "a basketball player from the San Antonio Spurs was admitted with a concussion, and some curious staff members inappropriately perused his records." At the end of the article, the issue comes up again. Writer Katherine Eban Finkelstein was chatting with Dr. Reed Gardner, the chairman of "medical informatics" at LDS, and his wife when "the vexing issue of medical confidentiality arose and Gardner's wife Jackie, brought up the recent infraction that her husband has been fretting about. 'It's like what happened with that basketball player,' she said—and, unthinkingly, she named him. Gardner reddened and lowered his fork. "You said it," he replied, mortified. "I didn't."

But the cautionary lesson of the exchange is unmistakable. Even the most secure of databases has the single irreparable flaw: the human factor. From a technical point of view, it does not seem unreasonable to ask how hospitals can be certain their medical systems would be secure when hackers have already shown they can crack computer systems at the CIA and Pentagon? Even if they could erect the ultimate firewalls, the most serious threat is not the hacker, but the authorized user and the insatiable curiosity of our species.

THE CRADLE-TO-GRAVE ID

If the courts have provided few protections, Congress has also been slow to act to protect medical privacy—at least, where nonmembers of Congress are concerned. In 1982, after a reporter filed a Freedom of Information Act request for a list of prescription drugs supplied by the National Naval Medical Center to the Office of Attending Physician of Congress, Senator Howard Baker took to the floor of the Senate to denounce what he called an "intolerable invasion of personal privacy." The senator insisted that "The interest of patients in the absolute confidentiality of medical information is paramount." But a mere two years earlier, Congress had rejected a bill that would have assured such privacy to average citizens. Over the next two decades—despite growing concerns—Congress would repeatedly fail to pass legislation protecting medical privacy.[30] Prospects for legislation improved after the passage of the Kennedy-Kassebaum bill, which required the federal government to develop privacy standards as a result of pressure from the European Union.

But if the past patterns of privacy legislation hold, any bill that survives the process will be unlikely to solve the problem, and may even make it worse. One overriding concern is that bills that purport to strengthen privacy protections may actually undermine them, by preempting tougher state laws or by leaving gaping loopholes that allow politicians to claim success, while leaving patients naked in the coming data storms.

The privacy proposals unveiled by the Clinton administration in September 1997 did little to assuage such fears. While proposing new privacy standards, Health and Human Services Secretary Donna Shalala also acknowledged the changed landscape for medicine. "Today, the revolution in our health delivery system means that instead of Marcus Welby, we have to place our trust in entire networks of insurers and health care professions," she said, echoing the language of managed-care executives. What she wanted to do, she said, was "balance the protection of privacy with our public responsibility to support national priorities—public health, research, quality care, and our fight against health care fraud and abuse." Shalala's formulation marked a radical retreat from traditional understandings of medical privacy. In the past, it was believed that the government must have a "compelling public interest" before it could invade our medical privacy. Shalala was proposing a much lower "balancing" test.

Even on paper, Shalala's balancing test would put patients on the losing end of any conflict with law enforcement. The Shalala plan proposed giving law-enforcement officials the right to examine anyone's medical records with virtually no limits on how they could use such information or how and whether they could disseminate it. Indeed, her proposal would have made it easier for investigators to get someone's medical records than to get records about their movie rentals or cable-television habits—all protected by federal law. Not only would federal investigators not need a court order to examine medical files, they would have no obligation to ever inform patients of the intrusion. Nor would Shalala's plan have given patients any chance to challenge the disclosure of their medical information.[31]

The issue of trust was magnified by the furor over the universal identifier number. Even though medical privacy was honored more in the breach than in reality under the older, paper-based, balkanized system, patients still enjoyed what the Supreme Court in a different context referred to as "practical obscurity," because no one entity held all of their information. Part of its inaccessibility was the fact that the data was spread around, not easily accessed or analyzed. The National Identifier would change all of that: "That information will be irrevocably integrated into a cradle-to-grave medical record to which insurers, employers, government and law enforcement will have access," said, A.G. Breitenstein, the director of Health Law Institute.[32]

The requirement for the patient identifier had been included in a 1996 law, virtually without the public noticing it and certainly without much public debate. But, once publicized, no other single issue catalyzed as much concern over medical privacy.[33] "Think of the identifier as a dog tag that you wear from cradle to grave," the Center for Public Integrity complained. "The tags would allow every provider in the health-care industry—doctors, hospitals, insurers, nursing homes, and the like—to employ one common number for billing."[34] Editorial comment was overwhelmingly negative, much of it echoing fears that the ID number and the national medical database it would make possible smacked of Big Brother. The *Chicago Tribune* called it "a frightening concept, unjustified by any necessity." Other critics argued that personal medical records should be for private use—and were, frankly, none of the government's business. Even former government officials weighed into the debate. Bernadine Healy, the former director of the National Institutes of Health, noted that while government does many things well, "keeping secrets is not one of them." The abuse of FBI and IRS files should be cautionary lessons for anyone contemplating entrusting the federal government with custody of information about the sexual practices, sexually transmitted diseases, impotence, abortions, depressions, drug use, illnesses, and medications of individual citizens.[35]

There were, however, even wider implications. If the medical database were ever linked together with data about personal finances or criminal-justice records, a society of total surveillance would suddenly become an alarming prospect. While Americans have long resisted the idea of a formal national ID number, the medical ID would not only become such a number, but it would be far more powerful than any proposal ever offered. Despite repeated and heated denials that it would be misused, Americans watched as the Social Security number gradually evolved into a virtual national ID number—used and demanded for purposes far beyond its original intention.

A universal patient ID number might go even further. As privacy consultant Robert Gellman warned, the new number would be used for medical purposes only in the very beginning. Eventually, it would be a single national identifier used for "all governmental and private purposes."[36]

Why?

For starters, verifying identity is increasingly important and difficult. Many of the current documents are less than reliable, and institutions have had to deal with a rise in what is known as "identity theft." The patient identifier would be the new, improved, and universally trusted alternative. In time, the new number would be used not simply by the health-care establishment, but also by supermarkets, where a large percentage of prescriptions are filled. Inevitably, employers would also want to use the patient ID number, notes Gellman, since they are the primary source of health insurance and they would use the number to make it easier to track health information about their workers. Government would use the patient ID for welfare programs, public-health departments, and fraud and abuse prevention. The IRS would need the number to check on the deductibility of health-care costs, and law enforcement would need to use the numbers to access medical records needed in investigations. Because they also provide health care, schools would also begin using the universal identifier, as would credit-card companies, which allow customers to pay their medical bills with credit.

Originally, Gellman reminds us, the Social Security card was never in-tended to be used for identification purposes, but it is now needed for everything from getting a loan to applying for a job. "My guess," predicts Gellman, "is that the health identifier would make the Social Security number obsolete within a few years." Eventually the health ID card could become "an internal passport," raising the specter of a nation in which po-licemen can demand your "papers."

"People will not be able to use a credit card, cash a check, fly on an air-line, check into a hotel, go to school, or enter or leave the United States without showing the card," writes Gellman. "Anonymous health care may no longer be available."

In the past, such threats have alarmed Congress into reacting by pass-ing privacy protections. But the political landscape has changed and now seems permanently tilted against privacy protections. Even as public out-rage about the patient identifier built, the House of Representatives passed a "Patients Bill of Rights" that actually stripped away some of the few protections patients do enjoy. The bill wiped out many of the tougher state privacy laws and opened the doors to much broader access to medical records. Under the legislation, which was not enacted, doctors, hospitals, insurers, and pharmacists were given permission to release personal med-ical data to anyone involved in "health operations," a wording so vague as to render any privacy protections moot. Nor, under the legislation, would patients be given the right to deny such access.[37]

"There is no real money constituency in favor of privacy," says the Center for Public Integrity's Bill Hogan, "and there is a lot of money in fa-vor of invading it."[38]

7

■

The Secrets in Your Genes

Science seems determined to raise the ante, especially as scientists unlock the secrets of human heredity and genetics. The Human Genome project, which began in 1990, is an extraordinary fifteen-year effort to decode the human DNA by mapping and sequencing the twenty-three pairs of human chromosomes in the nucleus of every cell. Ultimately, scientists hope to identify and understand the 50,000 to 100,000 genes that comprise the human genome. It is hard to overstate the quantum leap in scientific knowledge represented by the project. In the past, scientists would focus on a single gene or protein for weeks or months; now they are analyzing billions of bits of information every day.

These discoveries are enabling scientists to develop new ways of detecting and treating hereditary disorders, which may number in the thousands. We already know that errors in the genes we inherit from our parents are responsible for diseases like cystic fibrosis, Duchenne muscular dystrophy, and Huntington's disease. They can also predispose us for certain kinds of cancer, autoimmune disorders, diabetes, glaucoma, and heart disease. As our knowledge expands, some scientists foresee a day, not too far distant, when it "will certainly be possible to identify those defective genes in individuals and a future 'probable health history' complete with numerical assignments to the probabilities."

How far will such knowledge take us?

In the science-fiction movie, *Gattaca*, a person's fate is fixed from the moment shortly after birth when a single drop of blood is tested genetically. An entire medical profile, complete with a future history of diseases, infirmities, and probable date of death is instantly revealed; a profile that would determine what jobs, status, and social rank the child would enjoy.

Each person's identity became a matter of blood and urine samples. Even one's love life is determined genetically, as potential mates ran tests on a strand of hair to get a profile of strengths and weaknesses that would put a pregenetic dating service to shame. In the movie's futuristic world, the law bars discrimination based on genetic makeup, but no one seems to pay the slightest attention. Genetically enhanced supermen hold the most coveted roles in society, and individuals unfortunate enough to be born without enhancements seem disproportionately to have jobs cleaning up the trash. In *Gattaca*'s world, genes literally are destiny (except for the individuals bold enough to steal another's genetic identity). Of course, this dystopian nightmare is an exaggeration. But the reality is hardly reassuring: For many of us, genetic data is the most personal information science is capable of producing—a virtual road map of an individual's makeup, a blueprint of the human personality, a future diary of our medical history. Equally troubling, genetic research has the power to provide a universe of information about ourselves over which we have limited control and of which we may not even be aware.

Of course, such knowledge could change the entire nature of medical care, from reacting to and treating sickness, to preventing people from getting sick in the first place. But the promise does not come without a very sticky price. A swab of tissue, a blood sample, even saliva provides clues not merely about our susceptibility to diseases, but our life span, even our personalities. Might we eventually be able to decode genetic information that profiles our artistic abilities, our aggressiveness, our willingness to take risks, whether we are shy, extroverted, romantic, or dangerous? Can our genes tell if we are sociable, altruistic, or intelligent? Can they predict our sexual orientation? Whether we are prone to alcoholism, impulsivity, or drug addiction? And how far are we willing to go to manipulate our genes? If we had the technology, would we want to delete those genes that might lead to cancer? What about the genes that might predispose us to moodiness? Or other undesirable personality traits? Would we want to engineer our children: Select their hair color? Their height? The color of their eyes?

Genetic information is not only exceptionally sensitive, Lawrence Gostin argues, but also unique in "the sheer breadth of information discoverable; the potential to unlock secrets that are currently unknown about the person; the unique quality of the information enabling certain identification of the individual; the stability of the DNA rendering distant future applications possible; and the generalizability of the data to families, genetically related communities, and ethnic and racial populations."[1]

But the privacy of genetic information is threatened precisely because of its sensitivity. As it becomes more useful, it will be more widely disseminated. As it becomes more accurate, it will become more valuable.

It is not difficult to imagine how useful and even valuable such knowledge would be—for banks that might want to know their customers' life spans before issuing loans; to insurance companies who want more reliable underwriting data; to landlords in screening tenants; to employers making hiring decisions. Schools, adoption agencies, and other bureaucracies would also find the information useful—always, of course, with the best of intentions.

Under the cover of compassionate and benign intentions, genetic information could be used widely in schools; for example, to identify children who might be prone to dyslexia or so-called "fragile X syndrome," or who might benefit from early intervention or special-education programs. Schools might also become clearinghouses for noneducational purposes, providing genetic information to social-service agencies or public-health services. We can easily imagine the various helping professions arguing that such information could help them deal with health problems by signaling them which children need early speech or physical therapy or helping them identify children who pose potential disciplinary and emotional problems. But, as Laura Rothstein has written, the danger is that such information effectively strips the entire family—and not simply the child—of genetic privacy.[2] The use of such intimate and sensitive information poses other dangers as well. Genetic information that labels a child could set in motion a process of self-fulfilling prophecies, in terms of lowered expectations. Will children be steered away from challenging careers? Or college? Will they be seen as products of their genes? Will other factors like home life or personal motivations get lost in the genetic diagnosis? And will children with similar problems, but lacking genetic markers receive the same attention and the same level of services?

GENETIC DISCRIMINATION

For many of us, the dilemma of genetic testing is that doing the right thing can be the wrong thing. Getting tested to find out our medical risks may put us at risk of losing jobs or insurance. The new science, which was supposed to open doors for new treatments, has actually resulted in doors being closed. The promise of safety has turned out to be chancy.

There is already evidence that many patients who might otherwise benefit avoid genetic testing for fear that the results might damage their insurability or employability. One study of 332 people who belonged to support groups for families with genetic disorders found that 17 percent of the participants withheld genetic information from their employers. A 1997 phone survey found nearly two-thirds of the respondents saying they would refuse genetic tests if they knew their insurer or employer would have access to the results. And researchers trying to study how to keep women with breast cancer gene mutations healthy found that almost one-third of the high-risk women refused to participate in the study, specifically because they feared the loss of their privacy and thought that it might lead to some sort of discrimination.

The evidence suggests their fears are not groundless.

The television program *60 Minutes* reported the story of a woman whose parent developed Huntington's disease. A genetic counselor urged the woman to get herself tested, since she had a 50 percent chance of inheriting the specific gene that caused the disease. The counselor also cautioned the woman to make sure that she secured both health and life insurance *before* she was tested, since a positive result would probably preclude her from obtaining insurance in the future. Somehow this information got back to the woman's boss. At first, her supervisor seemed sympathetic and supportive. But when the test revealed that the employee did, in fact, have the mutated gene, and she shared this information with her boss, she was fired. (In the eight months before the firing, the woman had been promoted three times and had received outstanding ratings on her performance.) None of her siblings will now be tested for Huntington's disease, even though they are obviously at risk. Having seen what happened to their sister, they are simply too frightened that the test could cost them their jobs and their insurance.

A report by the U.S. Department of Labor turned up similar cases of genetic discrimination:

> One individual was screened and learned he was a carrier of a single mutation for Gaucher's disease. His carrier status indicates that he might pass this mutation to his children, but not that he would develop

Gaucher's disease himself. He revealed this information when applying for a job and was denied the job because of his genetic mutation, even though it had no bearing on his present or future ability to perform a job.

During a job interview with an insurance company, a 53-year-old man revealed that he had hemochromatosis [a metabolic disorder in which iron pigment is deposited in the tissues] but was asymptomatic. During the second interview, he was told that the company was interested in hiring him but would not be able to offer him health insurance because of his genetic condition. He agreed to this arrangement. During his third interview, the company representative told him that they would like to hire him, but were unable to do so because of his genetic condition.[3]

Although these are admittedly anecdotal, there is evidence that discrimination is actually quite widespread. A 1996 study reported in *Science and Engineering Ethics* found that a survey of 917 individuals at risk of developing a genetic condition and of parents of children with such conditions found 200 cases of genetic discrimination. A paper presented in 1997 at the annual meeting of the American Society of Human Genetics reported that a survey of physicians, patients, and genetic counselors had identified 550 people denied insurance or jobs because of genetic information.[4]

Given the sensitivity of such data, one would expect the medical profession to have developed a strict ethic of confidentiality when dealing with such information. Instead, the science of genomics seems to have outrun the development of a reliable ethical compass, even for professionals in the field. And, indeed, genetic science poses some of the most poignant, and perhaps ultimately irresolvable, challenges to privacy. Faced with evidence of genetic disorders, for example, what should be kept private and who should be told? An individual may want to withhold evidence of a genetic disorder from his employer, but does he have the right to withhold such information from a brother or sister who may face the same risk? What are the ethics of telling or not telling a child? And at what age?

Eugene Pergament, who is both a professor of OB-GYN at Northwestern University's Medical School and director of Northwestern's program in genetic counseling, illustrates the dilemma by posing the following case: Through an affected son, a mother is diagnosed as a carrier of the gene that causes hemophilia. This means that the mother's sisters are also at risk of having sons with hemophilia. What are the ethical obligations of the clinical geneticists in this case? Should they inform the woman's siblings, who face a fifty-fifty chance of also having affected sons? Most clinical geneticists, Pergament says, would not override patient objections to inform family members. "The overriding responsibility of the clinical geneticists remains with the patient and not to any other family members and certainly not to society because of the public-health effects of the mutant gene."[5]

But not all physicians share this attitude. Doctors, midwives, and hospital residents were presented with a hypothetical case of a patient who tested positive for Huntington's disease. They were asked whether they would breach confidentiality by sharing this information with relatives of the patient, who might also be at risk. "A surprising 83 percent of health professionals felt that they should inform this relative *even if the patient requested privacy,*" [my emphasis] Pergament writes. Patient privacy fared only somewhat better among geneticists. Less than one-third (32 percent) said they would maintain confidentiality; 34 percent would tell their patient's relatives if asked; and a remarkable 24 percent would violate their patient's confidentiality even if they were not asked. In sharp contrast, 65 percent of patients surveyed believed that physicians should maintain patient confidentiality *despite* explicit and direct inquiries by at-risk individuals; only 22 percent believed that doctors should breach confidentiality if they were asked directly; only 8 percent thought physicians should seek out the at-risk individuals with the information.[6] The paradox, Pergament noted, is that "although patients, physicians and clinical geneticists operate on the premise that medical and personal information should be kept confidential and private, a significant portion of each group appears willing to violate that privacy when presented with specific examples." What accounted for this willingness to violate basic principles of doctor-patient confidentiality? Has the incredible progress of the Human Genome Project fundamentally changed the rules of the game? Whatever, the reason, Pergament wrote: "Both patients and physicians, including clinical geneticists, appear unaware of or unwilling to recognize the potentially catastrophic consequences of failing to maintain strict confidentiality when confronted with specific clinical genetic problems."[7]

This lack of consensus may prove troublesome, as both the public and private sectors move ahead with creating vast new databases built on the collection and analysis of DNA.

A NATION OF SUSPECTS

Besides employers and insurance companies, law enforcement has found DNA evidence to be particularly powerful as an investigative tool. DNA analysis has been a special boon to forensic science, which now comes close to being able to absolutely identify specimens from any suspect or individual in cases involving rape, murder, and kidnapping. Seeking to exploit the power of DNA evidence, law enforcement has moved aggressively to create massive data banks of DNA material. Some of those DNA databases are composed of individuals who have committed certain violent crimes, containing hundreds of thousands of samples. By 1996, forty states had enacted laws creating forensic DNA databases, and many of them required felons to provide blood and saliva samples for DNA identification testing. In 1994, Congress enacted the DNA Identification Act that made millions of dollars available to the states for DNA analysis, in exchange for which the states followed federal uniform guidelines that made a national DNA database both possible and inevitable. The FBI was also authorized to establish CODIS (Combined DNA Identification System), a national computer network that is able to identify suspects that would never have been linked to specific crimes prior to the new technology.[8] The FBI's DNA database went into operation in October 1998.

There are already signs that the scope of the DNA databases will be expanded. Although many were originally limited merely to sex offenders, there has been a gradual creep toward expanding the circle of suspects whose samples are kept. Some states now require samples to be taken from even nonviolent felons, including only drug or white-collar offenses. Eventually samples might be taken from other groups, including juveniles and those arrested, but not convicted of crimes.* "I think the trend is that ten years from now all felonies will be covered," says M. Dawn Herkman, chief of the FBI's Forensic Science Unit in Washington. So far, the courts have not shown any widespread willingness to apply Fourth Amendment protections to DNA data-bank laws.

Jean McEwen, an associate professor at the Boston School of Law,

---

*Louisiana already allows DNA to be taken from anyone arrested for a crime. Virginia, Wyoming, New Mexico, and Alabama require that all convicted felons provide DNA samples. Since 1996, New York State has required anyone convicted of any of twenty-one separate offenses to provide DNA samples.

notes that there is a danger of "surveillance creep" in which everybody in the population, perhaps at birth, eventually will be required to provide a DNA sample to the state, which could then use it as our new national identifier, effectively replacing the Social Security number or even the universal patient identifier.[9] It is not inconceivable that there will be proposals to begin taking samples from new immigrants, welfare recipients, and people in various drug and alcohol programs. Already the FBI's Heckman says, "We recommend that all violent felonies, burglaries, juveniles and retroactivity for people on parole be included."[10]

Clearly, such databases are an unparalleled boon to law enforcement and have already cut down the number of unsolved crimes. But, as McEwen notes, "On the other hand, a population-wide DNA data bank could fundamentally alter the relationship between individuals and the state, essentially turning us into a nation of suspects."[11] In Britain, where police have been even more aggressive in their use of DNA-profiling, authorities have been known to ask and even require every resident of a town to provide DNA samples to help narrow the field of suspects in high-profile cases.[12]

At present, forensic DNA typing does not test samples to determine genetic predispositions or other tests; they are used strictly for identification and matching purposes. But if the DNA data has limited use, the same cannot be said for the samples from which that information is drawn. If the samples—whether they are blood, or tissue, or saliva—are kept and disseminated, they could be tested for a complete genetic profile. Beyond the identification power of the DNA data, major privacy issues are raised by the question of the retention and control of the samples themselves because they "contain a potential wealth of genetic and other medical information." The concern is that the samples could be retested for many years in the future, for reasons having nothing to do with why they were collected in the first place. "A tissue database, in other words," writes McEwen, "has the capacity for dramatic self-expansion; people will have supplied the samples with no idea of the extent to which the samples may reveal personal information."

Such concerns lead the National Academy of Sciences to recommend that the samples taken from offenders for the DNA identification be destroyed "promptly" after analysis. This does not seem likely to happen. There are simply too many reasons (and temptations) to keep the samples on hand. Alabama already grants access to its DNA databanks for non-law-enforcement purposes, authorizing the use of its samples for "educational research or medical research or development."[13]

By far the largest DNA data bank to date is maintained by the U.S. military, which requires all of its personnel to provide samples to the DNA Specimen Repository. By 2001, the Defense Department is expected to have more than three million samples. The purpose of the data bank is humanitarian; the DNA can be used to identify the remains of missing soldiers. Although the Defense Department plans to keep all of the samples for fifty years, it revised its policy in 1996 to permit members of the armed services to have their samples destroyed when they leave the military. "But as with the DNA samples housed in state crime labs," Jean McEwen notes, "the samples in the military's repository are inherently subject to being used for purposes other than those which they were collected."[14] For example, it would be possible for the military to expand the use of these data banks from mere identification to the routine investigations of crime. And what if science were to definitively identify the so-called "gay gene" one day? Would the DOD possibly begin to test for sexual orientation? To address such concerns, the DOD clarified its policy in 1996 to provide that the samples cannot be used without consent for any purpose other than the identification of human remains, except in the case of a subpoena for the investigation or prosecution of a felony.

But the government is by no means alone in compiling DNA data banks. Commercial data banks are also growing rapidly. In some ways, these may pose an even greater threat to privacy, because those samples that are kept for medical, as opposed to merely identification purposes, are used to reveal much more sensitive information. Moreover, in the clinical data banks, the name, address, and other personal medical information about the depositor is likely to be included.

Beyond that, perhaps the largest source of DNA information is not kept in any formal data bank at all. Any place that keeps blood or any other tissue samples is a potential gold mine of genetic information. This might include blood banks, or the screening cards many state health labs keep on newborn infants. The cards, which are kept after testing the blood spots on the cards for PKU, McEwen notes, "collectively constitute an enormous inchoate DNA bank."[15]

"In fact," McEwen writes, "because DNA may be found wherever biological materials are present, even such places as post offices (where DNA may be found on millions of licked stamps), barbershop floors (where DNA may be found in hair roots), and manicure salons (where DNA may be found in clipped fingernails) these phases can be viewed as at least potential DNA 'banks.'" Perhaps more troubling, "even ordinary medical records that maintain genetic information are potential DNA data banks." Computerization of such records makes it nearly impossible to control the flow of this information. "To an insurance underwriter, even a reference in a medical record to the fact that a person has banked his or her DNA in a particular disease-related bank could trigger suspicion that a genetic disorder runs in the family. This deposit, in turn, could be used as a basis to deny coverage or at least to require DNA testing before issuing a policy."[16]

GENETIC LOOPHOLES

Despite the high stakes, there is no comprehensive federal law that provides workers or anyone else with protection against the invasion of genetic privacy. As an analysis by the Labor Department noted in 1998, the few protections that do exist are incidental, "narrow in scope," and "not well established." Although the Health Insurance Portability and Accountability Act of 1996 did prohibit health plans from using any health status, including genetic information, as a basis for denying or limiting coverage, the law did nothing to stop the gathering or use of such information for noninsurance purposes.

Similarly, the Americans with Disabilities Act bars discrimination based on disability, but the law continues to allow preplacement medical exams of unlimited scope, including genetic testing. The ban on preemployment inquiries into possible disabilities does not prevent the voluntary disclosure of medical information about an applicant by a third party or by the applicant himself. Although the law bars employers from withdrawing a job offer after the employee undergoes a preplacement medical exam, nothing prevents employers from gathering genetic data on their employees. Policymakers have reasoned that there is no reason to block employer access to such information since the employer is prohibited from using that information inappropriately. That means, according to Mark Rothstein, that company medical officers may require that individuals consent to giving blood samples as a condition of employment but "the employers need not disclose what tests are being performed on the blood and need not disclose any test results." Moreover, it is legal under the law for employers to require—again as a condition of employment—that applicants sign a release authorizing the disclosure of all of their medical records, including family histories, and the results of genetic tests. Nor does the law prohibit company medical officers from sharing medical information with management, including diagnostic results about employees.[17]

How do doctors reconcile this with the Hippocratic Oath, or other traditions of doctor-patient confidence?

At least one group seems to have responded by dumbing down its statement of medical ethics. In 1976, the Code of Ethical Conduct of the American Occupational Medical Association (AOMA) would have forbidden disclosing specific medical findings to nonmedical personnel within a company. But that code was revised in 1993 to add the words "except in compliance with laws and regulations." As Mark Rothstein remarks, "In effect, the revised code provides that disclosures are ethical if they are legal. The paradoxical result is to establish the minimum standards of the ADA, and antidiscrimination law, as the ethical norm of a medical specialty college."[18]

PROTECTING GENETIC PRIVACY

If genetic information is the ultimate private fact about us, how should it be protected? Does it deserve extraordinary protections, over and above those provided to less-sensitive medical information? Can it be separated from the rest of our medical data?

Advocates who believe that genetic information deserves special protection argue that "control of and access to the information contained in an individual's genome gives others potential power over the personal life of the individual by providing a basis not only for counseling, but also for stigmatizing and discrimination."[19] For example, a genetic test that identified a risk that an individual might suffer from Alzheimer's disease in the future has devastating personal, financial, and social consequences. As three legal experts recently noted, the very diagnosis that one might be prone to Alzheimer's "is itself a signal event, a labeling through medical records that can set in motion the snuffing out of one's civil self, even if the individual never contracts Alzheimer's."[20]

DNA is not simply another piece of data or medical information, say advocates of special protection, but is, in fact, "the human essence"—what makes individuals special and irreplaceable. The authors of the Genetic Privacy Act—George Annas, Leonard Glantz, and Patricia Roche—argue:

"To the extent that we accord special status to our genes and what they reveal, genetic information is uniquely powerful and uniquely personal, and thus merits unique privacy protection."[21]

They offer three reasons for treating genetic information as even more sensitive than other medical information. First, they describe a person's genetic profile as a sort of "future diary" because it "describes an important part of a person's unique future and, as such, can affect and undermine an individual's view of his/her life's possibilities. Unlike ordinary diaries that are created by the writer, the information contained in one's DNA, which is stable and can be stored for long periods of time, is in code and is largely unknown to the person. Most of the code cannot now be broken, but parts are being deciphered almost daily." Second, genetic information does not simply involve a single individual. By definition, genetic information "divulges personal information about one's parents, siblings, and children." And third, they note, there is a long and dismaying history of discrimination and stigmatization based on genetics.[22]

But they seem to claim too much, and too little. The danger here is that we both overestimate and underestimate the privacy implications of genetic information. As powerful as the knowledge of our genes may be, the reality is that even the most advanced genetic test does not have a lock on predicting our future. At best, it merely provides us with probabilities, which can be affected and changed by a host of other factors and choices we make. A disposition to alcoholism does not mean that we become alcoholics; a gene that raises our cholesterol does not mean we will develop heart disease. Diet, exercise, and medication may be as significant as anything written in our genes. "Our genes no more dictate what is significant about our lives than the covers and pages of a blank diary dictate the content of what is written within . . .," notes medical ethicist Thomas Murray. "The content we must write ourselves."[23]

We also risk falling into the trap of reductionism—of seeing ourselves as reduced to our genetic makeup. But our genes are not us. They are neither the human personality nor the human soul. They are extraordinarily powerful and information about them is exceptionally sensitive. *But so is other information about us.* And as powerful as the information from genes may be, other medical information may actually be far more telling. For example, a medical record that indicates we have been diagnosed with hepatitis B or tested positive for HIV has far more predictive value than any genetic test.

The point here is not to debunk genetic information, but to point out that it is not unlike other medical information in its sensitivity. "Genetic information is special because we are inclined to treat it as mysterious, as having exceptional potency or significance, not because it differs in some fundamental way from all other sorts of information about us," notes Thomas Murray, the director of the Center for Biomedical Ethics at Case Western Reserve University School of Medicine.[24] By focusing exclusively on the threat to privacy posed by genetics, we might unintentionally compromise other efforts to protect medical privacy in general.

The reality is that much of what we consider routine medical information has a genetic component, including our family histories. As the science advances, it seems likely that genetic testing and information will increasingly be integrated into everyone's medical records as a standard part of diagnostic tests and medical profiles. Genetic information is already so deeply embedded into the practice of medical underwriting that it seems both impractical and unlikely that any attempt to somehow screen it out or segregate the material could ever be adopted in the real world. As a practical matter, doctors would have to edit each and every medical record, chart, and history, to delete any reference to family histories or other genetic information. This would not only be time-consuming, and expensive, it would likely prove to be impossible. "Genetic information," writes Mark Rothstein, "is deeply ingrained in medical information, and if there ever was a time when the two could be separated, that time has passed."[25]

The answer is not to leave genetic information unprotected, but to create protections for *all* medical information, including genetic data. Indeed, most attempts by state legislatures to protect genetic privacy have proven to be weak and inadequate. Though some of them limit the use of genetic information in the provision of health insurance, they do not extend the protections to life or disability insurance. Part of the problem is that while many of the laws limit the ways in which employers can use the information, they do not actually restrict access to the information. But, as Rothstein argues, if the goal of such legislation is to ensure privacy, then the focus of legislation cannot be limited simply to how the information is used—it must be on restricting *access* to the information in the first place. Most of the legislation seeks to prevent unlawful, inadvertent, and unauthorized disclosures of genetic information. Although that is a laudable goal, a much more significant problem is the *authorized* disclosure of genetic information. As a condition of employment or insurance, individuals can still be required to execute a release authorizing the disclosure of medical (including genetic) information. Notes Rothstein: "All the procedural measures in the world will not protect the confidentiality of the information under these circumstances."[26]

HARD CASES

Medical privacy is not an absolute right. There are some cases where its violation may, in fact, be justifiable, most notably in those cases where the public's health or safety is at risk. One of the thorniest questions is whether and how to protect the confidentiality of patients with AIDS. Clearly, when officials require AIDS patients to disclose the names of their sex partners, they are invading their privacy. But if such information can be used to prevent the spread of the disease and save lives, such an invasion might be justified. Critics of mandatory reporting requirements respond that such rules do little to prevent HIV infections because they may, in fact, dissuade people from being tested or from being treated by a health-care system that will betray their confidentiality.

Any reasonable resolution of this conflict will require a careful balancing of the interests that would include the narrowest possible use of such information. Information about patients' HIV status could be sharply limited only to their partners and to those who will come in direct physical contact in a medical setting. Aside from those individuals, privacy protections should be tightly observed.

The debate over AIDS confidentiality highlights the challenge to organized medicine. No system that drives patients away from medical care can be considered "efficient," and no practice that induces patients to avoid testing or treatment can fairly be described as an advance in medicine. Despite the gibes of critics, protecting privacy does not have to involve a Luddite attack on the new technologies. To the contrary, there are legitimate high-tech enhancements of medicine that need not sacrifice individual medical privacy. Dr. John R. Lumpkin, the director of the Illinois Department of Health, presents the following scenario. It is 2:00 A.M. in a busy emergency room. "A middle-aged man arrived complaining of severe pain in the abdomen. In the rush to come to the hospital the family brought as many medications as they could find, but were not sure if they got them all. He had been treated in a number of local hospitals, and his stomach bore the surgical scars of those visits."[27]

The doctor would need to know—quickly—what medications the man was really taking. What might doctors find beneath the scars? It would be in the interest of the patient, his family, and the doctor to be able to immediately access all of this man's records before treatment. Lumpkin presents this case study as an argument for centralized databases and universal identifiers. But the same function could be performed by datacards in which the same medical information is encoded—but which is under the exclusive control of the patient. At least as far as individual treatment is concerned, the datacard would provide physicians with the same immediate access to medical information, without sharing it over a network or including it in a national database. The good news is that technology that threatens to destroy medical privacy could ultimately become a tool to restore control to individual patients.

There are some hopeful signs that the medical profession itself may yet rise to the challenge to its traditions and ethics. The Massachusetts Medical Society has endorsed six basic principles of patient privacy and confidentiality:

1. The patient has a fundamental right to privacy and confidentiality in his/her relationship with a physician. It is the physician's responsibility to do his/her best to protect the patient's privacy and confidentiality. Patient-physician relationships should be governed by mutual trust, respect, courtesy, honesty, and confidentiality.

2. Privacy and confidentiality are the privileges of the patient, so only he or she may waive them, in a meaningful and non-coerced fashion. Release of information for a specific purpose such as insurance payment should not require waiver of the total right to privacy and confidentiality.

3. An individual's rights to privacy and confidentiality should not be compromised. Statutory and regulatory exceptions should be specific and narrowly defined.

4. Conflict between a patient's right to privacy and a third party's need to know should be resolved in favor of the patient's privacy and confidentiality except where that may result in serious harm to the patient or others.

5. The development and acceptance of new information technologies should include measures that strengthen, not jeopardize, patient privacy and confidentiality.

6. Physicians have an ethical responsibility to understand issues of privacy and confidentiality, educate their staffs, and make reasonable efforts to inform their patients of these issues.[28]

Guidelines similar to these could provide the basis for the reassertion of the medical profession's ethical obligations to protect patient confidentiality. Too often, the profession has been either a willing participant or a compliant collaborator in undermining the traditional patient-doctor trust. Medical professionals who recognize the dangers of sacrificing privacy for cost containment or "efficiency" can make common cause with patients—a potentially powerful and influential alliance. There is, however, only so much that the medical profession can do on its own. Not even the most strongly worded principles have the force of law. Here, Congress needs to act at least as forcefully as it has to protect the privacy of video rentals.

Many states have adopted medical-privacy laws, but the current marketplace and technological developments require federal legislation. In an age where sprawling managed-care companies straddle state lines and medical datawebs cover the country from coast to coast, only uniform standards have any reasonable prospect of assuring patient confidentiality. The danger, of course, is that federal legislation could actually weaken some of the existing tough state privacy laws. But this can be addressed by not making such legislation preemptive. On the contrary, new federal protections should provide a minimum baseline for privacy, which states would be free to enhance if they chose.

To be meaningful, any medical-privacy law would have to be comprehensive in scope; guarantee patient access; provide strict need-to-know limits on third-party access; and provide for substantial criminal and civil fines for any actual or attempted unauthorized access or use of medical information. Federal legislation should also bar the use of personally identifiable medical information for research purposes or for electronic databases without the explicit consent of the patient.[29]*

---

*The Electronic Privacy Information Center's suggested guidelines for medical privacy legislation:

SCOPE: Legislation must cover all medical information, wherever it is collected, stored, processed, transferred or used, no matter the form. Legal coverage should not be limited to only medical information collected in the provision of health care but should include information collected for financial, educational, employment, marketing, and other reasons.

PATIENT ACCESS: Patient should have full access to all personally identifiable medical records. No records should be kept secret. Record keepers should be required to notify patients that they maintain records. Patients should have the ability to correct or remove any inaccurate, irrelevant or out-of-date information. Any card-based data system must allow consumer access to all personal information contained on the card.

ENFORCEMENT AND OVERSIGHT: Substantial criminal and civil fines should be imposed for actual or attempted unauthorized access, disclosure, or use of medical information. Individuals should be able to enforce rights and obtain damages and related costs in civil court. An independent agency should be created to conduct oversight and enforce the provisions of any federal medical privacy law.

THIRD PARTY ACCESS: Third party access to medical records should be strictly limited to a need-to-know basis. Law-enforcement officials should be required to obtain a warrant after showing a compelling government interest for each piece of information sought. Civil litigants should have to show a compelling interest for each piece of information. Privileged communications should never be disclosed. Use of medical information by employers or for marketing purposes should be prohibited.

NATIONAL DATABASES: The creation of electronic databases of unified clinical records without the consent of the patient should be prohibited. Psychiatric records should not be included in any system of electronic records.

RESEARCH RECORDS: Use of personally identifiable information for research purposes should require consent from the individual. New technologies that create pseudo-anonymous records should be used for any personally identifiable information. Research records should not be used for any other purpose and should be protected from disclosure by warrant or subpoena.

SECURITY: Medical information should be protected by the best available physical and electronic security. Records in storage or transit should be encrypted. Audit trails should track each access to an individual's file. Access should be limited to data relevant to the matter at hand.

IDENTIFICATION NUMBER: The Social Security number should not be used as a patient record identifier. The number that is used for record identification should not be used for any other purpose. Any health-care card issued should not be used for any other purpose, particularly not for determination of employment eligibility or for personal identification.

PREEMPTION: A federal medical privacy law should set a minimum level of protection for medical record privacy. . . . No state statute should be preempted."

From: "Principles for Federal Privacy Protection of Medical Records," Electronic Privacy Information Center, October 30, 1995.

8

■

Big Brother at the Office

Perhaps you have had the famous Freudian dream, in which you suddenly realize that you have gone to school or work, but have forgotten to get dressed. Whatever the classic analysis might be, the dream is a stark metaphor for the modern American workplace. Many of us are naked, at least in the sense that we have few protections of our privacy. On some occasions, workers find the metaphor to be literally true: some employers have installed video cameras in locker rooms and restrooms, a practice that is legal in all but a handful of states. But the invasions of employee privacy are actually far more widespread and intrusive. No federal law makes it illegal for an employer to gather and compile highly personal information about employees, even if it is unrelated to the job they do. It is perfectly legal for your boss to monitor your family life, check up on the organizations you belong to, delve into your medical history, and even do background checks on your personality traits and education.

Employers can listen in to your phone calls.
They can read your e-mail—even if your message is marked "private."
They can listen in to your voice mail.
They can monitor what is on the screen of your computer and what you have left on your hard drive.
They can install software that monitors the number of keystrokes you perform per hour, and measures the time you are away from your workstation.
They can make you urinate into a cup to test for drugs.
They can read your credit reports, and look at your medical records.

They cannot give you a polygraph test, but they can probe your innermost thoughts with psychological tests.

They can share information about you with creditors and government
agents.[1]

The violations, however, are not all one-way. Disgruntled employees
have been known to wear concealed wires or hidden recorders to tape conversations and meetings with coworkers and managers. One San Francisco
employment lawyer estimates that as many as one-fifth of his clients tell
him that they have secretly recorded conversations in their offices. Even
though many of these tape recordings violate state laws, some judges appear to overlook the invasions and have allowed aggrieved workers to
introduce the tapes as evidence.[2] Ironically, new developments in employment law have actually helped shape the current climate of mistrust. Because of the rising tide of litigiousness, employers have a limited ability to
get honest and thorough information about employees from past employers (a negative letter of recommendation is an invitation to a lawsuit). They
may also be forbidden by law to ask about certain problem areas in an applicant's past—including arrests. An unintended consequence of such protections has been that employers have become subtler, more creative, and
more roundabout in their approach to learning about their employees.

Strictly speaking, the tradition of delving into the private lives of employees is not new in American business. In its early years, the Ford Motor
Company pioneered corporate paternalism by scrutinizing the home life
and personal finances of its employees to determine if they were worthy to
receive profit-sharing bonuses. Representatives of Henry Ford's "Socio-
logical Department" visited homes of employees to determine whether
they gambled, drank, had dirty homes, an unwholesome diet, or sent
money to foreign relatives. Following in his footsteps, business continues
to argue that its ability to probe into the background of employees is both
a fundamental right and a business necessity.

Federal law provides little protection to employees for several reasons:
first, though public employees enjoy some minimal Fourth Amendment
protections, those rights do not extend to the private sector. Second, Congress has been reluctant to enact privacy rules for private businesses, even
going so far as exempting employers from laws protecting the confidentiality of electronic communications. "When most Americans go to work in

the morning, they might just as well be going to a foreign country," says Lewis Maltby, of the ACLU, Workplace Rights Project, "because they are equally beyond the reach of the Constitution in both situations. And unfortunately, federal law does very, very little to fill this void."[3]

How widespread are such practices?

One survey found that two-thirds of the nation's largest corporations hire private investigators to gather information about employees' private lives. Another recent poll of 906 large and midsize employers found that more than one-third of them conduct one or more kinds of electronic surveillance on their employees. If any kind of electronic monitoring is included—including the number of keystrokes by data-entry workers, phone logs, and videotaping to deter crime—the proportion rose to 63.4 percent.[4] In 1993, *MacWorld* magazine estimated that 20 million workers were being monitored through computers on their desktops.[5] A widely publicized survey of eighty-seven Fortune 500 companies with a combined 3.2 million employees found that 75 percent said they collected information about employees beyond what workers voluntarily provide and almost half did do so without informing the employees. More than two-thirds reported hiring private investigators to do background checks of their workers; more than one-third (35 percent) said they used medical records to make decisions about employees. The vast majority acknowledged that they shared information about their employees with government agencies and creditors.[6]

New technologies promise even more sophisticated workplace monitoring. A Virginia company is now marketing artificial intelligence software that automatically scans employee's e-mail for "offensive language."[7] A New Jersey company has developed a system to monitor whether employees at their restaurant wash their hands after going to the bathroom.[8] Given trends in litigation employment law—which hold employers liable for everything from employee honesty to sexual harassment—the level of intrusiveness is likely to keep rising.

YOU'VE GOT MAIL . . .

One of the cases that underlined the vulnerability of employees and the lack of legal protections was *Shoars v. Epson America, Inc.*[9] Like many American companies, Epson had an extensive e-mail system, which was administered by a woman named Alana Shoars. Feeling that confidentiality was essential to the new network, Shoars assured her colleagues at

Epson that the company's e-mail system was private and their passwords and communications secure.

They were not.

When Shoars discovered that one of the company's executives was eavesdropping on electronic messages, she confronted him—and was promptly fired. Because the incident occurred in California, Shoars had high hopes that California's constitutional protections of privacy gave her an advantage when she sued Epson for wrongful discharge, slander, and for invasion of privacy. But Epson, like other employers, insisted that since the company owned the e-mail system, it had the right to control it and to monitor how it was used. Since the company provided the equipment, the software, and the network, they reserved the right to ensure that their employees used electronic mail strictly for business purposes.[10]

Privacy activists like Philip R. Zimmerman, the legendary creator of PGP (which stands for Pretty Good Privacy), an encryption system, challenge the argument that because companies own equipment, they should have the right to control and monitor its contents. "I use a company pen," says Zimmerman. "If I use it to write a letter to my wife, does that mean they can read the letter?"[11] But that was precisely what Epson was claiming. As it turned out, there was no California law protecting the privacy of e-mail. Shoars tried to argue that the violation of e-mail privacy was covered under the state's older laws dealing with wiretapping, but the trial court rejected her argument. The court also rejected her argument that Epson's snooping violated California's broader constitutional right of privacy. In a setback for the privacy rights of the state's employees, the court ruled that the constitutional right of privacy only protected *personal* information. The court saw no reason to extend privacy protections to "business-oriented communications." Nor did federal law provide any help. When Congress passed the Electronic and Communications Privacy Act to cover e-mail communication in 1986, it explicitly exempted employers. Thus, even though Shoars felt she had a sound commonsense basis for her case— Epson's promises of confidentiality, the use of passwords that seemed to promise privacy—Epson's snooping was protected by law.

Indeed, the U.S. Supreme Court has granted employers a good deal of leeway in their prying into employee activities. In 1987, the Court ruled in favor of a supervisor in a public-sector workplace who searched one of his employee's files, office, and desk, ruling that the worker had no reasonable expectation of privacy at his workplace.[12] Since public employees have greater constitutional protections against unreasonable searches and seizures than workers in the private sector, the clear implication of the ruling was that private companies had been granted even broader license to search employees' work areas and communications.

Apparently, executives at Pillsbury were also reading workers' e-mail messages back in 1994, when they came across a private message from Michael Smyth to one of his colleagues. Unaware that his slam was captured in the company's electronic net, Smyth wrote that his bosses were "back-stabbing bastards." Pillsbury promptly fired Smyth for what it said was his "inappropriate and unprofessional comments." Smyth sued for wrongful discharge, claiming that he had been promised that his electronic communications would be kept private—a claim denied by Pillsbury. In January 1996, a federal judge threw out Smyth's case, ruling that *even if* the company had promised that the messages were confidential, the "defendant's actions did not tortiously invade the plaintiff's privacy."[13]

A study by the Society for Human Resource Management found that 80 percent of the organizations surveyed used e-mail, but only 36 percent had policies for its use, and only 32 percent had written privacy rules.[14] That may be changing, as more companies begin to protect themselves by explicitly informing employees that their e-mail may be subject to surveillance. Such surveillance is also likely to become even more aggressive, especially given the aggressiveness of litigators who not only subpoena every piece of document and piece of paper, but have also learned that deleted e-mails can be accessed and used against companies at trial. Chevron, for example, had to pay $2.2 million to four women in a case that involved offensive e-mail and interoffice mail. Among other things, the company found itself liable for some of its employees using the e-mail to transmit documents like "25 Reasons Why Beer Is Better Than Women."[15]

THE NO-PRIVACY ZONE

In the 1970s Congress created the Federal Privacy Commission, which studied the issue of employee privacy in depth. Business groups lobbied the commission against recommending federal legal protections, insisting that they should be allowed to develop their own voluntary policies to protect employees from privacy abuses. Commission Chairman David Linowes, a professor at the University of Illinois, has conducted follow-up studies to determine how well business has done in protecting privacy. His conclusion is that voluntary regulation has been a dismal failure. Not only do businesses continue to collect detailed and highly personal information, but they often also fail to ensure the accuracy or the confidentiality of those files.

"The amount of unsubstantiated and irrelevant information that finds its way into files is amazing," complained Linowes. "Rumors, poison-pen letters, things that appeared in newspapers. We found many errors that resulted in terrible abuse. Employees should be allowed to correct errors, but 24 percent of companies do not allow corrections."

Employees under review or who are being considered for promotions might come under special scrutiny, which might include attempts to learn more about their character, past behavior, spending habits, friends, and associates. In one case found by Linowes, a man had been denied promotion because his file described him as "known to have used drugs." It later turned out that one of his neighbors had told company investigators that he had "heard" he had once tried marijuana. Another woman's personnel file included grade-school report cards and evaluations from her third-grade teacher, including a note describing the woman's mother as "crazy." That note reportedly led her employer to question her mental soundness. Another executive's file included his complete medical records, including the fact that he had complained to his doctor about recurrent headaches. A scribbled notation that the man "seems to have difficulty managing finances" may have cost him a promotion to a job supervising company budgets.[16]

At the Lawrence Berkeley Laboratory, which is operated jointly by state and federal agencies, employees were routinely tested—without their knowledge—for a variety of traits, ailments, and conditions. Black employees were tested for the sickle-cell trait; female employees were tested for pregnancy. Other employees were routinely tested for syphilis, without ever being told the tests were being conducted or informed of the results. The lab defended its practices by arguing that the tests were simply part of its general mandatory medical examination. Because employees were also asked to fill out a questionnaire that asked questions about venereal disease and menstrual problems, the laboratory argued, the employees should have expected that they might also be tested for such problems.

Although a federal district judge threw out the case, the Ninth District

Court of Appeals, reversed the decision, ruling that the procedures violated both the federal and California privacy rights of the employees. "One can think of few subject areas more personal and more likely to implicate privacy interest than that of one's health or genetic makeup," the court ruled. "[I]t goes without saying that the most basic violation possible involved the performance of unauthorized tests—that is, the nonconsensual retrieval of previously unrevealed medical information that may be unknown even to the plaintiffs." In particular, the tests for syphilis and pregnancy were "highly sensitive, even relative to other medical information." The Appeals Court also rejected the claim that filling out the questionnaire had given the laboratory the go-ahead for the other tests. "The fact that plaintiffs acquiesced in the minor intrusion of checking or not checking three boxes on a questionnaire doesn't mean that they had reason to expect further intrusions in the form of having their blood and urine tested for specific conditions that correspond tangentially if at all to the written questions." (The court pointed out that pregnancy is neither a "venereal disease" nor a "menstrual disorder.")[17]

Although the Lawrence case may be an extreme example, Linowes found that 38 percent of the companies surveyed do not inform employees of types of records maintained on them; 44 percent do not tell personnel how records are used; and nearly 60 percent fail to inform employees about their policies of providing information to the government. Besides that, 18 percent don't tell their employees what records they can see and 42 percent have no policy for conducting periodic reviews of their record-keeping system. He was also troubled by the lack of solid policies to correct recurrent errors in the dossiers. Nearly one out of four companies (23 percent) had no policy to forward corrections to anyone who received incorrect information within the past two years.[18] "With information being transmitted across the country and abroad at the speed of light," noted Linowes, "an error in one record can be propagated a hundredfold instantaneously. If no effort is made to forward a correction, this is detrimental to both the recipient organization and the individual."*

---

*Stung by the failure of private industry to voluntarily protect employee privacy, David Linowes now supports legislation that would protect workers by (1) allowing only minimum intrusiveness into personal affairs of a person, eliminating data that is irrelevant

. . .

One of the few recommendations of the Privacy Commission that did result in federal legislation was the proposal to limit the use of polygraphs by private employers. By 1987, employers were administering nearly 2 million polygraph tests a year to applicants, using the procedures to probe into their religious, political beliefs, sex lives, and union affiliations. In response, Congress passed the Employee Polygraph Protection Act, which bars the use of lie detectors to screen new hires. (Although businesses can still employ lie detectors on their workers if they have a "reasonable suspicion" of wrongdoing.)[19]

In place of polygraphs, though, some employers have turned to psychological tests, which set new standards for stripping employees naked.

SO HOW'S YOUR SEX LIFE?

Sibi Soroka applied for a security job at a Target Store in California; a job that involved maintaining surveillance of customers to catch suspected shoplifters. As part of the application process, Soroka was required to take a psychological test designed—or so the company insisted—to measure whether he had good judgment and emotional stability, qualities that the store believed were especially important for the position he sought. Security guards are not armed, but they do carry handcuffs and are authorized to use force against suspects. Target executives were persuaded that the test they used, known as the "Psychscreen," would weed out unstable employees who might put both their customers and other employees at risk or would otherwise disrupt the store's operations.[20]

Made up of more than 700 questions, Target's Psychscreen was a combination of the Minnesota Multiphasic Personality Inventory and the California Psychological Inventory, tests that had been used in the past to screen out "emotionally unfit" applicants for jobs like police officers and air-traffic controllers, as well as nuclear power-plant operators. As Soroka sat down to take the test, the administrator told him and the other applicants to make sure they answered *every* question.

___

to the decision at hand; (2) permitting individuals to see data about themselves, upon which a decision is based, and (3) creating mechanisms for enforcing confidentiality, when informational privacy is expected. Specifically, Linowes would allow punitive damage, capped at $10,000, for workplace-privacy violations.

Soroka's discomfort, however, grew with nearly every page. The test not only included what he regarded as standard psychological questions, but also inquired into his religious attitudes and included questions that went into extraordinary detail about his sexual orientation and sex life. Some of the true-false questions he was instructed to answer included:

"I feel sure that there is only one true religion. . . .

"I have no patience with people who believe there is only one true religion. . . .

"My soul sometimes leaves my body. . . .

"A minister can cure disease by praying and putting his hand on your head. . . .

"Everything is turning out just like the prophets of the Bible said it would. . . .

"I go to church almost every week.

"I believe in a life hereafter. . . .

"I am very religious (more than most people). . . .

"I believe my sins are unpardonable. . . .

"I believe there is a God. . . .

"I believe there is a Devil and a Hell in afterlife."

If these questions seemed outrageous violations of his privacy, Soroka was absolutely appalled by what the Psychscreen wanted to know about his sex life:

"I wish I were not bothered by thoughts about sex. . . .

"I have never been in trouble because of my sex behavior.

"I have been in trouble one or more times because of my sex behavior. . . .

"My sex life is satisfactory. . . .

"I am very strongly attracted by members of my own sex. . . .

"I have often wished I were a girl. . . . (Or if you are a girl) I have never been sorry that I am a girl. . . .

"I have never indulged in any unusual sex practices. . . .

"I am worried about sex matters. . . .

"I like to talk about sex. . . .

"Many of my dreams are about sex matters."

As chance would have it, Soroka was able to have a friend come to the test site, and together they were able to take the test to a copying store, where they photocopied it. Eventually he sued, charging Target and its parent company, Dayton Hudson, with discrimination, later adding charges that the Psychscreen violated his constitutional right to privacy, invaded his privacy, and required him to disclose confidential medical information, among other grounds. He also sought a preliminary injunction to block Target from using the test.

Target defended its policies vigorously, pointing out that under the testing procedures, the answers would be scored by the psychology consulting firm known as Martin-McAllister. The firm rated applicants on five traits: emotional stability, interpersonal style, addiction potential, dependability, and reliability, and whether or not they would have a tendency to follow the rules. According to the company, Target never saw the specific answers applicants provided to the questions in the survey, but merely got the ratings and a recommendation from Martin-McAllister about whether or not to hire the applicant.

But Soroka's lawyers were able to present their own expert testimony that the test was "unjustified and improper." Moreover, they presented evidence that the test was often wrong and had resulted in more than six out of ten qualified applications for the security jobs being denied jobs because of faulty test results.

Soroka lost at the trial-court level but won in the California Court of Appeals, which declared that California's state constitutional right of privacy extended to both public and private employers and that it protected job applicants as well as employees. It recognized that some invasions of privacy might be justified under some circumstances, but it ruled that there must be a "compelling interest" and must be closely related to the actual nature of the job to pass constitutional muster. In using the "Psychscreen," Target could meet neither test. "While Target unquestionably has an interest in employing emotionally stable persons to be [security officers], testing applicants about their religious beliefs and sexual orientation does not further this interest," the appeals court ruled. Target appealed to the California Supreme Court, where it was joined with a case challenging NCAA's drug-testing program for student athletes. (The court eventually ruled against the athletes, saying that the NCAA's health and safety concerns outweighed what it said were the "diminished" privacy expectations of anyone who went out for a college athletic team.)[21] Before the high court got a chance to rule on its case, however, Target agreed to settle out of court. It did not admit liability; however, it set up a $1.3 million fund to be divided among applicants who had taken the Psychscreen, and agreed to drop the test from its requirements for security-job applicants in California.

Although Soroka's case resulted in at least some vindication of his privacy claims, it is unclear whether the result would have been the same in a state other than California.

FIRST, YOU HAVE TO PEE INTO THIS CUP. . . .

For many employees, the most obvious and direct challenge to their privacy comes in the form of drug tests. One of the paradoxes of privacy protection is the way the courts have applied the Fourth Amendment's protections against unreasonable search and seizure. An individual's home is protected against entry by any government agent. Those agents cannot seize his property or papers without an express court order. Courts have ruled repeatedly that the Constitution does not merely protect places, but also people, and thus the Fourth Amendment's protections also apply to any other invasive proceedings, including strip searches. Private entities have even less access than the government to a man's home and person; under almost every circumstance, the entry of a private home or the intrusion into a person's physical security by a private citizen is a crime. Although there are procedures for intrusive disclosures through the discovery process in a civil trial, no one except the government has a right to invade the privacy of the home—and even then, the right is tightly circumscribed.

But in the area of workplace law, the equation is turned on its head. In most contexts, private employers have far more power than the government to violate the privacy of their workers. Put another way, an individual is protected more effectively from the government than from his employer because the protection against warrantless searches does not extend to the private sector. The result is that the same action that would be deemed an unconstitutional violation of your rights when done by the government, is perfectly permissible if done by your boss—including wiretapping, reading your private e-mails, and drug testing.

The courts have repeatedly found that drug tests are a significant invasion of privacy, violating not only the Fourth Amendment, but also the Fifth Amendment's protection against self-incrimination, and the Fourteenth Amendment's protection of due process and privacy. Because those protections are not absolute, some forms of testing have been upheld, including those in which there is a "reasonable suspicion" that someone has been under the influence of drugs. Another exception is for random testing of government employees in jobs involving the public safety, and of some student athletes.

In general, though, the courts have ruled out blanket or random drug tests without any reasonable justification. "By analogy," Judith Decew writes, "although United States banks are surely concerned to ensure that their employees are not embezzlers, that worry does not entitle them to search all bank employees and their homes on the chance that they may uncover a dishonest employee."[22] But since the constitutional protections against unreasonable searches do not extend to private businesses, employers *are* able to search the urine and blood of their employers on the chance they may be using drugs.

For many workers the requirement that they submit to drug tests is the most obvious and direct challenge to their privacy. One study found that 80 percent of the companies in the survey tested their employees for drugs, and millions of Americans are required to urinate into cups, jars, and bottles every year as a condition of their employment. Although Supreme Court Justice Antonin Scalia has called drug testing a "needless indignity," it has widespread support and illustrates the problems of balancing privacy concerns with other priorities. Supporters of drug testing point to the overwhelming evidence that drug use not only exacts a societal cost, but also hurts the productivity of American business. Recent government estimates put the cost of drug abuse to the nation's employers at $60 to $100 billion a year in property damage, absenteeism and tardiness, reduced productivity and quality, higher costs for health insurance and worker's compensation, employee theft, and the turnover of workers. Many of the nation's largest and most prestigious corporations require pre-employment tests; the list includes more than one-quarter of the Fortune 500 corporations and such trendsetters as the *New York Times*, IBM, Exxon, Federal Express, AT&T, and Lockheed. Obviously, the most compelling justifications of drug testing involve jobs that affect safety, such as railway workers and airline pilots. But the vast majority of people tested are not in the classic "safety-sensitive" jobs.

What no one seriously questions, though, is the fact that drug tests involve a considerable loss of privacy, ranging from puncturing the skin to obtain blood to actually watching a person give a urine sample (in order to ensure that nothing is substituted). Beyond the physical intrusion, drug tests may reveal a good deal more medical information about the person subjected to such tests. Judith Decew notes that such tests can reveal information about the person's use of birth-control, pregnancy, epilepsy, manic-depression, diabetes, heart disease, even schizophrenia medications. In addition, it is also not always clear who has access to the results of such tests. Nor is it obvious that the tests—upon which so much rides for an individual in terms of employment, insurance, and reputation—are all that accurate.*

Clearly, there is a necessary tradeoff between privacy rights and the public safety when it comes to the issue of drug testing involving jobs whose performance puts the public at risk. Testing blood donors, or air-traffic controllers, or railway workers seems to pass any reasonable balancing test. But, at a minimum, employers should inform applicants and employees in advance and in writing if submitting to a drug test is a condition of employment. Moreover, they have an absolute moral obligation to maintain strict confidentiality and to ensure the accuracy of initial tests and to run confirmatory tests if a positive result is obtained. Employers who have specific reasons to suspect that an individual might be or have been impaired while on the job should similarly be able to require a test; but there seems little justification for blanket or preemptive drug tests. Once again, the law has had unintended consequences. As Walter Olson re-

---

*Critics claim that many of the drug tests have error rates as high as 60 percent. Moreover, the tests cannot determine whether a worker is actually under the influence of a drug at the time, nor do they measure how any specific drug might impair a person's performance. Decew notes: "Positive cannaboid results have been obtained from urine samples of people who have taken anti-inflammatory drugs such as ibuprofen (Advil, Motrin, and so on) or naproxen, and similar medications might affect the results of tests for barbiturates. Cold remedies such as Contac or Sudafed can mimic the presence of amphetamines, and positive tests for morphine can be obtained from those who have taken drugs containing codeine, including many popular cough syrups."

ported in *The Excuse Factory,* the Americans with Disability Act has made it quite tricky for employers faced with suspected drunks on their staff. The courts have said that the federal government as an employer has a positive duty to confront workers who might be intoxicated on the job. But such is the state of litigation, Olson notes, that "if employers do lead glazed-looking workers into the personnel office and pull out a Breathalyzer, they set themselves up for suits over privacy invasion, defamation, and similar outrages." Unfortunately, such a legal climate may make it more prudent to test everyone rather than focus on problem employees.

WORKING FOR PRIVACY

The transparent workplace raises several nagging issues for privacy rights: If society respects and values privacy, can it tolerate a situation that denies any privacy protections for the place where we spend one-third of our lives? Can we pretend that we can still have privacy if we have no right to protect ourselves against violations by people who have economic power over us? For most American workers a choice of their privacy or their livelihood is no choice at all.

Employers are not bound by the same constitutional limit as government; the Bill of Rights was created to restrict the powers of government, not the powers of private citizens. But even so, constitutional protections of privacy/information rights are not irrelevant. Infringements of privacy by an employer necessarily affect those rights vis-à-vis the rest of society. When it comes to information, the walls between private and public are increasingly porous. Given the fluid nature of information, what good are our protections against government intrusion if employers are given carte blanche to probe our lives and share that information with those same governmental agencies? It is also important to remember that employers have not resorted to draconian surveillance techniques out of sheer ill will. Rather, businesses can make a compelling case that the current legal climate gives them little choice whether or not to monitor their employees. Society's penchant for litigiousness has forced companies to assume a defensive posture. Over the last several decades, the trend has been toward creating new classes of legal actions that customers, partners, and workers can bring against companies. Not only do they face a raft of potential lawsuits and complaints from employees—for discrimination, for sexual harassment, for unfairness of every sort—but they also find themselves held liable for their employees' conduct and action. Such laws make it difficult to dismiss problem employees, and give businesses powerful incentives for ever-increasing levels of surveillance, if only for self-preservation. From a practical point of view, any protections of employee privacy may have to be counterbalanced by shifting more responsibility from companies to individual employees.

Legislation should probably begin with the most egregious violations, including electronic monitoring, video surveillance, and medical information. At minimum, companies should be encouraged to adopt the so-called fair-information practices. This would mean that personal information be used only for the specific purpose for which it was gathered; that employees be able to see information about themselves; and they should be given a chance to correct any incorrect information that might be in their files.

But there are definite limits to the power of legislation. More hopeful, however, might be changes in the marketplace itself, as companies begin to use privacy policies to compete for customers and employees. Increasingly, businesses will find that protecting employee privacy is not only an attractive option for employees, but gives those employers with the strongest assurances a clear competitive advantage. Just as customers will gravitate toward merchants who prove reliable and trustworthy in handling their data, so valued employees will be attracted to environments that promise to treat them with respect and reticence.

PART 3

■

The Snoop Wars

9

■

The Government's War on Privacy

Historically, the greatest threat to personal privacy has been the State. It still is. Jealous of its own secrets, the government covets ours.

As great as the challenge posed to privacy by employers, marketers, and the medical field, governments combine an apparently limitless appetite for information with unprecedented power to obtain such information. Ironically, though, the same technologies that have done so much to erase privacy also provide some prospect of being able to protect it. This has raised the anxiety of the intelligence agencies, who fear that communications might not be as transparent or as easy to intercept as they had hoped.

Ultimately, that is what the keyhole wars are all about. The government's assault on privacy is waged on three fronts:

1. Government intelligence agencies insist on having a built-in trapdoor in the nation's information infrastructure so they can easily intercept and listen in one and/or read personal communications.
2. As those systems become more secure, law enforcement demands that it be given access to any keys to codes that seek to keep information private and secure.
3. Intelligence agencies continue to wage their decades-long campaign to weaken the privacy and security precautions available to private citizens. Limiting our ability to use encryption technology remains a top priority for much of the federal government.

Although issues like "digital telephony" (the FBI's wiretap initiative) and the fight over encryption sometime seem of interest only to netzines and other wonks, the issues are central not only to any discussion about the shape of the Information Age, but also the future of privacy. Much of the communication that now occurs electronically once took place face-to-face: behind closed doors, in a field, in bedrooms and living rooms, far from prying eyes or ears. This was considered a basic freedom: men and women could engage in discussions about politics, or finance, or their personal lives, free of surveillance, monitoring, or censorship by others, including the police or other agents of the state. Increasingly, however, our lives are played out in the electronic world. We use electronic communications not only to buy things, but also to decide what we read and what we watch. Cyberspace is where many of us gather to hear the news, debate politics, find new loves, explore our individual tastes.[1] And, occasionally, it is where criminals plan their crimes.

In other words, what once took place behind locked doors now occurs on-line. But here is the rub: The same technology that threatens to erase the private also holds the promise of restoring it. Digital communications are more difficult to tap than over-the-wire communications and encryption—scrambling or encoding data and other communications—theoretically makes it impossible to read those communications even if they are intercepted.

This makes some government agencies unhappy because the new technologies greatly increase the ability of individuals—including criminals—to assure the privacy of their communications. By invoking fears of drug cartels, kidnappings, and international terrorism, the FBI has sought the power to be a fly on the wall in the new information age. The agency wants to build a peephole into every electronic wall. In effect, their proposals would require all of our systems of communications to be equipped with an unblinking surveillance camera that can be turned on under the proper circumstances. Beyond that, they want the keys to every door, every file cabinet—the code to every private communication in the electronic age.

WIRETAPS AND PRIVACY

Debates over the government's ability to wiretap private conversations are not new. In 1928, a case involving wiretapping and government surveillance resulted in one of the most famous and influential defenses of the right of privacy. That year, the U.S. Supreme Court ruled in *Olmstead et al.*

v. *United States* that the Fourth Amendment prohibition of unreasonable search and seizure did *not* apply to wiretapping phone conversations.[2] But the case inspired a dissent by Justice Louis Brandeis, who used it as an occasion to expand on his 1890 article, which is widely credited with establishing the tort of privacy. In *Olmstead,* Brandeis insisted on the constitutional basis of the "right to be let alone." But what makes his dissent so prescient was his discussion of the implications of modern technologies, which seemed to so befuddle his colleagues.

Brandeis insisted that the Court update the Constitution's protections against unreasonable searches and seizures to accommodate new technologies that were scarcely even imagined:

> When the Fourth and Fifth amendments were adopted, "the form that evil had therefore taken" had been necessarily simple. Force and violence were then the only means known to man by which a government could directly self-incrimination. It could compel the individual to testify—a compulsion effected, if need be, by torture. It could secure possession of his papers and other articles incident to his private life—a seizure effected, if need be, by breaking and entry. Protection against such invasion of "the sanctities of a man's home and privacies of life" was provided in the Fourth and Fifth Amendments by specific language.

"But 'time works changes, brings into existence new conditions and purposes,'" Brandeis noted. "Subtler and more far-reaching means of invading privacy have become available to the government. Discovery and invention have made it possible for the government, by means far more effective than stretching upon the rack, *to obtain disclosure in court of what is whispered in the closet.*" Scientific progress was unlikely to be satisfied simply with the technical capability to tap someone's phone.

With extraordinary foresight, Justice Brandeis wrote: "Ways may some day be developed by which the government, without removing papers from secret drawers, can reproduce them in court, and by which it will be able to expose to a jury the most intimate occurrences of the home." He specifically had in mind the development of psychology and related social sciences which "may bring means of exploring unexpressed beliefs, thoughts and emotions." Brandeis insisted that the Constitution protected the essential value of privacy, whatever the specific means that were adopted to invade their privacy.

"It is not the breaking of his doors, and the rummaging of his drawers, that constitutes the essence of the offense," Brandeis argued, "but it is the invasion of his indefeasible right of personal security, personal liberty and private property, where that right has never been forfeited by his conviction of some public offense—it is the invasion of this sacred right which underlies and constitutes the essence of [the judgment].

"Breaking into a house and opening boxes and drawers are circumstances of aggravation; but any forcible and compulsory extortion of a man's own testimony or of his private papers to be used as evidence of a crime or to forfeit his goods, is within the condemnation of that judgment." Noting that the court had previously ruled that a sealed letter entrusted to the mails was covered by the amendments, Brandeis wrote, "There is, in essence, no difference between the sealed letter and the private telephone message." As one federal judge had remarked: "True, the one is visible, the other invisible; the one is tangible, the other intangible; the one is sealed, and the other unsealed; but these are distinctions without a difference."

In fact, Brandeis went on to argue, wiretapping was actually a more serious breach of personal privacy than the opening of sealed letters. "Whenever a telephone line is tapped, the privacy of the persons at both ends of the line is invaded, and all conversations between them upon any subject, and although proper, confidential, and privileged, may be overheard," Brandeis wrote. "Moreover, the tapping of one man's telephone line involves the tapping of the telephone of every other person whom he may call, or who may call him." Referring to the abuses of power by the British Crown that had led to the Fourth and Fifth amendments, Brandeis declared: "*As a means of espionage, writs of assistance and general warrants are but puny instruments of tyranny and oppression when compared with wiretapping.*"

But Brandeis was not content to simply draw a narrow legal point. He wanted to establish the central place of privacy in the constitutional scheme. The Framers, he wrote, undertook "to secure conditions favorable to the pursuit of happiness. They recognized the significance of man's spiritual nature, of his feelings and his intellect. They knew that only a part of the pain, pleasure and satisfactions of life are to be found in material things. They sought to protect Americans in their beliefs, their thoughts, their emotions, and their sensations. They conferred, as against the government, the right to be let alone—the most comprehensive of rights and the right most valued by civilized men. To protect that right, every unjustifiable intrusion by the government upon the privacy of the individual, whatever the means employed, must be determined a violation of the Fourth Amendment."

It was "immaterial," Brandeis wrote, that such intrusions were in aid of law enforcement or for other beneficent reasons. "Experience should teach us to be most on our guard to protect liberty when the government's purposes are beneficent. Men born to freedom are naturally alert to repel invasions of their liberty by evil-minded rulers. The greatest dangers to liberty lurk in insidious encroachment by men of zeal, well-meaning, but without understanding."

THE KEYHOLE WARS

In January 1994, Vice President Al Gore outlined the administration's vision of the information superhighway to an enthusiastic audience in Los Angeles. He embraced proposals for a deregulated system with open competition and universal access. Media coverage was extensive and generally sympathetic, but lost amidst the enthusiasm for the brave new information world was Gore's signal to the law-enforcement community that it would play a central role in the development of the National Information Infrastructure. Sandwiched between his more libertarian themes, Gore promised that the White House would work to ensure that the superhighway would "help law-enforcement agencies thwart criminals and terrorists who might use advanced telecommunications to commit crimes."[3] On the Air Force 2 flight out of Los Angeles after the speech, privacy advocate John Perry Barlow asked Gore what this meant for the administration's policy regarding cryptography—the encoding of electronic communication to ensure their privacy and security. As Barlow later recounted, "He became as noncommittal as a cigar-store Indian. 'We'll be making some announcements . . . I can't tell you anything more.'"[4]

The vice president's uneasiness may have reflected the fact that the administration had definitively cast its lot with the intelligence agencies in the ongoing struggle over privacy. The administration would not only embrace proposals to mandate that the telecommunications industry build in special trapdoors for agencies to listen into digital communications, but was intent on pushing the so-called Clipper Chip, which would go into every phone and computer and would enable the government to decode any electronic communication. Law-enforcement agencies argued that their peepholes would be used only to fight terrorists and catch drug dealers, while protecting the privacy of law-abiding Americans. But as Barlow later quipped, "trusting the government with your privacy is like trusting a Peeping Tom to install your window blinds."[5]

Skeptics of government goodwill could turn to a long list of abuses. From 1940 to the early 1970s, intelligence agencies routinely opened and read the mail of individuals under suspicion. Sometimes agencies like the CIA opened mail at random, despite federal laws that make tampering with the mail a crime. Prominent activists, from Eleanor Roosevelt to Martin Luther King Jr., were also subjected to bugging and wiretaps. In King's case, the planting of microphones enabled J. Edgar Hoover to probe into virtually every corner of the civil-rights leader's private life. Perhaps most famously, the Nixon administration illegally wiretapped four journalists and more than a dozen government officials, ostensibly to search out leaks to the media. Though the taps never uncovered the source of the leaks, they netted a huge amount of delicious gossip about personal problems, sex habits, and delicate personal relationships. At one point, the FBI actually wiretapped a sitting member of the U.S. Supreme Court—William O. Douglas—and agents listened in on the conversations of Chief Justice Earl Warren and Associate Justices Potter Stewart and Abe Fortas.

For more than two decades, the FBI monitored the NAACP, maintaining dossiers on key officers and board members. In 1963, before his death, John F. Kennedy authorized the IRS to turn over tax records to the subversive-hunting House Un-American Activities Committee. Similarly, law-enforcement agencies kept close tabs on groups they regarded as potentially subversive, entering the office of the Socialist Workers Party more than 200 times, and photographing nearly 10,000 documents between 1941 and 1976. In 1986, the SWP won a court judgment of $264,000 for the campaign of bugging, wiretaps, and surreptitious entries. More recently, the Clinton White House was found to have somehow obtained roughly 900 raw FBI investigative files of former administration officials. At the same time, the IRS has been accused of a host of abuses, from staffers snooping through confidential tax returns, to accusations that the

IRS targeted critics for retaliation.[6] One notable case involved Gregory Millman, who wrote in the September 1991 issue of *Corporate Finance* that the IRS has failed to collect billions of dollars in taxes owed by major corporations. Fearing that the reporter had obtained sensitive insider information from someone in the agency, the IRS launched a probe of Millman. According to author David Burnham: "Almost immediately, without informing Millman, the IRS obtained from the telephone company a list of all the numbers the reporter had dialed from his phone. But then the IRS cast a much wider net, requesting telephone companies all over the country to provide it with the toll record of all the telephone calls made by those persons whom Millman had called."[7]

The 1960s and early 1970s were a high-water mark of concern over the growing violations of privacy. As early as 1964, Vance Packard declared, "The expectation that one has a right to be let alone—the whole idea that privacy is a right worth cherishing—seems to be evaporating among large segments of our population." As many as 14 million Americans were being scrutinized in some sort of security check.[8]

In April 1971, the U.S. Senate's Subcommittee on Constitutional Rights—known as the Ervin Committee—exposed a vast system of spying on civilians by the military. Tens of thousands of card files and dossiers of potential "dissidents" were kept on file by the Military Intelligence headquarters at Fort Holabird, Maryland.[9] Three years later, Ervin's committee reported that fifty-four federal agencies operated no fewer than 858 databanks that contained more than a billion separate records on American citizens. Eighty-four percent operated without any explicit legal authorization, and fewer than one-third of them notified citizens that they were collecting information about them.[10]

Even before it was consumed by Watergate, the Nixon administration took an extraordinarily expansive view of the government's power to conduct surveillance. Attorney General John Mitchell authorized wiretaps on grounds of national security, making the novel claim that the presidency carries with it the "inherent" power to do whatever the occupant of that office thinks that he needs to do to protect national security. Rejecting the Nixon-Mitchell claim, Judge George Edwards of the Sixth Circuit Court of Appeals, used the occasion to remind the litigants of the historical antecedents of privacy protections. "It is strange, indeed," Edwards wrote, "that in this case the traditional power of sovereigns like King George III should be invoked on behalf of an American president to defeat one of the fundamental freedoms for which the founders of this country overthrew King George's reign."

"Fear of surveillance, no less than fact," Alan Barth later wrote, "produces in the national community a chilling influence on the exercise of those liberties which are the indispensable basis for self-government." His comments were echoed by Senator Ervin himself, who said: "When people fear surveillance, whether it exists or not, when they grow afraid to speak their minds and hearts freely to their government or to anyone else, then we shall cease to be a free society."[11]

PEEPHOLES

Even though it would be the most zealous advocate for the idea, the notion of government peepholes did not originate with the Clinton administration. Beginning in the early 1990s, under the Bush administration, the FBI had quietly tried to persuade telecommunications companies to voluntarily provide FBI-friendly backdoors in their technologies. But the campaign, dubbed "Operation Root Canal" within the agency, proved unsuccessful.[12] Instead of giving up, the FBI began to instead push legislation that would have required all providers of electronic communication to provide immediate, real-time interception of all communications. The new law would also have covered computer networks as well as phone companies. Critics immediately denounced the proposal, questioning whether it was needed and warning that the proposal could actually weaken computer security by creating new holes. The proposal would have required companies installing new lines to get permission from the Department of Justice, which could deny a request if the system was not sufficiently easy to wiretap. An editorial in the *Washington Post* denounced the legislation as "an assault on progress, on scientific endeavor and the competitive position. It's comparable to requiring Detroit to produce only automobiles that can be overtaken by faster police cars."[13] More damning was the finding of the GSA, the government's primary purchaser of communications equipment, that the FBI's trapdoor proposal "would make it *easier* for criminals, terrorists, foreign intelligence [spies] and computer hackers to electronically penetrate the phone network and pry into areas previously not open to snooping."[14]

"O U R   O N L Y   I N I T I A T I V E"

Faced with opposition from the telecommunications industry and the public, the legislation died. But the FBI's interest was unabated. When Bill
Clinton came into office, anxious to establish an image of being tough on
crime, he was receptive when the FBI told the incoming administration
that the wiretap proposal was "not their top initiative, it was their only initiative."[15] Setting the tone of much of the debate that was to follow, FBI
Director Louis Freeh said he wanted legislation that "would require telephone companies to build into their new digital systems a technical capability that would allow continued electronic surveillance. . . ." Freeh
acknowledged that in 1993, only 976 criminal wiretaps had been ordered
obtained by law-enforcement agencies at any level and less than half of
those by the feds.* But, he insisted, "without federal legislation, federal
law enforcement will be crippled and the national security endangered."

"Without an ability to wiretap," he warned darkly, "the country will be
unable to protect itself against foreign threats, terrorists, espionage, violent
crime, drug trafficking, kidnapping, and other crimes."[16]

In August 1994, the administration introduced the FBI bill. The new
legislation succeeded in splitting the industry opposition, by limiting
coverage to "common carriers" and expanded the prohibition on the interception of cell-phone conversations to cordless phones and other communications that had been scrambled to protect privacy. But the legislation
required that the telecommunications industry change its technology to allow for the immediate interception of calls and their transmissions to a remote government facility where agents armed with warrants could listen.[17]
The law also required the companies to have enough capacity to meet
every surveillance order on demand. In return the government promised
as much as $500 million to cover their costs.

Supporters of the legislation argued—and continue to maintain—that
the legislation merely maintained the balance between law enforcement
and personal freedom provided in the Constitution. That balance, they insisted, was threatened by the new technology because it would put many
communications beyond the ability of law enforcement to access even with

---

*In 1997, federal and state judges approved, 1,186 requests for wiretaps. Nearly three-
quarters of those requests were for drug investigations (*New York Times*, May 20,
1998).

a bona fide court order. Even with the new trapdoors, they insisted, agents would still need a warrant approved by a judge before a wiretap could be approved. So, they argue, nothing had really changed.

This was decidedly *not* how civil libertarians and privacy advocates saw it.

The American Civil Liberties Union charged that the legislation "created a dangerous and unprecedented presumption that government not only has the power, subject to warrant, to intercept private communications, but that it can require private parties to create special access. It is as if the Government had ordered all builders to construct new housing with an internal surveillance camera for government use."[18] Privacy advocates, including Marc Rotenberg and David Sobel of the Electronic Privacy Information Center, urgently tried to make the case that the legislation broke dangerous new ground. In a letter to Senator Malcolm Wallop, they warned that the nation's communications infrastructure "has never before been designed with the stated purpose of facilitating the interception of private communications." Not only would the bill require that vulnerabilities be intentionally built into the system, but the legislation itself "represents a fundamental change in the law's approach to electronic surveillance and police powers generally.

"While we as a society have always recognized law enforcement's need to obtain investigative information upon presentation of a judicial warrant, we have never accepted the notion that the success of such search must be guaranteed. . . ."[19]

Privacy concerns were not only the questions raised by the legislation. Despite the urgent, anxious warnings of dire consequences if the tapping bill was not passed, the *New York Times* reported in March 1994 that there were "no instances in recent years where the FBI agents had encountered any technology-based problems in conducting wiretaps." In September 1994, Roy Neel, the president of the United States Telephone Association testified that "we are now aware of any cases where FBI has been unable to perform wiretaps because of technological restrictions." The FBI later insisted that it had encountered such barriers, but was able to cite only ninety-one incidences. Rejecting the FBI claim that the law simply restored a predigital balance between rights and security, Neel described the wiretap proposal as "a level of surveillance capability unprecedented in

terms of immediacy, breadth of application or capability for routine surveillance of individual citizens."

Opposition to the legislation drew an unusual collection of liberals and
conservatives, both fearful of the precedent the legislation would provide.
The reaction of editorialists was similarly negative. "The FBI's fix—requiring phone companies to build easily tappable systems—raises the unsettling image of forcing a phone company to design its 'home' so that the
police can easily enter. . . ." the *New York Times* wrote. Under the head-
line, "Keep Snoops Off-Line," *USA Today* slammed the proposal: "Here's
an idea that ought to chill your enthusiasm for the new information superhighway: the government wants to build it with bugs so agents can check
what you're saying and doing." The editorial writers cast the proposal in
Orwellian terms:

> Government agencies could build an electronic profile of anyone who
> picks up a phone or activates a computer modem. Privacy advocates
> say such profiles could include bill-paying records, political leanings,
> sexual preferences, and travel itineraries. They could include intimate
> e-mail messages and notes dictated to an electronic personal assistant.
> Calls to 900 numbers would be on file forever. The vast amount of in-
> formation about every one of us now available on computer would be
> compounded exponentially.[20]

Joining the chorus of opposition, the *Charlotte Observer* said the
FBI's wiretap bill "represents a shift in the American citizen's historic relationship with government. Whatever the gain in investigative inconvenience, insisting that electronic envelopes be equipped with built-in traces
and government operated zippers is contrary to the whole idea of a private
life."[21]

Such concerns, however, were no match politically for the FBI's warnings. Escalating his rhetoric, Freeh warned that without a wiretap–friendly telecommunications system, his agency "may be unable to
intercept a terrorist before he sets off a devastating bomb . . . unable to
rescue abducted children before they are murdered by their kidnappers."
Against such rhetorical pyrotechnics, personal-privacy concerns seemed to
be very weak tea indeed.

Brushing aside those concerns, Congress passed the FBI bill with extraordinary alacrity. The House Judiciary Committee approved the bill on October 4, 1994; the full House adopted it on October 5. The Senate Judiciary Committee approved the legislation the following day; and the full senate gave it final approval the next day. President Clinton quietly signed it into law on October 24, 1994.*

DROPPING THE NEXT SHOE

The ease with which the wiretap bill was passed was a chilling precedent for future struggles over privacy on the information superhighway. Clearly, the FBI's trapdoor into the superhighway provided merely the first opening. During the fight over the wiretap legislation, the ACLU warned that despite the bill's exemption of on-line services, the ultimate target was on-line communications. Given the new presumption that "industry has the affirmative responsibility to create special technical capacity for the government to snoop," the ACLU asked, was there "any real doubt that the FBI will be back in the years to come asserting that its ability to intercept communications has been thwarted by easily available encryption" and that it would also push for an easy backdoor to encoded communications?[22]

For many privacy advocates, the ability to have private communications in the electronic era is *the* privacy issue of the next decade. Indeed, the stakes could not be higher: Even as intellectual property becomes more valuable, it has become more vulnerable, as communication becomes more mobile and more easily interceptible. Moreover, the lines between the various forms of communication continue to blur as voice, data, and visual communication are bundled together, sometimes wireless, sometimes over common carriers.[23]

With all of the eyes watching and ears listening, what possible assurance can we have that any of this can be kept private? The answer is encryption.

---

*Five years later, opponents continue to oppose both the FBI's specific proposal and the $500 million appropriation for implementing the law. Despite the opposition, Attorney General Janet Reno told Congress that the Justice Department and the FBI "will avail ourselves of all lawful mechanisms available to force the implementation of the wiretap law."

10

■

Breaking the Code:

The Fight over Encryption

First a layman's primer on encryption. The technology itself may be mind-foggingly complex, but its applications and significance are relatively easy to understand. Despite its techie-trappings, cryptography is the essence of privacy in the electronic world.

Essentially, encryption enables anyone to send an electronic communication that can be read by only the person to whom it is sent. It provides security for everything from voice communications and e-mail to the electronic transfer of funds. Without encryption—or encoding—electronic communications such as e-mail are comparable to sending a postcard; such communications are open and easily read by third or fourth parties. Encryption is the envelope, the seal that keeps the communication private. It is also the reasonable guarantor of security for everything from health records to fund transfers to love letters.

Historian David Kahn traces the private use of encryption back four millennia to the ancient Egyptians. The Hebrew scribes of the Old Testament's Jeremiah also used a cipher, and Julius Caesar pioneered the use of codes for military purposes. "It must be that as soon as a culture has reached a certain level," Kahn has written, "probably measured largely by its literacy, cryptography appears spontaneously—as its parents, language and writing, probably also did. The multiple human needs and desires that demand privacy among two or more people in the midst of social life must inevitably lead to cryptology wherever men thrive and wherever they write."[1]

Encryption can also be a powerful tool to conceal plots and nefarious deeds. But as Carl Ellison notes, the same can be said of any arrangement that allows individuals to be sheltered from public scrutiny. "It is true that cryptology can give privacy to individuals trying to meet electronically (by videoconferencing, conference calls, etc.)," he writes, "but individuals have always had both an opportunity and a right to privacy. Sometimes this is achieved by meeting in a closed room or an open field. Sometimes it is achieved through cryptology. Citizens used this privacy to make love, to confess to a priest, to confer with a lawyer, to meet in various Anonymous twelve-step groups, to hold business meetings, to plan new inventions or product releases, to plan sales strategies, to have a pleasant chat with friends, and to engage in innumerable other innocent pastimes. In addition to this, some individuals use privacy to plan criminal activities.

"It would help law enforcement greatly," Ellison notes, "if every conversation in the last category were relayed directly to the appropriate agency to be tape recorded and used both to guide investigations and to be presented as evidence in an eventual court trial. However, there is no way to achieve this selective privacy."[2]

The most adamant advocates of encryption are the so-called cypherpunks, such as Eric Hughes. The author of the "Cypherpunk's Manifesto," Hughes has little faith in voluntary self-regulation, or the restraint of government.[3] His analysis is electronic-age realpolitik. "We cannot expect governments, corporations, or other large, faceless organizations to grant us privacy out of their beneficence. It is to their advantage to speak of us, and we should expect they will speak." But he also rejects European-style legislation or regulations that seek to protect on-line privacy because such regulations defy the fundamental and immutable laws of information in an information society.

"*Information does not just want to be free, it longs to be free . . . ,*" declares Hughes, "*information is fleeter of foot, has more eyes, knows more, and understands less than Rumor.*"

What this means is that if we are to expect any privacy we can count neither on the goodwill of our neighbors, the restraints of the powerful, nor the power of law. We are on our own; it is up to individuals to find creative ways of communicating and dealing with one another in ways that allow for anonymity.* But the very technology that erodes privacy also

---

* Hughes distinguishes privacy from secrecy. "A private matter is something one doesn't want the whole world to know, but a secret matter is something one doesn't want any-

provides the possibility of a strong privacy unknown to previous genera-tions. "People have been defending their own privacy for centuries with whispers, darkness, envelopes, closed doors, secret handshakes, and couri-ers. The technologies of the past did not allow for strong privacy, but elec-tronic technologies do." The bulwarks of the new strong privacy, Hughes declares, are cryptography, anonymous mail-forwarding systems, digital signature, and electronic money.

LOCK AND KEY

Until quite recently, encrypting electronic communications on a routine basis was not practical. Under old encryption technology both the sender and the receivers needed to have the same secret key—one to encode the communication, one to unlock it and read it. The problem with this is that it is both cumbersome and vulnerable to attack. But the modern history of encryption began in 1976, when Whitfield Diffie and Martin E. Hellman developed an alternate—and much easier—approach to encryption. In-stead of two secret keys they proposed using a "public key" and a "private key." The public key, as its name suggests, is freely available and can be ac-cessed by anyone who wants either to use or copy it. This is what you would use to send a communication. When the intended recipient gets your message, though, he must use his own private key—which no one else knows—to unlock the code. Another way to understand how this works, suggests Bruce Schneier, is to think of the two codes as a lock and key. "The world doesn't need a new lock design for every front door. It is enough to have one lock design, and hundreds of thousands of different

---

body to know. Privacy is the power to selectively reveal oneself to the world." For Hughes, the key to privacy in the electronic age is making sure that each party to a transaction has the knowledge only "of that which is directly necessary for that transac-tion." That requires we reveal as little as possible. "When I purchase a magazine at a store and hand cash to the clerk, there is no need to know who I am."

The key to assuring privacy in an open society, is the availability of "anonymous transaction systems"—a notable example of which is cash. In an electronic age, cryp-tography and its related technologies would serve the save function.

"Privacy in an open society also requires cryptography. If I say something, I want it heard only by those for whom I intend it. If the content of my speech is available, I have no privacy. To encrypt is to indicate the desire for privacy, and to encrypt with weak cryptography is to indicate not too much desire for privacy. . . ."

keys."[4] The advantage of the public and private keys is that there is no special handling required, no transmissions of code words, or numbers. The same technology can be used to verify the identity of both senders and recipients, by creating a digital signature.

The keys are codes generated by computers; they can be numbers, strings of numbers, words—it does not really matter. What does matter is the length of the key. Simply: The longer the key, the more bits, the harder it would be to crack the code and thus the safer the communication. In the world of cryptography, *bits matter*. A code that uses a 56-bit key, for example, could probably be cracked in a matter of hours; one that used an 80-bit key would take 10^7 years, a 112-bit key would take 10^{17} years and a 128-bit key would take 10^{22} years to crack.[5]

ENTER THE SPOOKS

The resurgence of academic interest in encryption in the mid–1970s was paralleled by increasingly aggressive efforts by the nation's intelligence establishment to slow and/or control the new technology. Not surprisingly, the agency most intimately involved in the issue was the National Security Agency, which undoubtedly boasts the most sophisticated code-breaking technologies and the most advanced information-gathering apparatus in the world.

NSA richly deserves its hyper-spooky reputation. Even the most intrusive technologies for invading privacy pale in comparison to the NSA's surveillance systems, such as Echelon, which is operated in conjunction with intelligence agencies in Great Britain, New Zealand, and Australia. Even for a century that has grown used to being watched and listened to, the implications are disconcerting. "Within Europe," a report to the European Parliament declared, "all e-mail, telephone and fax communications are routinely intercepted by the United States National Security Agency, transferring all target information from the European mainland via the strategic hub of London, then by satellite to Fort Meade in Maryland via the crucial hub at Menwith Hill in the North York Moors of the UK."[6]

Such watching and listening is clearly a major priority for intelligence agencies. According to a report by the conservative Free Congress Foundation, the Echelon site at Menwith Hill in Great Britain is the largest spy station in the world, with a staff of 1,400 NSA personnel and 350 staffers from the UK Ministry of Defense.*[7] The report to the European Parliament described Echelon as a worldwide surveillance apparatus that "stretches around the world to form a targeting system on all of the key Intelsat satellites used to convey most of the world's satellite phone calls, Internet traffic, e-mail, faxes and telexes." The system works by positioning ships, satellites and intercept stations across the globe—in New Zealand, Hong Kong, the United States, Australia, and Great Britain—which have the capability of capturing nearly every satellite, microwave, cellular, and fiber-optic communication on the planet. Wrote analyst Patrick Poole: "Having divided the world up among the UKUSA parties, each agency directs their electronic 'vacuum-cleaner' equipment towards the heavens and the ground to search for the most minute communications signal that traverses the system's immense path."[8]

What makes Echelon especially noteworthy is that unlike many of the other electronic spy systems developed during the Cold War, Echelon is designed "for primarily non-military targets: governments, organizations and businesses in virtually every country." The report to the European Parliament described Echelon as operating by "indiscriminately intercepting very large quantities of communications" and then analyzing all of the data using extraordinarily sophisticated artificial intelligence technology which listens, reads, and sifts the communications for key words, phrases, names, or places to "tag." Once tagged, the intercepted communications are captured, transcribed, and then forwarded to the intelligence agencies of the countries that might find them of interest. Each of the five countries in the system gets to contribute to the so-called "dictionaries" used by Echelon to identify special words and phrases in the intercepts. But the truly Orwellian power of the Echelon system is its capacity to filter, decrypt, and analyze the messages it captures. Echelon reportedly uses futuristic com-

---

*Writes Patrick Poole: "The backbone of the ECHELON network is the massive listening and reception stations directed at the Intelsat and Inmarsat satellites that are responsible for the vast majority of phone and fax communications traffic within and between countries and continents. The twenty Intelsat satellites follow a geostationary orbit locked onto a particular point on the Equator. These satellites carry primarily civilian traffic, but they do additionally carry diplomatic and governmental communications that are of particular interests to the UKUSA parties."

puters systems like the Silkworth system at Menwith Hill, which employs voice recognition, optical-character recognition and data-information engines to sift the messages. Other systems can "flag" an individual's voice pattern, so that the surveillance system can capture every conversation that person makes.

How might such powers be abused? We do not need especially active imaginations to imagine the possibilities. There have already been suggestions—some from whistle-blowers—that Echelon's technology was used to intercept real-time telephone conversations involving a United States senator and possibly a congressman.[9] In late 1998, the NSA was forced to acknowledge that Diana, Princess of Wales, whose file ran to 1,056 pages, was among those caught in its surveillance web. Though Diana was not a specific target, NSA's eavesdropping dragnet was so comprehensive that it picked up hundreds of *mentions* of the princess, apparently right up until the moment of her death.[10] The *London Observer* has reported that Echelon's data net has also snagged communications involving such groups as Amnesty International, Greenpeace, and a missions organization known as Christian Aid. But the possibilities for using such intercepts to win a business advantage may be even more tempting than political snooping. As the stakes of world trade grow, the edge provided by insider information about strategies, prices, and terms is increasingly invaluable.

In 1995, the *New York Times* reported that both the NSA and the CIA station in Tokyo had provided crucial detailed information to the U.S. trade representative whose negotiators were locked in difficult talks with Japanese car companies. A Japanese newspaper subsequently charged that the NSA was monitoring confidential communications among Japanese companies.[11] In 1994, intelligence agencies intercepted phone conversations between a French company and Brazilian officials who were in the market for radar systems.[12] The reports from the intercepts were forwarded to the American competitor, Raytheon Corporation. Other reports have linked NSA intercepts to negotiations over satellite deals involving Indonesia and oil and hydroelectric deals in Vietnam.[13]

As if that were not enough, European Union states, the parliament report said, have also signed a memorandum of understanding in 1995 agreeing to set up an international phone-tapping system that would include forcing network and service providers to install easily "tappable" systems.

THE NSA CAMPAIGN

Despite these extraordinary powers, the NSA was deeply worried that the spread of powerful encryption technology might interfere with its ability to watch and listen. At the urging of the security agencies, the U.S. government has treated encryption technology the same as it treats dangerous munitions, and has jealously restricted its export—even though it is easily available from vendors around the world. In the early 1970s, the government tried to control the market for encryption by setting the national standard—known as the Data Encryption Standard, or DES—at a mere fifty-six bits. One does not need to be a computer scientist to realize that the standard was set at a level that the NSA would have little trouble decoding. Indeed, in 1998, a group of cryptographers cracked the DES in less than three days using a machine they built for less than $250,000, proving that the government's standard could be decoded both quickly and cheaply.[4]

Under Director Bobby Ray Inman, the NSA also tried to put a damper on the development and dissemination of cryptographic know-how to the public by targeting academic research. At one point, an NSA operative went so far as to suggest that the NSA had exclusive control over the funding of research into encryption, but he later backed off. In an attempt to classify even those encryption products designed by nongovernment research, the NSA next tried to limit the ability of American scientists to present papers at scientific conferences, citing the 1951 Invention Secrecy Act. When two of their first targets, Professor George Davida of the University of Wisconsin and freelance researcher Carl Nicolai, received an order from the NSA declaring their work classified and ordered them not to discuss it in public, the two researchers not only refused the order but went public with the NSA's heavy-handed threat. Faced with publicity and brewing academic backlash, the agency backed off and rescinded its order, which it claimed was a mistake.[15]

Inman's next gambit was to declare encryption a threat to national security and call for limits on the public dissemination of encryption. "There is a very real and critical danger that unrestrained public discussion of cryptographic matters will seriously damage the ability of the government to conduct signals intelligence," he insisted.[16] The scientific community was outraged. "If you want to win the Indianapolis 500, you build the fastest car; you don't throw nails on the track," gibed the president of Association for Computing Machinery. Undeterred by the criticism, Inman asked the American Council on Education in 1983 to conduct a study on the limits on academic research on the subject. The ACE panel rejected the idea of restrictions on the dissemination of technical information on encryption, but endorsed the voluntary submission of papers to the NSA. So repugnant was the notion, however, that no scholars outside the agency itself permitted the NSA to vet their work.[17]

Throughout the 1980s the NSA pushed hard not only to keep the encryption genie in the bottle, but also to have a hand in the developing telecommunications superstructure.° Its clout would become apparent in the fight over the Clipper Chip.

THE CLIPPER CHIP

One of the early drafts of the wiretap bill would have explicitly banned the use of any encryption not authorized by the government. But in 1991, the Justice Department, NSA, and CIA had to agree that a flat ban on encryption would prove too controversial. So it was dropped for the time being.[18] But it was never off the table.

°In 1984, the Reagan administration gave the agency broad authority over computer security by designating the NSA—rather than the National Bureau of Standards—as the national manager for Telecommunications and Automated Information Systems Security. A second directive in 1986 gave the NSA even wider powers, which it seized with considerable vigor and enthusiasm. During the mid-1980s, the NSA used its new authority to send agents to visit private companies, including Lexis/Nexis, DIALOG, CompuServe, as well as financial institutions. Mead Data Central, the parent company of Lexis/Nexis reported one visit by five government agents, representing CIA, the NSA, and the FBI.

In part because it had overstepped its boundaries, in 1987 Congress passed the Computer Security Act, reaffirming the National Bureau of Standards as the point-agency for protecting the security and privacy of nonclassified information. Although the legislation was designed to reaffirm civilian control, the NSA continued to play a central role in the issue, both undermining and co-opting its rival agencies.

†In a memo to Defense Secretary Dick Cheney, the director of the CIA and the attorney general, Brent Scowcroft, President Bush's National Security Advisor, noted that "Success with digital telephony [the wiretap bill] will lock in one major objective; we will have a beachhead we can exploit for the encryption fix; and the encryption access options can be developed more thoroughly in the meanwhile."

Unfortunately for the intelligence agencies, both the technology and the marketplace threatened to outrun the NSA's ability to control the process. In September 1992, AT&T announced that it would begin to market a telephone encryption device called Surity 3600, which would sell for $1,100. The FBI and other agencies were both surprised and alarmed and, for a time, considered threatening AT&T with legal action if the company did not drop the idea of marketing a scramble-phone. But AT&T's move also provided the government with an alternative.

If the spooks could not ban nongovernmental encryption outright, the next-best option was to control the market for encryption technology. To do that, they would have to force the marketplace to accept the NSA's own encryption devices, which would enable private citizens and businesses to keep their communications private and secure from everyone . . . except the government. The technology the agency had in mind was known as Skipjack, but it was code-named "Clipper."[19]

The NSA "Clipper" would scramble any communications, *but the government would hold the key to them all.* After intense discussions between AT&T and the Justice Department, the telecommunications company agreed to drop its own device and instead adopt the Clipper for its new phone. In return, the company hoped, the government would make the NSA technology the new national standard.

That is exactly what President Clinton did. The final decision to go ahead with the Clipper Chip was made at a March 31, 1993 meeting attended by the vice president and the attorney general as well as the NSA, the CIA, and the Office of Management and Budget. A little more than two weeks later, the president announced his support for the Clipper as the new national standard, which was quickly followed by an order from the Justice Department for 9,000 new Clipper phones from AT&T. Under the guidelines issued by the Justice Department, the keys to the Clipper would be held by two government agencies with ties to the intelligence agencies and law enforcement. In theory, the agencies would release the "escrowed" keys only when they received the proper order, but under the Justice Department's rules they would be exempt from any sanctions for violations of the procedures. Individuals whose communications were intercepted would have had no rights to object or even to suppress the data.[20]

If Clinton thought that the market-based gambit would be accepted, he was quickly undeceived. Reaction was immediate and overwhelming. A Time/CNN poll found 80 percent of the public opposed the idea of the Clipper proposal.[21] The *Christian Science Monitor* editorialized: "The government should not be in the business of asking manufacturers to build secret backdoors into their equipment, particularly when government holds the keys."[22] And *Business Week* asked: "Will the Information Super-highway enable the federal government to become a high-tech snoop on a scale undreamt of in George Orwell's worst nightmares?"[23] Perhaps the most devastating critique came from columnist William Safire, who described the Clipper as a proposal that "we turn over to Washington a duplicate set of keys to our homes, formerly our castles, where not even the king in olden times could go."

"The clipper chip . . . would encode, for Federal perusal whenever a judge rubber-stamped a warrant, everything we say on a phone, everything we write on a computer, every order we give to the shopping network or bank or 800 or 900 number, every electronic note we leave our spouses or dictate to our personal digit-assistant genies.

"Add to that stack of intimate data the medical information derived from the national 'health security card' Mr. Clinton proposes we all carry. Combine it with the travel, shopping and credit data available from all our plastic cards, along with psychological and student scores. Throw in the confidential tax returns, sealed divorce proceedings, welfare records, field investigations for job applications, raw files and CIA dossiers available to the Feds, and you have the individual citizen standing naked to the nosy bureaucrat."[24]

Ignoring the scope and vehemence of the public opposition, the Clinton administration nevertheless announced on February 4, 1994 that it was formally adopting Clipper as a "voluntary" government standard. The "voluntary" part was largely for political cover because the Justice Department and the NSA continued to push manufacturers hard to adopt the Clipper standard, hoping to create a large enough market to make Clipper the de facto national standard—relegating other forms of encryption to the fate of the Betamax. At the same time, NSA began a campaign to convince other countries to adopt the Clipper standard themselves. Understandably, however, many of the foreign governments were more than a little reluctant to use a chip in all of their communications whose key was held by the NSA.

The effort was a nearly complete bust. Many of the AT&T devices bought by the federal government in the first flush of enthusiasm for the Clipper reportedly gather dust in government warehouses.[25]

THE HAPPY-FACE CLIPPER

The failure of Clipper did not mark the end of the government's attempt to limit private encryption. Beating a tactical retreat, the administration decided that nongovernmental encryption would be permitted . . . as long as the keys to every code were handed over to a "trusted third party" instead of a government agency. However, both the software and "third parties" would have to be certified by law-enforcement and intelligence agencies if the software was to be exported. Shortly after Vice President Gore outlined his support for "key escrow," privacy advocate Marc Rotenberg labeled the new policy "Clipper with a happy face."[26]

Apparently assuming that it would never occur to lawbreakers to find ways of avoiding insecure communications, the FBI began pushing legislation to make key-escrow systems mandatory—in other words, making it illegal for Americans to encode their communications without handing over the keys to a government-approved agency. And the administration's briefing papers bluntly declared that government lawyers had concluded after studying the issue that "Americans have no Constitutional right to choose their own method of encryption."[27]

In practical terms, the proposed laws would mean that every computer or system that used a security code would have to give a copy of that code to a government-approved third party. That would affect every set of medical records, as well as every cash machine, vending system, and on-line communications system. The idea of "key escrow" was an example of technological wishful thinking and legal chutzpah. Technically, it assumed that a system could be designed so that (1) it would provide security and safety for the "keys" handed over to third parties without creating nightmarish new system weaknesses, and (2) there was a practical way of also assuring that the government could get "covert access, ubiquitous adoption, and rapid access to plain text." Experts questioned both assumptions. "Keyholders" would have to manage literally billions of codes, which would be changing daily. Holding them accountable for failures or lapses would either be extremely difficult or simply impossible.

The proposal also marked a novel approach to the relationship between citizens and their government. For two centuries, the Fourth Amendment had protected citizens against unlawful searches and seizures. But now the administration was not only demanding that citizens, in effect, hand over keys to their front doors and personal files, but it would also make them criminals if they refused to comply. Storing or keeping any information in a way that the government could not easily read would now be a federal crime.*[28]

The administration's policy received another rude setback in mid–1996, when a panel of the National Research Council issued a 450–page report which not only endorsed the wide use of privacy-enhancing encryption, but warned against the passage of any new laws restricting encryption. The report by the NRC's Committee to Study National Cryptography Policy even suggested that it was the government's own antiencryption policies that might pose the greatest threat, because weak encryption not only made business, but also the nation itself more vulnerable to mischief. "If cryptography can protect the trade secrets and proprietary information of businesses and thereby reduces economic espionage (which it can), it also supports in a most important manner the job of law enforcement. If cryp-

---

*Gore's new policy also continued to sharply restrict the expert of encryption technology, limiting any codes to a mere sixty-four-bits. As Rotenberg noted, the administration was "trying to force America's software companies to include government-sought key-escrow features in its software as the price for export approval." Under the federal regulations, the government continued to treat encryption as munitions technology—treating it the same way it would a machine gun—and therefore subject to severe export restrictions. The logic of the ban apparently was that U.S. companies would be reluctant to create two different brands of software—one for domestic sale, another for export—and that they would therefore market only weak encryption systems. But the fact was that encryption was easily available throughout the world. There were numerous free encryption programs, including PGP—which stands for Pretty Good Privacy—which was offered free over the Internet. In 1993, an international study found more than 350 different encryption products from foreign companies in twenty-two different countries. By June 1996, Trusted Information Systems found that the number of encryption products had risen to 532 products from twenty-eight countries. Commenting on the futility of the government's efforts, Bob Kohn, general counsel for PGP, quipped: "The export law is like building a chain-link fence in the middle of the ocean to keep the water out." (Ashley Dunn, "Governments and Encryption: Locking You Out, Letting Them In," *New York Times,* October 8, 1997.)

tography can help protect nationally critical information systems and networks against unauthorized penetration (which it can), it also supports the
national security of the United States."[29]

Underlining the extraordinary and exceptional nature of the government's attempt to regulate encryption, a survey found that the United
States was virtually alone among free, industrialized countries in attempt-
ing to control the right of its citizens to keep their digital communications
and information private. Countries that had followed the FBI's lead and
imposed domestic controls on encryption included China, Pakistan, Rus-
sia, Singapore, Israel, and Belarus. Although France also had a quite re-
strictive policy, the government there announced plans to ease its controls
to "allow French companies to fully enter the marketplace of electronic
commerce currently dominated by U.S. companies." Other than that, almost every democratic, industrialized country in the world permitted their
citizens to use, manufacture, and sell encryption technology without any
legal limits.[30] In late 1997, the European Commission explicitly rejected
proposals to restrict cryptography or set up key-escrow systems. Taking a
radically different tack than American law-enforcement agencies, the EC
report argued that "restricting the use of encryption would well prevent
law-abiding companies and citizens from protecting themselves against
criminal attacks. It would not, however, permit criminals from using these
technologies."[31]

But the FBI continued to push hard for limits. During a congressional
hearing, FBI Director Louis Freeh declared: "[W]e're in favor of strong
encryption, robust encryption. The country needs it, industry needs it. We
just want to make sure we have a trapdoor and key under some judge's authority where we can get there if somebody is planning a crime." Moreover, the political dynamic seemed to favor the FBI. "When it comes right
down to it," reporter Brock Meeks wrote, "your privacy rights don't stand
a snowball's chance in hell of outweighing pictures of dead babies or pieces
of dead babies." And Freeh was not at all shy about invoking images of
rampant terrorism that might be unleashed in an encrypted world. "The
FBI," Freeh insisted, "cannot and should not tolerate any individuals or
groups . . . which would kill innocent Americans, which would kill America's kids."[32]

The bombing at the 1996 Olympics and the crash of a TWA flight to

Paris (which was, for a time, believed to be the work of terrorists) gave extra momentum to sweeping counterterriorism measures that would have dramatically increased the government's surveillance capabilities.*[33]

Freeh clearly viewed the spread of encryption with alarm. "The drug cartels are buying sophisticated communications equipment . . ." he warned Congress. "This, as much as any issue, jeopardizes the public safety and national security of this country. Drug cartels, terrorists, and kidnappers will use telephones and other communications media with impunity knowing that their conversations are immune from our most valued investigative technique."[34] Not only was the administration seeking tougher controls on encryption, it also sought authority to allow multi-point—also known as "roving"—wiretaps—a shift that would allow the government to wiretap *individuals* as well as locations.

The political appeal of the FBI's warning became apparent in the congressional debate over legislation regulating computer privacy. Civil libertarians, the computer industry, and privacy advocate had rallied around a bill proposed by Congressmen Zoe Lofgren of California and Bob Goodlatte of Virginia, known as the "Safety and Freedom through Encryption Act" (SAFE) that would have outlawed key escrow and would have eased the government's control on the export of the technology. Initially, the bill seemed headed for easy passage; it was cosponsored by more than 250 members of the House and was easily approved by the House Judiciary and International Relations Committees. But when Congress returned from its August 1997 recess, supporters faced a full frontal assault from the FBI and the Clinton administration. FBI director Freeh pushed hard for his own proposal to manage key escrow and toughen the export controls and, in mid-September, he won a stunning victory against the forces of computer privacy.

In the space of a week, the house National Security Committee voted to actually toughen export controls on encryption and the House Select

---

*The Clinton administration specifically announced: "We will seek legislation to strengthen our ability to prevent terrorists from coming into possession of the technology to encrypt their communications and data so that they are beyond the reach of law enforcement. We oppose legislation that would eliminate current export barriers and encouraging the proliferation of encryption which blocks appropriate access to protect public safety and the national security."

Committee on Intelligence passed legislation that appeared to create government controls over virtually every kind of software in existence. Not only did the committees endorse legislation requiring every computer user to supply the government with a set of spare keys, it also outlawed the use of *any* program that could not be easily accessed and read by government agents. The legislation was so sweeping that critics warned that it would "effectively outlaw software as we know it." Ratcheting up the pressure on Congress, Freeh had urged the tougher legislation in a series of "classified briefings" behind closed doors. That secret testimony, which emphasized the threat from criminals and terrorists, persuaded House members to opt for the most extreme antiprivacy proposals on the table.[35]

Taken literally, the Freeh plan would have banned the use of any code system that his agency could not easily break. As Peter Wayner noted in the *New York Times*, "The latest approach is to ban virtually everything and presumably let the prosecutors decide what qualifies as encryption." He noted that one early version of the proposed ban on codes was so sweeping that it "would seem to include all computers, paper, chalkboards, cereal-box decoder rings, writing instruments, and the arms of baseball managers telling their players what to do."[36] After these setbacks, privacy advocates quickly recovered and the House Commerce Committee rejected the FBI plan on September 24, 1997.[37] Six months later, the FBI announced that—at least temporarily—it would no longer push for the encryption controls.[38] The agency's retreat came only weeks after the *New York Times* reported that the battle over encryption was threatening President Clinton's political support in Silicon Valley.[39] Rather than reflecting a change of heart on the part of the FBI and the NSA, the decision to back off (for the time being) seemed to be a response to political arm-twisting from the White House.

Despite continued jockeying over the issue of export controls, however, the issue was never definitively laid to rest, and the victory for privacy advocates rested on the shakiest possible political ground. A single terrorist incident would quickly revive the proposals, especially if the episodes occurred at a time when the political parties are vying with one another for the mantle of toughness on crime. Savvy privacy advocates also recognized that the defeat of the more radical antiprivacy measures pushed by the FBI had the effect of making other attempts to regulate encryption seem more moderate in comparison. One proposal—known as McCain-Kerrey—would not overtly mandate the use of key escrow, but would effectively have forced it as a national standard. Under the legislation, any network either created by the federal government or financed in any way by the government would be compelled to hand over its "key" to a government-approved third party.[40] On top of that, the government would be allowed to purchase only those encryption products that allowed easy access to the keys. What could not be accomplished de jure would be accomplished de facto.[41]

The history of the government's attempts to provide itself with a trap-door into the nation's communications system explains the intensity of the reaction to the Intel Corporation's decision to install a "unique identifier" in its new Pentium III chips and to the revelation that the Secret Service had been quietly bankrolling a private company that was buying up tens of millions of driver's-license photos to create a national database. In both cases, the government appeared to accomplish indirectly what it could not achieve directly.

As in the case of the Clipper Chip, law enforcement's best hope may now be for private technology companies to embrace new (government-approved) standards providing for easy government access to communication. Given the political realities, it is unlikely that the FBI could ever have persuaded Congress to give it the right to plant tracking devices into every personal computer. But no law prevents the Intel Corporation—or any other company that dominates the marketplace—from doing so, thus providing the government precisely the access to personal communications that it was unable to get through the front door. The only flaw in such a plan is its assumption that consumers will accept such standards. It also assumes that competitors will not exploit the decision of companies like Intel which choose to sacrifice their customers' privacy.

PART 4

■

The Exposure Culture

■

11

The Tell-all Society

Why do we have such a hard time taking privacy seriously? Perhaps one reason is the fact that many of those who complain most loudly about its violations are also among our greatest exhibitionists. Until our own time, every civilization has set out some boundaries for those things that can be shown and those that must be hidden. As James Twitchell notes in his book on shame, cultures tend to differ on what is considered private, but they share essential similarities. "No matter where you are, you will feel shame for haphazard public excretions, difficult-to-manage eating/suckling habits, nonreproductive sexual behavior, and strange to us, dying. A shame rule of thumb: if you do it in private, if covering/uncovering is important, or if the act is surrounded by a lexicon of expletives and euphemisms, you can guess that shame is near."[1]

But shame is not simply the invention of civilization. There are indications that it is encoded into our humanity. "Man," Nietzsche wrote, "is the creature who blushes."[2] Our need to cover and hide ourselves not only defines our sense of self, but creates the boundaries that separate public and private. It reminds us that there are parts of our lives that need to be protected and sheltered. It also reminds us that we need to be able to retreat to a sanctuary, zone of privacy, in order to be able to face the world under some circumstances. As Carl Schneider argues, shame cannot be understood without understanding the role of privacy, and vice versa. Privacy allows us to engage in intimate relations and to tap our creative sides without being distracted by shame or pride. "A life without privacy," notes Schneider, "is a life lived at high noon, devoid of darkening shadows."[3]

In sharp contrast, a recent front-page story in the *Wall Street Journal* declared: "Openness Has Now Become the American Mantra: Silence Is

Seen as Suspect." A subhead added: "Hard to Get People to Shut Up."[4] Indeed it is, especially since this orgy of pseudo-confession is so often regarded as testimony to the honesty and authenticity of the sharer. Under relentless battering from the therapeutic sensibility of our century, restraint and reticence—among the famous and obscure alike—are now regarded with something like distrust. Keeping one's dysfunction or family turmoil to oneself is not only regarded as suspicious but potentially unhealthy, whereas unburdening oneself—to a therapist, casual acquaintances, readers, or a national television audience—has come to be seen as a sign of healing. And even if the public occasionally expresses distaste for all of this, it still devours the details. Our appetite for self-revelation seems matched by an appetite for the chance to peep. As far as I can tell, no supermarket tabloid has gone out of business for lack of readership.

THE EXHIBITIONIST SOCIETY

One of the themes of the 1998 movie *The Truman Show*—described as "watching a film about a television show about someone's life"—is that our culture has become jaded by mere drama. The movie opens with the audience being told, "We've become bored with watching actors giving us phony emotions. We're tired of pyrotechnics and special effects. While the world he inhabits is to some extent counterfeit, there is nothing faked about Truman. No script, no cue cards. It isn't always Shakespeare, but it's genuine. It's a life."[5] Or sort of a life. The movie's main character is the unwitting star of his own television show, whose theme is nothing more than the fact that it captures and broadcasts every aspect of his existence. Everyone is in on the show, except for Truman.

But the movie leaves a nagging question. Why did the producers in the film feel they needed to go to such lengths to convince Truman he was living a private life? There are obviously many Americans who require no such fiction—they are more than willing to expose themselves in far more graphic ways than Truman's producers ever imagine. In 1998, the media was briefly agitated by reports that two teenagers planned to lose their virginity live on the Internet.[6] Though the story turned out to be a hoax, the fact was that their "sharing" of such an intimate moment would have been small beans by current Internet standards. There is *nothing* that someone is not willing to reveal or share about his- or herself.

The so-called net-cam pages on the Internet, such as Jenny-cam, chronicle the banal existence of a new class of cyberexhibitionists. By one estimate, there are more than 400 Web sites devoted to around-the-clock monitoring of the daily life of men and women who escape from what Frederick Exley called the "the blank anonymity of life."[7] The Web cams are a culture of total surveillance. The so-called Jenny-cam monitors the daily routine of a twenty-one-year-old Washington D.C. woman named Jennifer Ringley, who allows hundreds of thousands of thrill-seeking Web surfers to watch her eat cereal, do her makeup, talk on the phone, and occasionally disrobe. Apparently, this is sufficiently diverting for 10,000 customers to pay $15 for the privilege of updating a picture of the day-in-the-life of Jennifer.[8]

The new technology has been a syngeristic boon for both voyeurs and exhibitionists, most of whom are not professionals, but get their thrills precisely from being watched, doing everything from showing off their navels, to having sex on camera. But not always. Perhaps the most notable aspect of the new cyberexhibitionism is its grinding *ordinariness.* Often the sites seem less about exhibitionism than in exorcising fears about being alone, antidotes to anxieties of obscurity. One self-surveilling cyberexhibitionist describes himself "as a longtime freelance game designer" who informs potential viewers that most of the time he "will be working on-line at his Web site design business and/or chatting with friends."[9] All Geek. All the time. Live.

This is, of course, unfair both to geeks and to cyberspace, for the Net has no monopoly on self-exposure. The price of admission on daytime television shows from Ricki Lake to Jerry Springer is usually the willingness to surrender any morsel of privacy and shame. Personal revelations, confessions, pseudo-confessions, and exhibitionism are the very meat of the genre, from the embarrassing and graphic to the exploitation of deeply intimate moments (reunions, confrontations) on national television. Women without legs talk about the kind of sex they like; women confess having sex with their husband's friends; teenagers discuss their anatomies. Confessions beget confessions in a televised competition for the most shocking personal self-revelation. ("I slept with my mother. I slept with my father. I slept with both.") Surely, it was no surprise that Timothy Leary planned to broadcast his death live via the Internet, after sharing in excruciating detail his drug intake to anyone who logged onto his Web site.[10] Having grown used to the limelight, Leary had, in the end, only his death to offer on the altar of celebrity.*

The Victorians, of course, had very different views. Although often derided as prudes, their attitude toward privacy reflected their sense that the intimacies and depths of life were fragile, in need of protection. As Joshua Meyrowitz commented, "Our own age, in contrast, is fascinated by exposure. Indeed, the act of exposure itself now seems to excite us more than the content of the secrets exposed."[11]

This applies especially to our cult of celebrity. In the aftermath of Princess Diana's death, celebrities complained bitterly about their own struggles with the media. Perhaps seeing their own lives and frustrations writ large in the struggle over the princess's privacy, they joined in a chorus of denunciation of the culture that had stalked the princess to her untimely death.

Describing an assault by the paparazzi, actor David Duchovny explained, "You get this rage. You have no control. It feels like an assault. You start to shake, your heart races. And you know they want to get into a fight. They can't lose." Model Christie Brinkley complained about tabloids that reported she was a shopaholic. Once confined to supermarket tabloids, such stories are now widely reprinted in other papers, broadcast on shows like *Inside Edition,* and on the Internet. "They say that's the price you pay for fame. But the price tag keeps changing, and it's gotten worse." Ellen DeGeneres, who broke cultural ground as a lesbian entertainer, identifies the morbid fascination behind much of the celebrity watching. "People are so fascinated by fame they'll go on talk shows—and if they can't be famous, they want to see someone else fail."[12]

Of course, that's part of the entertainment value of the culture of exposure: the same media that can make a common person into a celebrity can also strip celebrities of their pretensions, showing us that they are

---

*Nor is it surprising that there are plans to create an entire television network devoted to addiction and recovery. The Recovery Network will be a "round-the-clock media showcase of addiction and anomie," which will feature people discussing everything from "alcohol to drugs, to depression, sex, obsession, eating disorders, family violence, compulsive gambling and sexual abuse." (Ruth Shalit, "Dysfunction Junction," *The New Republic,* April 14, 1997.)

really "just like us." As E. L. Godkin once noted, "The dragging down of the mighty has been a not unpleasing sport to the natural man in all ages."

While recognizing the "perverse symbiosis" between the media and the publicity machines of celebrities, actor Tom Selleck told *Newsweek,* "If it came to a choice between this invasion of my privacy and the media promoting my career, I'd say, don't help me. Stay out of my life. Public figures are not public property."[13]

One would hardly know this, however, from the gaggle of celebrities and wannabes who crowd the public prints and airwaves, vying with one another to confess addictions, sexual fantasies, marital problems, and eating disorders. Describing the dilemma of the postmodern celebrity, Christopher Lasch drew a distinction between fame and celebrity. Whereas fame is based upon noble and noteworthy deeds of the sort chronicled by biographers, in contrast, celebrity is evanescent, the stuff of tabloids and talk shows, which are more interested in "personalities" than actual accomplishments.[14] The fleeting nature of contemporary glory, wrote Lasch, adds poignancy to the anxiety of would-be celebrities. Postmodern celebrities cannot afford privacy because it risks obscurity, an intolerable fate for those who can measure their worth only by the pseudo-standards of the contemporary media.

Lest the new celebrities be ignored, the stakes are constantly raised. And the culture alternately is shocked by and applauds the continuing stream of confessions. Although psychotherapy provides a model for this sort of "sharing," it is one thing to air one's private demons in the privacy of a therapist's office, quite another to disembowel oneself on the *Jerry Springer Show.* It is the difference between seeing a lover unveiled before in a moment of intimacy and a Peeping Tom looking in the bedroom window from the bushes. Not surprisingly, the democratization of celebrity has raised the ante of self-exposure for the rest of us. The modern approach to healing is as much John Bradshaw and his mummery about healing the inner child as it is about Freud. Instead of honoring the instinct of concealment, we encourage confession, preferably in front of an audience that will embrace and accept you. If not a therapist, then a support group or a television audience.

Despite her martyrdom, the patron saint of this culture of self-revelation was Diana, Princess of Wales.

STALKING DIANA

Diana is widely regarded as a tragic victim of the war on privacy. Certainly, her privacy was violated in every conceivable manner, tapes of Diana's intimate phone conversations were leaked to the media, and paparazzi stalked her. She was watched by spy agencies, and journalists dissected her every move. Ex-lover James Hewitt published a humiliatingly detailed account of their affair, an act of betrayal that even if it stood alone, would have been a life-changing violation.

Hewitt's caddishness, of course, did not stand alone. Diana was the ultimate quarry. Vying with one another for circulation, the London tabloids were willing to pay enterprising and shameless photographers millions of dollars for capturing her in a private moment. The more private, the better. According to one report, the widely circulated photo of Diana embracing boyfriend Dodi al-Fayed netted the photographer more than $3.2 million, more than enough incentive to drive the press to even more fervid excesses. Photographers would hide in trees and bushes or masquerade as window washers. Even their language seemed to capture the brutish nature of their assault on her. Sounding for all the world like rapists, they called taking Diana's picture "doing Di," while rapidly snapping pictures of her was "to smudge," "to whack," "to hose," "to rip," or "to bang" Diana. When she became upset and lashed out at photographers or fled them, the photographers called it "being looned," a not-so-subtle hint that they regarded their prey as unstable.[15]

The public simultaneously deplored the brutishness of the media and devoured every morsel it fed them.

THE PRINCESS CONFESSES

Because of the tragic circumstances of her death, it is easy to forget that Diana set a new standard for conspicuous emotionalism and self-exposure. Starting in 1991, she began recording the story of her life and her troubled marriage for journalist Andrew Morton, who took pains to conceal Diana's actual involvement until after her death. Indeed, Diana seems to have approached her revelations in Morton's book almost as a form of therapy, pouring out her vulnerabilities to the journalist's tape recorder. Morton submitted written questions to Diana "about every aspect of her life," and admitted later that he was "stunned by Diana's candour . . ."[16] Although Diana was destined to become a martyr of intrusive, predatory journalism, she was also a willing participant in the media's dissection of her life. Largely as the result of her own revelations, the public came to know what drugs she took, which psychologists and spiritualists she consulted, the size of her waist, the frequency of her vomiting, her 1982 attempt at suicide by throwing herself down a flight of steps, her therapies, and her various emotional turmoils. Perhaps not fully aware of the contradiction, she counted a number of journalists and editors as "confidants."* Throughout her final years, she "confided" details of her married life and her romances to these journalists, often with full expectation that they would be emblazoned across the front pages of British newspapers. As one commentary noted after her death, the media's relationship with Diana "was at times symbiotic rather than parasitic." She was not above leaking stories of her own romances to make other suitors jealous. And as much as she came to resent the media, she went on BBC to discuss her failing marriage and admitted her affair with James Hewitt, opening virtually every aspect of her life to scrutiny. Diana even publicly described how she told her sons that she and

---

*Although she famously described being hounded by paparazzi as "worse than sexual abuse," Diana was also not above using those same photographers to make her own point. Vacationing in St. Tropez with her sons William and Harry, as a guest of Mohammed al-Fayed, Diana was at first annoyed at the boatloads of paparazzi that flocked around her. Her children reportedly were actually alarmed, and feared for her safety. Diana's response was to make herself available to the photographers on her own terms. Each morning the princess and the two princes would appear on the beach where they "cavorted willingly in full view of the photographers." The resulting pictures of Diana thoroughly enjoying herself in a bathing suit were devoured by much of the world press. Reportedly, the paparazzi were so grateful for her cooperation that they sent her one hundred red roses. Not coincidentally, the explosion of public attention coincided with and completely overshadowed her ex-husband's birthday party for Camilla Parker-Bowles. She had trumped her rival by sacrificing her privacy.

As her fateful romance with Dodi al-Fayed intensified, Diana continued to try to manipulate the media's coverage. As she disported herself on al-Fayed's yacht, the *Jonikel,* with Dodi, Diana actually tipped off photographers about her "secret" rendezvous, occasionally hand-picking the photographers who would have access to these private moments. In the final days of her life, Diana herself passed word to fashion photographer Mario Brenna who was able to shoot roll after roll of the princess and Dodi frolicking together in the surf. Later, she let photographer Jason Fraser know the exact time and locations along the French and Italian coasts where she and Dodi would be sailing. Again, the results were seemingly intimate shots of the couple romping together on a Jet Ski.

Charles were splitting up. She also talked publicly about how she and her sons discussed their father's relationship with her rival, Camilla Parker-Bowles, surely one of the most private moments of her life.

Diana's penchant for self-revelation seems to have been contagious. Even the disclosure of the most trivial details had become the coin of the realm. Diana's sister-in-law, the Duchess of York, went so far as to share with the readers of her own autobiography that she had gotten plantar warts after wearing a pair of shoes she had borrowed from Diana, an embarrassing detail that infuriated Diana and resulted in a marked cooling of their friendship.

It did not escape Diana or others that much of her popularity stemmed from her willingness to confess her unhappiness. Surely, Diana would have been famous and popular had she been more discreet, but it was the poignancy of her personal story that made her of the brightest star in the constellation of late-century celebrity. Diana was not only a role model, but also a patron of the therapies that appealed so much to the disappointed and the injured. She was the first post–Oprah member of the Royal Family and, as such, was the exemplar of the new ethic of sharing, openness, and self-revelation. Her depressions, panics, and griefs were meticulously shared, documented, and reported. Justifying her decision to tell all to Andrew Morton, she described herself as "desperate," at "the end of my tether." "I can't stop weeping," she said of herself on one occasion. A friend described her "crying, sobbing, wailing." One sometimes suspects that if Winston Churchill never had an unpublished thought, Diana never had an unreported cry.

"Diana was news when happy," a commentator noted in the *London Times*. "She was bigger news when unhappy." Indeed, he suggested, the "more reckless Diana became with her happiness, the more she acquired the aura of a patron saint. She tore at her scar tissue. She bared her feelings to the cameras and enraged the respectable."[17] Much of her appeal arose from her willingness to tear open the vulnerabilities of her life. She was the ultimate talk-show guest, the fairy-tale princess whose life was as messed up as any viewer's. Describing Diana as "the paradigm unhappy woman of today," the *Times* commentator noted that "her illnesses, her turbulent emotions, her infidelities, her fascination with publicity, fame, health and shopping, struck a chord with people from all walks of life. . . ."

"She was the spokesman for those with impossible husbands, worried about their appearance, wrestling with divorce, careers, children, trying to match impossible expectations."[18]

After her death, Morton wrote that the princess's funeral marked "the passing of the old order, the ascendancy of a new ethic, which Diana so vividly personified."[19] What, precisely, was that new order? Certainly, it included a more human face for royalty, but it also marked a sea change in attitudes toward reticence. Even the normally sanguine English expressed anger at the royal family for their failure to engage in the sort of public emotionalism that Diana had personified. Diana's legacy stigmatized such restraint, which came to seem cold, even callous.

Even in death, Diana embodied our ambivalence about privacy. The day of her funeral, one caller to MSNBC confessed that she shared the outrage over the media's intrusions into the late princess's life, but found herself wanting the cameras in the church to show her the faces of the two grieving princes. She wanted to *see* them.

No one seriously objected to efforts to protect the privacy of Diana's children, but the lack of public emotional display by the royal family became a major issue, as even the British came to feel that they were somehow entitled to displays of public emoting. English restraint had become a sign of coldness and, worst of all, to our modern sensibility, a lack of sincerity. Paradoxically, the same public infuriated by the press's invasion of Diana's privacy bayed for public weeping from her survivors. Few seemed to have recognized the contradiction, at least at the time.

THE POSTMODERN CELEBRITY

Indeed, Diana was hardly exceptional in her willingness to expose herself. The idea of stripping oneself of secrets—family, personal, and sexual—is not only a cardinal doctrine of twelve-step programs, but colors the attitudes of society at large. What was meant to be whispered in the closets is now shouted from the rooftops, and each confession implicitly puts more pressure on others to also "share" lest they be seen as elitist or repressed. Perhaps that explains why J. D. Salinger is regarded as an eccentric crank for insisting that privacy and obscurity are a writer's most sacred possessions, while Roseanne Barr gets her own talk show.

Diana's approach to self-revelation and, ultimately, her celebrity appeal contrasted dramatically with Jacqueline Kennedy Onassis and Princess Grace. Like Diana, they also dealt with difficult personal issues, but chose to be far less forthcoming. Reportedly, Jacqueline Kennedy Onassis's early admiration turned to active disapproval of what she saw as Diana's public "disemboweling" of herself. No stranger herself to violations of privacy, Jacqueline Onassis felt no obligation to become a participant in her own deconstruction.

Perhaps Diana was so feckless with her privacy because it was her public rather than her private life that was the source of her self-esteem. In public she was admired and in control, while her private life was apparently a mess, a tangle of doubts, frailties, and confusion. Though most people draw strength and sustenance from private life and use it to create moral capital for their public personas, Diana seemed to draw confidence from her public image, using her celebrity persona to compensate for her private confusion. Public success became the balm for private unhappiness and perhaps a reason for what amounted to the self-immolation of her private life in leaks, confessions, and self-disclosures. In this respect, Diana was also the very model of the postmodern celebrity.

THE PRIVATE CELEBRITY

There is a certain paradox in celebrities who have spent their lives exposing themselves, only to wax indignant because they have been exposed. They are natives of a world that trades in the manipulation of images, where *seeming* is more important than doing. So their complaints often ring hollow.

But such complaints are also hauntingly familiar with their sense of powerlessness, of violation, and the loss of control that accompanies any assault on privacy. With all due allowance for the differences, celebrities wrestle with many of the same questions that confront those of us who are less notorious: What price are we willing to pay for living our lives in the modern fishbowl? Do we waive our private lives every time we go on-line? When we speak out on political issues? When we buy a product? Call a talk show? Make a phone call? Or are victimized by a crime? Can public figures also lead private lives? Or have they inevitably and irrevocably become public properties?

Put another way: When someone offers themselves to the public for scrutiny, can they legitimately close certain doors or pull some shades on their lives?

If we take privacy seriously, the answer has to be yes, even for the most flagrant exhibitionist among us. If I invite you into my living room, that does not mean you have a right to go into my bedroom uninvited. If I show you my family photo album, I have not given you permission to peep at me in the shower. I can open the door so far and no farther.

Of course, it is not so simple, especially in the age of total exposure. Public figures need to recognize that it is far easier to leave doors closed than to try to close doors that have been flung open. To the extent that celebrities or public persons of any sort are willing to expose their intimacies and faux-intimacies for personal or professional advantage they risk eroding their privacy altogether. Realistically, can Ellen DeGeneres have much expectation of privacy for her sexuality? What about Madonna? Or Dennis Rodman? In contrast, the dignity and reserve of Katie Couric in the wake of her husband's death was an almost startling counterpoint of grace, and was generally rewarded by both respect and reticence about her private life.

Unfortunately, reticence cannot always protect privacy, as witness Jackie Onassis. But the relentless exploitation of the personal inevitably invites further incursions—as witness Bill Clinton.

12

■

Clinton's Bedroom:

Privacy and Sex

It's not their business.

——Monica Lewinsky to Linda Tripp

It's nobody's business but ours.

——President Bill Clinton, August 17, 1998

Despite the title of this chapter, the nation's debate over Bill Clinton's right to be let alone did not involve his bedroom. Perhaps that would have made for a simpler dilemma, or at least one in which the lines could be drawn with somewhat more confidence. Instead, the question of the president's privacy dealt with what he did in a hallway off of the Oval Office, a place that was both private and public. It is not going too far to say that the entire relationship took place on the razor's edge of private and public.

Lewinsky once complained that while she was getting her "Christmas kiss" from the president in the doorway to the study off the Oval Office, Clinton "was looking out the window with his eyes wide open while he was kissing me and then I got mad because that wasn't very romantic."

Clinton explained to her, "Well, I was just looking to see to make sure no one was out there."

As Clinton told the grand jury, he did not want to be observed, remarking that anyone who did would have been an exhibitionist. "I tried to do it where nobody else was looking at it."[1]

OF PRESIDENTS AND PRIVACY

Clinton's sex scandals became a Rorschach test on social values, ranging from attitudes toward infidelity to the relationship of private character to public duty. But the undercurrent of much of the debate was the question of whether the president's conduct was private, and thus, whether the investigation of that conduct was an invasion of Bill Clinton's right to be let alone.

Although the nation's opinion leaders were appalled by Bill Clinton's lack of contrition in his first apology to the nation (the first of what was to be many), clearly many Americans responded sympathetically to the president's plea for personal privacy. Despite the growing evidence that the zone of privacy was shrinking under relentless media, political, technological, and legal assault, Clinton insisted, "Even presidents have private lives." Referring to his sexual indiscretions, Clinton said, "Now this matter is between me, the two people I love most—my wife and our daughter—and our God . . . Nothing is more important to me personally. But it is private, and I intend to reclaim my family life for my family. It's nobody's business but ours."[2]

This did not bring the matter to an end. But Clinton raised a larger and more urgent question: Did even presidents have private lives? And was it anybody's business what they did in those lives? In this context, Clinton was quite right: There is a right to a private life, even for presidents. I would go even further and say that the private life is essential for the existence of the public life. The erosion of privacy does not simply undermine private life; it cripples public life as well. The public realm easily overwhelms the private. But in Clinton's case, we see the corollary that the private can also overwhelm the public. Private life needs protection because of its smallness and its fragility. But Clinton's case reminds us that public life also needs protection from the private, lest it be trivialized.

For better or for worse, Clinton's case threatened to frame the growing debate over privacy at a time when public ambivalence was more acute than ever. At the most obvious level, the scandal threatened to change the basic norms of sexual privacy, in part by polarizing discussions of the issue. Clinton's critics argued that sexual conduct and personal character were crucial for judging a man's public character. On the other hand, many of his defenders openly applauded the public "outings" of the indiscretions of other public figures, especially those of the Republican persuasion. By decade's end, the danger was that the private lives of public figures might now be whipsawed by both Clinton sympathizers and foes. Media standards seemed especially to be in flux. After the story of Congressman Henry Hyde's three-decade-old affair was made public, media pundits and politicians alike bemoaned the violation of his privacy, and lamented the state of politics that had led to the use of private indiscretions as political ammunition. But the fact was that the story *was published* and repeated. By the newly emerging standards of media propriety, a story of steamy or seamy private doings need only be published by a single outlet to become the subject of general media reporting and comment. In January 1999, the airwaves of conservative talk radio buzzed with reports of an investigation by the supermarket tabloid the *Star* into the possibility that President Clinton had fathered a love child, while the mainstream media provided a forum for porn publisher Larry Flynt to accuse a Republican congressman of sexual indiscretions. At one time the mainstream media would have paid little if any attention to either the tabloid or the pornographer, much less treated them as bona fide sources. But by century's end, they had become an unavoidable part of the information chain. As it turned out, the story of the love child fizzled when a DNA match turned up negative, but only after it had been reported in the *Drudge Report,* the *New York Post,* and dozens of talk shows. Even as a nonstory, though, it was a notable milestone in the shift in media standards because the only source for the tale was a tabloid, *which had not yet even published the story.*

If the tabloid seemed a questionable source of information, Larry Flynt's *Hustler* fell even lower on the sleaze chain, yet his attack on the personal life of Representative Bob Barr was widely covered in major newspapers and news networks, even when he ventured beyond allegations of extramarital affairs. Both CNBC and CNN broadcast details of Flynt's allegations concerning an abortion by one of Barr's ex-wives, raising the possibility that the "outing" of private sex lives could extend to other reproductive issues as well.

Bill Clinton was not the first president to find his private life under siege. Other presidents have also found themselves under a microscope, and their private sexual lives have long been the subject of gossip, conjecture, and even controversy. Grover Cleveland's fathering of an illegitimate child became a campaign issue; Woodrow Wilson's second marriage was the subject of intensive and often-malicious speculation; Warren Harding made himself notorious for his own Oval Office escapades. Historians continue to debate the relations between Franklin Roosevelt and Lucy Mercer and between Dwight Eisenhower and Kay Sommersby.

Not even the Founding Fathers were exempt from malicious gossip. Whispers reported (falsely) that Alexander Hamilton was the illegitimate son of George Washington. Embroiled in scandals involving his sexual liaison with a married woman, Hamilton himself felt compelled to take out newspaper advertisements not to admit his sexual infidelities, but to defend his public virtue. Perhaps most famously, Thomas Jefferson was dogged by rumors that he had fathered a child with one of his slaves, Sally Hemings. For his own part, Jefferson was not above secretly subsidizing a scurrilous scribe named James Callender who spread malicious personal gossip about Jefferson's opponents. Turning on his onetime patron, Callender played a central role in exposing Jefferson's alleged sexual escapades.* By any measure, the sexual exploits of John F. Kennedy were more the stuff of the *Satyricon* than of Schlesinger (Arthur). But until Clinton, the Republic was able to go about its business, more or less undisturbed by the peccadilloes of a president.

Even so, public reaction to Clinton's sex life was notably different from that of the media and political elites. Many Americans evinced a remarkable willingness to look the other way, even as the scandal mounted. The depth of the public's sense of privacy was reflected by the number of Americans who felt that the president's privacy should be held so inviolate that they were willing to forgive even perjury to protect it. Liberal commentators expressed exasperation (at least initially) with the lack of concern over the president's prevarication; conservatives saw signs of moral myopia. But the public's reaction should also have been evidence that it regarded the entire question of privacy from a different vantage than the

---

*"By the time Jefferson ascended to the presidency, the private lives of public figures were clearly regarded as fair game by the press, and Jefferson, who had been active behind the scenes in paying off hired character assassins in the party wars of the 1790s, knew perfectly well that he could expect the same treatment." (from Joseph J. Ellis, *American Sphinx: The Character of Thomas Jefferson*, New York: Vintage Books, 1996, p. 255). Though many of President Clinton's defenders were quick to draw comparisons between Clinton and Jefferson, it would not perhaps be unfair also to note that Jefferson's journalistic hit-man, James Callender, was in many ways a precursor of Clinton's own James Carville.

Washington elites, and that it did so with a considerably heightened sense of urgency.

For years, opinion polls have shown that the public takes privacy very seriously. By overwhelming margins, the public feels that its privacy is being undermined. But such anxieties have not resulted in more than modest media attention or more than token legal protections. Some of the support for Clinton may have arisen from this frustration. In the public's mind, the connection between predatory media intrusions and the tragic death of Princess Diana was still strong. Many reacted viscerally to Linda Tripp's betrayal of Monica Lewinsky by secretly recording their conversations.

In more than one respect, Bill Clinton was a proxy for their own anxieties. If even the president has a right to privacy than so does any man. The public's willingness to extenuate Clinton's conduct was at least in part a plea for tolerance and protection of the fragility and failures in their own private lives. There is no mystery here. You have only to imagine how you would feel to have the most intimate details of your sex life broadcast across the world. Those most private moments, when we let down our guard, when we share our secrets, or express inarticulate emotions, all risk appearing absurd, even repellent if laid out in print, subject to the eyes and comments and judgments and gibes of people wholly unconnected with us. Most of us would draw the line at much milder invasions, including our relations with members of our family, the time we spend with our children, our religious faith, our reading and television habits and our salaries. Instinctively, the public recognized that privacy is so important precisely because it protects the most intimate, vulnerable parts of our lives. And few such areas are more vulnerable than sex. Most of us would be shocked and violated to know that we were being watched, or even overheard at such moments. Understandably, then, compelling anyone to disgorge those details to strangers, or to a grand jury, tapped deep wells of discomfort.

Instinctively, we also recognize the impossibility of discussing sex in public without changing the experience irrevocably. The reason why so many love notes seem silly is that, unless they were endowed with the affections of the parties, many of them are, in fact, clichés. Take away that human nuance—which is precisely what media coverage and legal proceedings do—and what is left is to genuine human relations what a fossil is to a living creature. Exposing any intimate relationship to a public audience not only flattens it; it almost invariably robs it of any individuality.

Like Greek dramas where the characters don masks, the exposed sexual relationship assumes a symbolic, assigned place in the public debate of the day. Because society's need to uphold its moral standard becomes more important than the needs of any individual private life, our privacy is offered up as a sacrifice to particular anxiety of the moment. The public agenda takes precedence over whatever impact the revelation might have on a family or the relationship itself.

BILL'S BOXERS

How ironic then that the president who wrapped himself so tightly in our anxieties about our privacy has done as much as any political figure to efface the lines between private and public. In many ways, the Clinton presidency was the apotheosis of the feminist slogan of the 1960s that the "personal is the political." Bill Clinton certainly seemed to think so.

Indeed, Clinton's political career was a running experiment in the blurring of the private, the personal, and the political. He not only pioneered the use of his feelings and his inner life as political tools and weapons, but also invited the public to ask questions of remarkable brazenness. In one memorable episode, Clinton was asked on an MTV show whether he wore "briefs or boxers." By some accounts, he blushed. But he also answered. In 1992, at the Democratic National Convention, Clinton went even further, sharing his emotional pain with a nationwide television audience: "I never met my father. He was killed in a car wreck on a rainy road three months before I was born, driving home from Chicago to Arkansas to see my mother. After that my mother had to support us. So we lived with my grandparents while she went away to Louisiana to study nursing. I can still see her clearly tonight through the eyes of a three-year-old: kneeling at the railroad station and weeping as she put me back on the train to Arkansas with my grandmother."[3]

Speaking to the same convention, his running mate, Al Gore invoked his six-year-old son's near-fatal accident. Four years later, he described his sister's death from lung cancer, turning an intensely private moment into a political score. In political terms, few public figures have gone as far into blurring public and private as Hillary Rodham Clinton, who has led the way in expanding the definition of those things that are everyone's business. Like feminist critics of the 1960s, Hillary Clinton argued that many of the areas of life that had previously been regarded as private were, in fact, profoundly political, including domestic arrangements, childbearing and child-care practices, as well as the relations between the sexes both at home and at work. Her book, *It Takes a Village*, may have many virtues, but a concern for personal privacy is not one of them.

Even before anyone had ever heard of Monica Lewinsky, critics remarked on the dangers of exploiting the intimacies of private life for political gain. Author Janna Malamud Smith noted: "The process of displaying private feelings to achieve public ends distorts them, and corrupts their meaning." Of course, Clinton and Gore did not invent the pseudo-confession, nor are they responsible for the more widespread tell-all culture that dominates our therapeutic society. But their political style marked a significant step in the transition of private disclosure once reserved for psychotherapy into the "public pseudo-confession of the political convention." It was perhaps not surprising that some of Clinton's strongest support in his time of troubles came from Hollywood, a tribe of exhibitionists who bitterly resent their own loss of control over their privacy. It was, in fact, a Hollywood producer who orchestrated Clinton's strongest and most adamant denial that he had ever had sexual relations with Ms. Lewinsky. It won plaudits for its appearance of sincerity. Months later, Clinton won similar plaudits for his very public acts of contrition and pleas for forgiveness, once again turning private moments of repentance into occasions for political redemption.

But as the political exemplar of the new age sensibility that valued confession, sharing, and faux-intimacy, Clinton seemed unaware that the politics of personal revelation carried the seeds of what he called the "politics of personal destruction." As Smith notes, "by using private feelings for public gain, Clinton set the stage for further invasions of his own privacy." As Bill Clinton was later to find, "once played *by* you, the personal thing is played *on you* ad nauseam."[4]

THE PERSONAL
AND THE POLITICAL

Clinton's problems did not begin with a consensual sexual affair. They began with a sexual-harassment lawsuit from Paula Jones, a state employee who alleged that her ultimate boss—the governor—had her summoned to a hotel room, where he propositioned her crudely. Although the case was eventually dismissed and settled out of court, the *Jones* case would have momentous political and legal repercussions. A unanimous U.S. Supreme Court gave Jones the right to proceed with her suit against a sitting president. The courts also struck down Clinton's repeated attempts to assert privileges, including confidential conversations with government lawyers and the Secret Service, establishing precedents that will haunt his less-libidinous successors.

Clinton's scandals cannot be understood without understanding the extraordinary shift in attitudes toward sexuality and sexual harassment over the last two decades. Modern sexual-harassment law is a direct product of feminist theorists, including Catherine MacKinnon, who were quite explicit in their suspicion and even rejection of the idea of personal privacy. Their claim—which has become enshrined in harassment law—is that the personal relations between employees were no longer, strictly speaking, personal. They were political and potentially fraught with legal risk. Looking, joking, propositioning, not to mention touching, groping, or trading favors for sex became a major preoccupation of both the public and private sectors. Many of the same pundits who claimed that the Lewinsky case was about "just sex" seem to forget that sexual harassment was always about sex. The leering supervisor (or the touching, caressing, leering supervisor) was no longer a private matter between the supervisor and the employee. Their desires, motives, interactions were no longer strictly personal. Inevitably, as the zone of law expanded, the zone of privacy shrank. Increasingly, individuals were compelled to reveal sexual habits, desires, and practices. Before Clinton was sued by Paula Jones, it was the case of Supreme Court Justice Clarence Thomas that defined the issue in the public mind and shaped public perceptions. Notably, his defenders never claimed that if the allegations were true, the former EEOC chairman's conduct should be considered a matter of his personal or private life.

THE SEX PRIVILEGE

In the wake of the Clinton-Lewinsky affair, writer Jeffrey Rosen has suggested that courts might want to recognize and enforce what he calls "something like a sexual privilege," which would be akin to the priest-penitent privilege or the attorney-client privilege, but which would specifically shield "innocent people from the need to answer questions about their legal, but embarrassing sexual activities."[5] Rosen also argued that the president should throw himself behind the shelf of constitutionally protected "zones of privacy." Leaning on the legal scholarship of Yale's Akhil Amar, Rosen wrote that citizens, including Clinton, who were asked such intrusive questions by a grand jury should be able to invoke the Fourth Amendment's privacy protections. Indeed, during his grand-jury testimony, Clinton seems to have followed—at least in part—advice by lawyer Nathan Lewin, who urged the president to invoke "the zone of privacy protected by the Fourth Amendment" as justification for refusing to answer highly personal questions.

As Rosen concedes, Clinton's lawyer in the sexual-harassment suit could have sought a protective order in the civil proceedings, but chose not to. Even so, he argued that the judge should have been more sensitive to Fourth Amendment concerns and should "have ruled out of bounds the entire inquiry into whether or not Clinton rewarded women who had sex with him."[6] But that is precisely the problem. If the issue was whether Clinton has used his public position, either as governor or president, to provide public rewards to public employees in exchange for sex, then, by definition, it was no longer a private matter, even by the most expansive understanding of privacy.

Moreover, the chances that the courts will recognize a "sexual privilege" are remote as long as sexual-harassment laws are enforced zealously and as long as courts find that the sexual history of individuals involved are relevant. Until 1986, the courts had enforced Title VII of the Civil Rights Act of 1964 as a protection for women against overt discrimination in hiring, pay, and opportunity in the workplace. But in 1986, the Supreme Court explicitly expanded the definition of discrimination to include sexual harassment. The decision marked a watershed in sexual politics as well as the workplace. The essence of the decision was that in certain contexts, sex was never private. Under the new doctrine, sexual harassment not only included demands or suggestions of quid pro quo involving sex, but also the presence of what the court described in 1993 as a "hostile environment." So unpredictable has that standard proven to be, that some employers have aggressively tried to protect themselves by "desexualizing" the workplace. In the mid–1980s, Chase Manhattan Bank went so far as to ban all touching of any kind in the workplace. Although the company has since eased up on the rule, the original policy had insisted that no employee touch any other employee, including even a pat on the back for a job well done.[7]

On college campuses the rituals of courtship were subject to even more searching ideological and legal interrogation. Relations that had once been subject to the traditional etiquette of restraint and respect were replaced with legalistic guidelines, including written codes that required men to explicitly ask and receive permission for every touch, loosened button, or kiss. The distinction between unwanted attention and rape; boorishness and abuse became increasingly uncertain. Coming on the heels of the sexual revolution, which had celebrated instinctual liberation, the result was understandably confusing. Academicians did little to clarify the matter. One Ivy League dean wound himself into rhetorical knots trying to explain his college's "No Means No" policy:

> A misreading of my "no means no" would be to put quotation marks around those words. When we say "No means no" and "The absences of a yes means no," that doesn't mean the absence of a verbalized yes means no. There is the courting, there is the initiation of an activity, and the response. It's the nature of the response that indicates the yes or the no. For example, if I am engaging in suggesting intimacies with somebody and touch that person, I don't need to get a yes, I don't need to ask permission. That occurs within the context of what's happened just prior to it. What is the response that I get to that? Does that suggest that it is accepted or not?[8]

In other words, call a lawyer before going out on a date.

The era of Kinsey gave way to the era of litigation as much of the fumbling, tentative, and inchoate protocols of sexual relations were written and rewritten by lawyers. Privacy was an early casualty. Attorneys in sexual-harassment cases routinely set out to demonstrate that the defendant's conduct had contaminated the working environment and often the only way to do so was to demonstrate his "pattern and practice" of harassment or abuse. For many defendants sexual-harassment law had thus become a hunting license for their likes, lusts, and loves.[9]

But the law also often cast a net so wide that it would involve innocent third parties, including women who had the misfortune to have had a consensual relationship with someone tangled in a lawsuit. In 1994, an ex-employee filed a sexual-harassment suit against Bob Guccione Jr., the son of the publisher of *Penthouse,* who was at the time the owner of *Spin* magazine. Seeking to establish a sex-for-favors pattern, attorneys called former girlfriend Celia Farber as a witness in the case. As she later recounted: "Over a period of almost three years, I was subpoenaed for thousands of pages of documentation, including every draft of every article I ever wrote, my entire academic records, love letters, diaries and documentation of any 'dates,' 'gifts,' or another physical remains of the affair." Even though she was not a party to the suit, protecting her privacy was not a high priority in the litigation. "An investigator called my first editor four or five times and asked him whether he ever saw me and Bob touch each other, whether we ever left the building together, whether we ever held hands."[10]

Despite this, Jeffrey Rosen believes that the federal judge should have exempted Bill Clinton from having to answer embarrassing questions. But as Judge Susan Weber Wright remarked during Clinton's fateful January 1998 deposition in Paula Jones's sexual harassment lawsuit, "I have never had a sexual harassment case where there was not some embarrassment."

Bob Packwood knew all about embarrassment. Years before Clinton's own sexual conduct paralyzed the capitol, Senator Packwood's decades-long pattern of accosting women had been dissected, analyzed, and documented. Over twenty-four years, inter alia, Packwood had grabbed a staff member by the shoulders and kissed her on the lips; grabbed another staff worker with both hands in her hair and kissed her, forcing his tongue into her mouth; grabbed a staff assistant, pinned her against a wall or desk, held her hair with one hand, bending her head backward, fondling her with his other hand, and kissed her, forcing his tongue into her mouth; ran his hand up the leg of a dining-room hostess and touched her crotch area; made suggestive comments to a prospective employee; kissed a baby-sitter and touched her leg as he drove her home.

At the time, there were few protests that the charges or the investigation violated Packwood's personal privacy. And, indeed, to the extent that the investigation focused on his unwanted and crude advances against staffers, it did not concern private conduct at all. But the Packwood investigation did set a precedent by giving a green light to sweeping invasions of privacy in cases involving sexual harassment and politicians. During the course of the probe, Packwood was forced to turn over thousands of pages of his personal diaries. The Senate Ethics Committee allowed Packwood to conceal some portions of the diaries that might involve strictly personal matters covered by attorney-client privilege and physician-patient privilege. Packwood was also permitted to mask out those diary passages that dealt with personal, private family matters, "despite the fact," the committee later sniffed, "that such entries were not protected by any recognized evidentiary privilege."[11]

Packwood also asked that he be allowed to keep private those entries dealing with consensual intimate relationships. These entries would theoretically involve women who had made no complaints against him and whose testimony would not directly bear on the charges that he had harassed and intimidated women. But the Senate committee flatly rejected Packwood's request, thus making every detail of his nonmarital sex life fair game. The scope of that investigation also widened quickly. In the course of reading the diaries, investigators stumbled upon other evidence of possible misconduct, including his private musings about his intention to seek a divorce and his concern to obtain income for his soon-to-be-ex-wife. When Packwood objected to the intrusions and tried to mask out diary entries "which relate to political, campaign, staff or similar activities and are wholly unrelated to the sexual misconduct/intimidation issues," the Senate took the case to federal court. In early 1994, Judge Thomas Penfield Jackson rejected Packwood's plea that rummaging through his private diaries constituted an improper search and violated the Fifth Amendment's protections against self-incrimination.[*] He ordered the diaries turned over to investigators, a blow that effectively destroyed Packwood's political career.

In January 1998, Bill Clinton found himself caught in this web. Under the existing law, Paula Jones's attorneys were well within their rights to probe into Clinton's sex life, or at least his sexual relations with past and present employees.

THE CASE FOR DISCRETION

Although many of the president's defenders argued that the law should protect us from having to discuss our sex lives, Jonathan Rauch advanced a somewhat more nuanced case for discretion based on culture.[12] Rauch asks us to set aside the legal and constitutional issues and look instead at the so-

---

[*]It was later determined that Packwood had tried to alter the diaries that he turned over to the Senate committee, a key fact in his eventual forced resignation. As a foreshadowing of the sexual-harassment probe of President Clinton, it is interesting to note that the special master who was charged with keeping the tapes and diaries was Kenneth Starr.

cial context of what he calls our "peculiar preference for hypocrisy" when
it comes to adultery. "Try a thought experiment," he suggests.

> You're at a dinner party. In full public hearing, someone demands to
> know whether you're cheating on your wife. Civilized norms require
> you to evade the question. But suppose the boor persists, demanding
> an answer. If you must answer, civilized opinion requires you to look
> him in the eye and say, 'Of course I don't cheat on my wife'—even if
> you do cheat on her. Moreover, civilized opinion is not angry with you
> for lying; it is angry with him for demanding to know. You are invited
> to the next party. He isn't.

Rauch insists that for a society that aspired to be "both free and faith-
ful," the tradition of lying about such matters "is not only hallowed but indispensable," because it is the only way to publicly declare adultery
intolerable, while, in fact, tolerating it.

In effect, Rauch is proposing what amounts to an etiquette of reticence, because it is a matter of simple manners not to pry too deeply, or
ask intolerable questions. We avoid the lie by avoiding the questions. It
would be a mistake to see this silence as a matter of "mere" manners, because etiquette is one of the contrivances that allows society to maintain its
often tricky equilibrium. Society can function only by selectively looking
away, pretending to believe things because the alternative is too messy and
painful. Dealing with straying spouses, Rauch says, the social etiquette requires that "If the adulterer and the spouse both prefer to hush up the affair, they lie, and no further questions are asked. Everybody pretends to
believe them, and the children slumber untroubled by sin."

Under the "ancient social compact," he argues, this is "what families
do." If Hillary pretends to believe Bill, "then we pretend to believe her."
We lie to protect the children, and also the social compact.

Rauch's argument is not a case for libertinism. Rather, it would be familiar and perhaps even congenial to the Victorians, who understood the
complexity and the delicacy of balancing public morals and private conduct. Supporters of the reticent sensibility would also have understood
Rauch's concern that once we begin promiscuously outing adulteries, society would not only be coarsened, but less able to stigmatize adultery, be-

cause it was too widespread. "People will drop civilized pretense and just say, 'Yes, I cheat, want to make something of it?' " Rauch predicts.

There are more than a few reasons to suspect that Rauch's warning needs to be heeded. Erik Erikson warned against imagining that public shaming was a route to "genuine propriety." Instead, excessive humiliation and shaming could lead to "defiant shamelessness." Indeed, as Clinton supporters pursued a "scorched earth" campaign against Republican critics by leaking information about their own affairs and indiscretions, the public reaction was increasingly numbed. Affairs were simply too common to be the source of outrage; and as the list grew to include men of considerable public integrity and respect, the reaction was less shame than indifference.

The Victorians would also have understood Rauch's point about the press and the law. While society has evolved as accommodation for private failings, both publicity and the legal machinery are crude and blunt instruments. The combination of sexual-harassment law, tort law, and the independent-counsel law, spurred on by the seemingly irresistible temptation to use the law to regulate ever-expanding spheres of life "took a bulldozer to the old deal."

"Alas," Rauch wrote, "today's prurient and intrusive workplace-harassment jurisprudence, with its bizarre combination of pinched sexual Puritanism and wanton legal promiscuity, set the law on a collision course with decency. Now the train wreck has happened." The end result, he warns, may be that we will come to a point where adultery is "condemned legally and excused morally—exactly the opposite of what ought to happen."

This is a far more formidable argument than some of Clinton's critics have recognized. At best, public humiliation is a questionable weapon of moral regeneration. It is hardly self-evident, after all, that the dramatically increased volume of publicity about sexual matters has made us a more prudent or decent society. Instead, it seems to have given the impression that such behavior is, in fact, far more widespread than it is in reality. Just as the increasingly graphic depictions of violence in the media run the risk of numbing our responses to such carnage, the constant drumbeats of exposure risk anaesthetizing our capacity for moral outrage.

But at a more fundamental level, Rauch is also right about the crucial role that privacy plays as individuals and society struggle with a moral balancing act. Privacy allows society to uphold moral and ethical principles

without resorting to medieval-style scourging and the stoning of miscreants. Rauch is also correct to point out the dangerous trend of replacing social accommodations with legal enforcement. Inevitably, as the zone of
legal sanctions grows, it constricts the zone of privacy. For much of the
past century, we have shrunk the social at the expense of the legal, turning
over matters once handled by families, neighbors, churches, and communities to bureaucrats or lawyers, who seldom have either the patience or
sympathy for the nuances of personal life, or an understanding of the com-
plexities of social arrangements. This comes very close to the heart of privacy and its essential character in American life.

But it does not answer the questions: Where do we draw the line?
What sense can we make of Clinton's story? Is it really an invasion of the
president's zone of privacy to raise questions about his veracity, his judgment, and his reckless conduct? Did Clinton have a reasonable expectation
of privacy when he was dallying with the intern? And finally, what does his
case say about developing an appropriate standard for judging the rele-
vance of public and private character?

THE PRESIDENT'S PRIVATE—
AND PUBLIC—LIFE

Was Bill Clinton's relationship with Monica Lewinsky a strictly private
matter that has no bearing on his public duties?

Clinton obviously did not think so. The Starr report chronicles the
president's growing anxiety and frenzied activities throughout 1997 and
early 1998 to cover up his involvement with Lewinsky, presumably because he thought that the country would be horrified by a fifty-one-year-
old president engaging in a sexual relationship with a twenty-one-year-old
intern. Already under criminal investigation, facing a sexual-harassment
lawsuit, and extraordinary media and political scrutiny of his personal conduct, Clinton understandably feared that the revelation of his affair with
Lewinsky would devastate his presidency. Unlike his predecessors—most
notably, John F. Kennedy—Clinton knew full well that he could not rely on
the discretion or the indulgence of the media. It seems reasonable to assume that he was well aware of the specific consequences that his private
acts with Ms. Lewinsky would have for his public duties.

After his efforts at concealment had failed and revelations of the affair
and the failed cover-up filled the airwaves, many of the president's sup-

porters pointed to the long-running relationship between French President Mitterand and his mistress (who bore his child out of wedlock) as a sign of a more sophisticated response to such behavior. But as Jean Bethke Elshtain noted, Mitterand's mistress's appearance at his funeral came as a surprise even to the sophisticated French. Why? Because Mitterand, in rather sharp contrast to Clinton, "had done it with a developed sense of rectitude and discretion." Mitterand did not disport with his mistress in the halls of state. "He did not have a staff assigned to facilitate assignations or to tidy up the messes," Elshtain notes. "By contrast, Clinton behaved recklessly in ways that were bound, sooner or later, to catch the public's eye."[13]

Most damning, the evidence suggests that Clinton too often saw his public role as a license to indulge his private cravings, and to protect himself from the consequences. A man who sent armed troopers to procure a date, and who dispatches White House aides to perjure themselves cannot plausibly claim privacy. Indeed, Clinton seemed to positively revel in dancing as close to the edge of private and public as he could. Consider the fact that Lewinsky was an intern entrusted to him; the disparities in age and power; even the location of the presidential indulgences—within earshot of the Oval Office itself—and Clinton's penchant for carrying on presidential business while being serviced by his private attendant. It seems inescapable that Clinton saw public office as a means to indulge darker private impulses. One enabled the other. There was no wall, no clear distinction. Inevitably, as Clinton had to know, a meltdown in his private life meant a meltdown in his public life as well.

The argument that Clinton's behavior was strictly private is similarly undermined by the way he mixed public duties with private indulgences. When the president lobbied a key congressman on the phone for a vote on Bosnian policy while he was having sex with Lewinsky, Clinton hopelessly conflated public and private moments. The obvious question is: *What could he possibly have been thinking?* Our policy in the Balkans was quite literally a matter of life and death—the issue was whether Congress would continue to provide funds for the peacekeeping mission, thus determining whether American men and women would be sent into harm's way in Bosnia. Needing the support of Congressman H. L. "Sonny" Callahan, Clinton spoke with him on the phone on November 17, 1995, while Lewinsky was performing an act of oral sex on him.[14]

If the sexual act was strictly personal and private, the plan to send troops to Bosnia was quintessentially a public matter. Few duties go more to the heart of the president's constitutional duties, his oath of office, or his status as commander in chief. Clinton was, of course, famous for his ability to "compartmentalize" aspects of his life, but his apparent limitless confidence in his ability to keep those aspects of his life in separate boxes devolved into something very like arrogance that led him into recklessness. Was this a private moment or a public one? Or are such distinctions impossible to draw with precision when we are talking about the president of the United States?

Even taking the most absolutist privacy position and accepting that even private figures deserve a zone of privacy—indeed, even accepting that sex in particular deserves extra discretion and protection—it is hard to ignore that even private sex sometimes has public consequences. It was Bill Clinton's duty to keep the spheres separate. The measure of his recklessness is his refusal to do so, except when it was too late to do so without sacrificing his credibility and his legal standing.

The private ceased to be private when Bill Clinton not only allowed it to become public, but to overwhelm the public aspects of his life. Until it had all but consumed his presidency, Clinton seemed not to understand why he needed to protect the one from the other. While the public was anxious to draw a sharp distinction between public and private life, ultimately, it was the president himself who undermined the distinction, with devastating consequences for both his private and public life. Despite his protestations, the issue turned not on his private conduct (he was never charged with adultery), but on his public behavior, including his concerted, orchestrated campaign of deception that enlisted not only his family members, but members of the White House staff. Clinton's repeated and conscious attempts to deceive raised the private matter to an issue with obvious and inescapable public consequences.

SEX, LIES, AND PRIVACY

So what *are* the standards for public figures in the post–Clinton age? Do they forfeit all right to a private life? Or should we decide that their private conduct is irrelevant to their fitness for office? Obviously, either extreme is a mistake. Turning public life into a no-privacy zone invites crude, vulgar intrusions that, in effect, become a tax on public involvement. But eliminating a zone of privacy also makes a genuine public realm impossible, because such elimination will make it both flat and fake. Even though we imagine that we are striking a blow for honesty and authenticity, in fact, public life would become increasingly inauthentic as even private emotions become increasingly stylized and choreographed for public consumption. Recall Milan Kundera's remark that any man "who was the same in both public and intimate life would be a monster. He would be without spontaneity in his private life and without responsibility in his public life."[15] In a fully transparent society, these are the only sort of men and women we would get in public life.

The other extreme, however, is equally unacceptable. No society can afford to ignore patterns of deceit, abuse, or recklessness in the private lives of men and women who aspire to offices of public trust.

So what is public and what is private? The answer is that "it depends." While the law often seeks a bright line, privacy concerns are being played out against a kaleidoscopic backdrop. Even our tolerant society demands adherence to the political, social, and aesthetic standards of the moment. But no one can ever be quite certain what those will be in the future. Not too long ago, youthful experimentation with marijuana would have been disqualifying; but not anymore. Might it once again carry a politically fatal stigma?

What will the anxieties of the future involve? Our willingness to help around the house? Whether we smoke? How much and how often we drink? Whether we use Viagra? Subscribe to the Playboy channel? Whether or not a woman uses birth control? How often we attend church? Or whether we have been treated in the past for depression? Or ever had a homosexual thought? Or engaged in premarital sex? Is a past abortion an issue? Have they tolerated unconventional behavior by our children? The answer to such questions might provide some voters with important information about a candidates' values. But public persons would still be fully justified in keeping such matters private. This nation is not as fanciful as it might seem.

Amidst the bitter partisan divisions over Bill Clinton's fate, it was perhaps easy to miss the remarkable consensus that Clinton's sexual conduct *alone* was, indeed, a private matter. (Although few of Clinton's defenders went so far as to call for the repeal or rollback of the sexual harassment laws that required him to answer questions about that conduct.) Even

Clinton's inquisitors, including Kenneth Starr and Henry Hyde, went to lengths to emphasize that their charges against the president did not concern "private" activities. Unfortunately, the Republicans weakened their case when the speaker-designate of the House of Representatives, Bob Livingston, resigned after he acknowledged extramarital affairs. Their "not-about-sex" message was further muddled when GOP presidential candidates joined in professions of marital fidelity, thus implicitly acknowledging that purity was a qualification for the office. More properly, they all should have said that it was not anyone's business as long as it did not affect their public duties.

The alternative is to concede that their private lives are public issues and thus open to searching scrutiny. The problem with that is that every politician who declares his purity puts pressure on others to do the same and legitimizes the inquiry into the most intimate corners of their lives. In doing so, they invite Larry Flynt into the mainstream of American politics. A veteran pornographer, who was not above wrapping himself and his scrofulous magazine in the pieties of the First Amendment, Flynt held Washington hostage with his million-dollar bounties for information about the private sex lives of prominent politicians. At the end of the twentieth century, privacy found itself confronted by the bizarre alliance of Jerry Falwell and Flynt—the neo-Puritans and the pornographers. Both of them would profess horror at being thus linked, but ironically, each made the other possible. Indeed, puritan and pornographer alike share the distrust of the private, which may explain the common cause made by Falwell and Flynt in turning private sexual morality into public matters.

But are they right? Is private adultery legitimately a public issue? Would the return of the scarlet letter lead us back to a stronger moral base?

Actually, a quite plausible case can be made that since the consequences of adultery and divorce are not strictly private and are, in fact, properly the public's business. The social implications of divorce are well documented. But almost by definition, society is the sum of individual private decisions. Does that mean that all of those decisions then are properly subject to public scrutiny? Indeed, if every private decision that affected society was a public matter, then nothing would be exempt, from our spending habits, to how we decorate our homes, to our diets.

The public/private dimensions of adultery, however, pose a more complicated dilemma. Adultery is an act that undermines the institution of marriage, a central pillar of our society. The wedding ceremony is a public event because it marks the community's sanction of a private relationship. But the public character of marriage does not mean that the details of the relationship of married couples are public. Quite the contrary, marriage is recognized universally as the most intimate of relationships, deserving special legal protections and privileges. No married person has an obligation to share marital confidences even with the closest relations.

But isn't marriage a contract? And isn't the breaking of a contract a matter of grave public importance?

As a pledge between husband and wife, before God and the community, marriage does indeed have elements of a contract that is sanctioned by the state. But the analogy of divorce to the breaking of a contract is, at best, strained. The relations between men and women are quite different from those between business partners, and the procedures for altering those arrangements are not only well established, but have been eased significantly in recent years. As most societies this side of the Taliban have learned, it is a futile effort to try to regulate individuals' loves, passions, attractions, and couplings as if they were business arrangements or unbreakable contracts. Such relations stand apart from much of the rest of our lives and although they have considerable impact on society as a whole, the ability of society to regulate and monitor them will always be limited in any society that respects individual freedom.

The final objection will be that adultery is a leading indicator of character. By definition, adultery is a breach of trust, but the historical record is far from clear that a man or woman who strays on a strictly personal matter cannot be trusted in other spheres of life. Moreover, society has other reasons for limiting the public's right to know about such affairs. Until recently, as Jonathan Rauch has noted, society had turned a blind eye to adultery; not as a way of providing moral sanction to straying spouses, but as a way of balancing social values with the need for discretion and tolerance. The significance of adultery and divorce rests in the damage they do to the fabric of intimate relations, especially those within the family. Until recently, society's innate wisdom had recognized that the revelation of adultery dramatically compounded that damage. Whatever good comes from the public's knowledge of such affairs is almost always outweighed by the hurt such revelations cause children, family members, friends, and the participants themselves.

Although it runs counter to the current spirit of the age, the case for discretion needs to be made once again. Both adultery and divorce are crises of intimacy, sexuality, and of our most intensely private personal relations. If we acknowledge that sex itself is a private matter, then it would seem to follow that other manifestations of those relationships of which sex is only a part also deserve protection. After all, we do not protect the privacy of sex because of the sanctified or special constitutional status of intercourse or other sex acts; we shield them because they are manifestations of the intimacies of life. It is not the physical act alone that is in need of protection, it is the *relationships* that lead to and shape such acts. In other words, we do not protect the intimacy of relationships because of sex; we protect sex because of the relationships themselves, perhaps especially when they are in turmoil or crisis.

Ironically, the struggle for privacy protections for gays may provide cover for politicians of very different orientations. Homosexuals are unusually vulnerable to privacy invasions especially in employment situations. But both gays and conservative politicians find themselves roughly in the same boat. They both risk having their sex lives offered up for public consumption by zealots anxious to expose that most unforgivable of all modern sins, "hypocrisy." Although there have been scattered episodes of "outings" by antigay activists, the worst threat to gay men or women who wish to keep their sexuality private are not homophobes, but gay activists who believe in "outing." Some of the militants believe as a matter of principle that all gays should come out of the closet; others target a specific class of private gays. "We're in favor of outing right-wing homophobes in society, the church and government who are hurting gays," says one activist.[16] The practice poses a dilemma for the media, as well, because the names of prominent politicians are often printed in "outing" publications, challenging the rest of the media to make a judgment whether to also publish the names. An obvious question is: Will the evolving rules be uniformly enforced or will there be an ideological test? Are gay conservatives fair game, but not left-leaning gays?

The same question will nag perfectly straight—even militantly heterosexual—public figures who may also find their private lives to be fair game in an era of sexual McCarthyism. As the closet doors are opened and standards are revised, we have already seen that conservative politicians including Henry Hyde, Bob Livingston, and Dan Burton are likely to come under especially searching scrutiny. The justification among the new class of media voyeurs will similarly be the search for "hypocrisy." While I was working on this book, I had occasion to discuss this issue with an investigative reporter for a prominent newspaper. I asked him specifically how he would have handled the story about Congressman Henry Hyde's thirty-year-old affair: Would he have pursued it? And would his paper have published it? He admitted that he did not know; nor was he sure any longer where the line was drawn. But as he considered the question, he suggested that reporters would be more likely to pursue stories of a public figure's sexual indiscretions if they had campaigned on "family values." Did this mean that reporters would pursue leads about Republicans and conservative Democrats, but not liberals? He insisted that this would not, but the question lingers. When no one really knows what the rules are, the risk is that they will be applied one way for people we like and another for those we dislike.

So far, the mainstream media seems to regard the sex lives of homosexuals as more or less off-limits, which raises the question of whether heterosexuals could someday appeal for the same level of discretion for themselves?

When the dust clears, we should hope for a strong bias toward separating private from public and granting public figures a generous zone of privacy. Deciding what is relevant and what is protected as a private matter requires us to use our judgment and to employ a nuanced standard that recognizes the foibles and frailties of individuals. Divorce may be a sign of personal failure, but it hardly is a disqualifying fact; medical information should be considered private, unless it directly affects the fitness of an individual for office. Whether or not one drinks should be relevant only if it has clear public consequences that affect the performance of one's duty. But this does not provide either the media or political opponents with a hunting license. There is information that the public would want to know, and which it would find relevant to their judgment of whether a candidate was qualified for a given office, that should nevertheless not be provided.

Lies will become less of an issue the more that public figures insist that "it's none of your business," and society begins to accept the legitimacy of such a claim.

Perhaps the best reason for respecting the privacy of public figures is the most practical. The scorched-earth tactics of the "politics of personal destruction" ultimately destroy not just politicians, but politics itself. Just as the politics of personal identity raises the "rage quotient" of politics, the attack on the private lives of politicians exponentially raises the level of rancor, bitterness, and plain brutishness. Not even a semblance of comity can survive such tactics because invading the home of an opponent is more akin to warfare than to the debate and deliberation of a democracy. Not only will the practitioners of such politics find themselves unable to get anything done, they will eventually forfeit the public's trust that they ever will or should make a difference. Nor will the champions of moral renewal fare much better. It is hard to see how youngsters will learn the difference between right and wrong by watching adults disrobing one another or triumphing over the destruction of their adversaries. This may be entertaining, but it is hardly edifying.

Although even public officials deserve a generous zone of privacy, they also have to recognize that in order to expect respect for their privacy, they must have an equal commitment to protecting the public from the private. Public persons are obliged to keep their private lives private, a requirement that may simply be too constraining for New Age politicians, even with the example of Bill Clinton before them. They should also practice a politics laden with at least some humility. Both sides in the culture wars should notice that though a posture of moral rectitude may be good for raising a family, or forming a church, it makes for very bad politics. All of us are in favor of righteousness. But, in general, we prefer our own righteousness, not our neighbor's. Even if we are churchgoers, we don't want our lives to be judged by the people in the church down the street, much less by people in government. And, in politics, this makes a huge difference. As much as voters may admire character and rectitude, they do not want to be hectored and nagged about it by politicians, even by politicians with whom they might agree on other issues. Voters who want their congressman to vote for the flat tax do not necessarily want him to regulate their sex lives.

■

PART 5

Toward a Right of Privacy

13

■

Privacy and Its Critics

Amid the muddled legal, political, and cultural landscape several things seem increasingly clear:

The struggle over privacy is the preeminent issue of the Information Age.

And, one way or another, there will be a revolution in personal privacy over the next several decades.

Personal privacy resonates with most of us. Whether explicitly or implicitly, we understand its relationship to freedom, autonomy, intimacy, and we sense its growing importance even as the walls of the Information Age close in on us.

More than a century ago, Louis Brandeis suggested that the pressure of modern life made privacy even more important than it had been for previous generations. "The intensity and complexity of life attendant upon advancing civilization," he wrote with Samuel Warren, "have rendered necessary some retreat from the world, and man, under the refining influence of culture, has become more sensitive to publicity, so that solitude and privacy have become essential to the individual." Leaving aside for a moment their reference to the "refining" influence of modern culture, the century since Brandeis and Warren wrote their landmark article has seen the development of new technologies that have permanently changed not merely the scope, but the very nature of intrusions into private life.

It is difficult to overstate what is at stake here. The erosion of privacy asphyxiates private life as it contracts the distance that separates individuals from one another and from the state. And yet neither Congress nor the courts have acted with any sense of urgency to protect privacy.

DESPAIRING SHRUG

Some critics might suggest that more has not been done to protect privacy because there is nothing to be done—the loss of privacy is a fait accompli, which we must simply learn to accept. They see the technologies of surveillance and the vast reach of the datawebs as a sign that privacy is obsolete, an early, but inevitable and unavoidable casualty of the age. But the obituaries for privacy are premature.

Even though the case for pessimism is formidable, it should be noted that it also comes at the end of a century rife with claims about the imminent demise of freedom, of democracy, of culture, of free markets, even the eclipse of history itself—predictions that have been frustrated by the failures of either history or human nature to conform themselves to the theories. Surely the fall of the Berlin Wall and the collapse of Communism ought to have given some pause to those who had argued for much of the last century that historical developments were inexorable and irreversible, and that they were certain they had chosen the winning side.

If we have learned anything at all, it is that the human spirit has a remarkable capacity to renew itself. New technologies may change the environment, but they do not change our idea of who we are or what we expect from life. Human freedom, dignity, and autonomy are made of hardier stuff than we sometimes imagine, and our history is largely the story of their remarkable persistence.

This is not to suggest that the new technologies do not pose a grave threat to privacy. Ultimately, though, it is man who determines the uses of technology, not the reverse. Even though fundamental human values may occasionally go into eclipse, every generation has the capacity to rediscover and regenerate what matters most. A century hence, there is every reason to believe that men and women will feel the importance of protecting their privacy as keenly as our own generation. Indeed, despite the obituaries for privacy, recent controversies—from the Clinton scandals to the public's reaction to the posting of Social Security information, the sale of driver's-license photos, and attempts by the government to install trapdoors or Clipper Chips in the nation's phones and computers—suggest that the public is not yet ready to surrender its privacy with a "despairing shrug." Politicians and businesses who ignore this fact do so at their own peril.

So what will it take?

There are no simple solutions. The modern world, with its disdain for reticence and its suspicion of privacy, did not emerge overnight. No single decision or piece of legislation shaped our culture's attitude toward privacy, and none—standing alone—will reverse that attitude anytime soon. We are the heirs of profound changes in technology, temperament, sensibility, and judgment toward religion, therapy, the role of the media, and the place of personality in society. All of them contribute to the present challenge to personal privacy. The struggle to preserve or restore that privacy will engage our politics, our legal system, and the culture. And its outcome is far from certain.

PRIVACY AND IT'S CRITICS

Privacy, of course, is not without its critics. There are those who dismiss privacy concerns on grounds of national security; or who insist that privacy be subordinated to efficiency or economic growth; to the cause of therapy, psychological health, or the exposure of hypocrisy. Indeed, our society's suspicion of secrecy is so ingrained that anyone arguing for stronger privacy protections can expect to be asked what they have to hide.

Privacy also tends not to fare well among the ideologues at both ends of the political spectrum; its philosophical antagonists range from social conservatives to radical feminists; and from the totalitarians of political correctness on the left to libertarians on the right. The irony here is that though some social conservatives regard privacy merely as an excuse to undermine traditional moral values, their counterparts on the left bring precisely the opposite charge: that privacy is an instrument for preserving patriarchal abuse and oppression. The result is that privacy finds itself whipsawed from both right and left. A short critique of the critics:

"FREEDOM FROM MORAL REGULATION"

By all measures, conservatives ought to embrace "the right of privacy" as a principle to sharply restrict government intervention into our lives. The right to be let alone is a powerful counterweight to those who would deploy the authority of the government to intrude into our personal affairs or disseminate personal information about us. But many conservatives have been reluctant to embrace the notion that there is a "right to privacy." Unfortunately, their hostility is largely a product of its connection to abortion. In effectively legalizing abortion, the Supreme Court relied on privacy rights, which it located in the Fourteenth Amendment's liberty clause. Critics on both the right and the left have expressed dissatisfaction with the court's reasoning in *Roe*. But the larger political legacy has been a permanent climate of mistrust among conservatives. For many of them, privacy was inextricably tied to a decision that came to symbolize an activist judiciary and social radicalism.*

But even beyond abortion, conservative legal scholars including Judge Robert Bork associate the right of privacy with a tendency toward libertinism and moral relativism. Bork is especially critical of the dissenters in *Bowers*—the case in which the Court upheld Georgia's antisodomy law—who invoked the right of privacy and declared "that a person belongs to himself and not others nor to society as a whole."[1] But, Bork argues, that can hardly be taken seriously. "In our view of morality and responsibility, no husband or wife, no father or mother act on the principle that 'person belongs to himself and not others. . . .' Here and elsewhere, some Justices have enunciated a position of extreme individualism, which amounts necessarily to an attitude of moral relativism. If all that counts is the gratification of the individual, then morality is completely privatized and society may make no moral judgments that are translated into law."[2]

Although Bork properly warns of the danger of giving judges the power to create new "rights" out of whole cloth, privacy is hardly a radical or subversive notion. Indeed, it was once regarded as an essential bulwark of society's traditional values. Without understanding the central role of privacy, Hannah Arendt argues, it is impossible to understand the historic and cultural importance of private property. Indeed, she grounds the right to property in its role as a guarantor of the right of privacy, making privacy

---

* It is not my purpose here to debate the merits of the abortion issue; others have done it more effectively and at much greater length. But the connection between abortion and privacy is not self-evident, nor has it gone unchallenged. The Court's decision in *Griswold* declared that the state had no right to interfere in the private decisions of a married couple. But as Duke University Law Professor William Van Alstyne notes, prior to *Roe*, "No one had supposed that even marriage would entitle one to destroy third-party life that one's own acts—albeit acts of marital intimacy—had brought about." One can certainly believe in a right of privacy that does not include the taking of another's life. Alstyne and others argue that *Griswold* does not imply the sort of rights invented in *Roe*.

and property inseparable. "Prior to the modern age . . . all civilizations have rested upon the sacredness of private property," Arendt wrote in *The Human Condition*.[3] "The four walls of such property defined both the sacred intimacies of private life and the public domain because they "offer the only reliable hiding place from the common public world, not only from everything that goes on in it but also from its very publicity, from being seen and being heard. . . . The only efficient way to guarantee the darkness of what needs to be hidden against the light of publicity is private property, a privately owned place to hide in."[4]

Nor would the Victorians have agreed that privacy was a cover for "the freedom of the individual from moral regulation." Far from seeing privacy as a solvent of social bonds, or a license for moral relativism, the Victorians regarded the privacy of the family and of the intimate details of personal lives as essential to preserving sacred values. In other words, privacy defined what we would now consider social conservatism.

It was no accident that the attack on the culture of Victorian values in the late-nineteenth and early-twentieth centuries was also an assault on such restraint. Critics of the reticent sensibility—sex reformers, political progressives, journalists, and other debunkers—understood they could undermine social order by attacking the culture of privacy which had "sought to shelter certain aspects of life from public scrutiny, publicity, and debate." Advocates for sex education and free love demanded an end to what they called the "conspiracy of silence," while Freud and his acolytes derided reticence on sexuality as evidence of repression, the cause of mental disorder, perversion, and neuroses. In art, realists sought to lift the veil on the dirty secrets of society, while advocates of privacy were reviled as snobs and hypocrites.

The new appetite of journalism for scandal fed the public's voyeurism, but also fed into a powerful leveling impulse, by tearing down distinctions and stripping public figures of their pretensions. Prying journalists, Rochelle Gurstein wrote, can effectively strip a man naked and reduce him to the lowest common denominator "by transforming the fragile activities of a person's private and intimate life into common property."[5]

Anarchists, bohemians, artists, and reformers of all stripes, who shared an animus for bourgeois values, eagerly joined in the attack on privacy. Claiming a higher purity than Puritanism, the critics of privacy challenged the code of restraint by insisting that the first step toward curing the ills of private and social life was exposing them. In that respect, they were forming the modern sensibility.

But what such critics shared, Gurstein writes was a "lack of awareness that intimate affairs, because of their frailty, cannot withstand the pressure of publicity; incomprehension that compromising anecdotes can only make sense in the larger context of a person's life story; and the naïve, misguided conclusion that all concerns for privacy signal efforts to cover up wrong-doing."[6]

What followed, of course, was a profound defeat for defenders of traditional values, and a remarkable transmutation of values. Exposure and intrusion into the intimacy of private lives, which had once been regarded as an outrage and a form of cultural pollution, now came to be hailed as symbols of health, enlightenment, honesty, and emancipation. And, as Gurstein notes, "reticence, once regarded as the very foundation of civilized life, came to be blamed as the root cause of personal misery, social evil, and impoverished national culture. . . ."[7]

How ironic, then, that one of the cultural bulwarks of social conservatism would come to be seen as a code word for moral relativism. In fairness, it is obvious that privacy no longer serves the role that it played a century ago. But has privacy become an excuse for irresponsible individuals to free themselves from moral regulation of any kind? Does the legal protection of privacy grant a license to individuals to shed all moral responsibility? Hardly.

Freedom from regulation and freedom from exposure equal freedom from morality only if we regard regulation and exposure as the only legitimate sources of morality, a position that few conservatives would hold seriously.

THE FEMINIST ATTACK
ON PRIVACY

Indeed, the most virulent ideological assault on privacy has come from the left, including feminists, whose shibboleth, "the personal is the political," has proven so fateful. Despite the role that privacy has played in the legalization of abortion, feminists have attacked the division between public and private hammer and tong. Catherine MacKinnon, one of the leading spokespersons for the movement, acknowledges that privacy is a central value in a liberal democracy, because it is designed to protect "an inviolable personality," and because it ensures "autonomy of control over the intimacies of personal identity." Privacy enables free, autonomous individuals to interact freely and equally. But when it came to women, MacKinnon argued, privacy served none of these ends, because it did not take into account their oppression and inequality. Because women were perpetual victims, MacKinnon argued, privacy was merely a device for shielding their inferiority and hiding their abuse and degradation.

"The right of privacy is a right of men 'to be let alone' to oppress women one at a time," MacKinnon declared. Far from protecting women, privacy actually "polices the division between public and private . . . that keeps the private beyond public redress and depoliticizes women's subjection with it."[8]

Democratic society separates areas that are subject to government control from those private zones where individuals are free to make their own choices and live their own lives. "The state does this by centering its self-restraint on body and home, especially bedrooms," MacKinnon writes. "By staying out of marriage and the family—essentially meaning sexuality, that is, heterosexuality—from contraception through pornography to the abortion decision, the law of privacy proposed to guarantee individual body integrity, personal exercise of moral intelligence and freedom of intimacy." But MacKinnon rejects such restraint, because women had no guarantee that they had access to such rights. There could be no "inviolable personality" protected by privacy because women were not inviolable. "For women the measure of the intimacy has been the measure of the oppression," she declaimed. "This is why feminism has had to explode the private. This is why feminism has seen the personal as the political. The private is public for those for whom the personal is political. In this sense, for women there is no private. . . . Feminism confronts the fact that women have no privacy to lose or to guarantee."[9] In her critique of privacy, feminist theorist Susan Moller Okin similarly argued, "The protection of the privacy of the domestic sphere in which inequality exists is the protection of the right of the strong to exploit and abuse the weak."[10]

How far did these critics propose to go? Were they arguing that because privacy was sometimes used to shield acts of abuse, therefore the very idea of personal autonomy and private life should be discarded? Because women did not genuinely enjoy a private life in modern society, did that mean there should be no distinction at all between private and public life? Would they do away with any private space? At least, in some extreme cases, the answer appears to be . . . yes.

Fleshing out her idea of a feminist utopia, writer Susan Schechter envisioned: "Family life would be open for community scrutiny because the family would be part of and accountable to the community." More specifically, she said, "community-based institutions could hear complaints and dispense justice, and community networks could hold individuals accountable for their behavior and offer protection for women."[11] This was a society where it would seem that literally everything was everybody's business. It was also a society that could quickly turn ugly. Personal choices were now political statements; one's private life became a statement of one's political commitments.

Critic Jean Bethke Elshtain described the feminist assaults this way: "The personal is the political. Nothing personal was exempt from political definition, direction, and manipulation—not sexual intimacy, not love, not parenting." As Elshtain noted, there was no way to square this belief with democratic notions of society. "The total collapse of public and private as central distinctions in an enduring democratic drama followed, at least in theory. The private sphere fell under a thoroughgoing politicized definition. Everything was grist for a voracious publicity mill; nothing was exempt, there was nowhere to hide."[12]

This is the essence of political correctness, which interrogates not only our ideology, but our attitudes, lifestyles, choice of friends, and taste in art. It politicizes personal decisions involving intimate relationships. While she was a graduate student, Patricia Boling writes, she found herself thinking about when and whether to have children and the impact of that choice on a future career. At her university, however, these were no longer "personal" decisions. Boling recalls that "I found myself and others subject to various forms of stereotyping and exclusion: 'You can't be a feminist because you have children.' 'You can't be a serious academic because you're a mother.' 'Straight women aren't really as feminist as lesbians.' 'Bisexuals can't join the Gay-Lesbian Support Group.'" Boling recalls that she felt both angry and insulted and began to question the claim that the personal was the political.[13]

But she was experiencing precisely what happens when the lines between private and public are erased. "In the society of total scrutiny, total accountability, and instant justice, the social space for difference, dissent, refusal, and indifference is squeezed out," Elshtain notes. Similarly, a politics based on personal identity, insisting that "my politics is about who I am," leads inevitably not only to more conflict, but also to greater emotional intensity. Disagreements are no longer about ideas or even interests—they are an assault on the self, on one's very being. Increasingly, though, identity politics insists on just this emphasis, grounding politics in personal sexual identity, race, or gender. Politics becomes the assertion of those identities; private identity "takes precedence over public ends or purposes; indeed one's private identity becomes who and what one is in public, and public life is about confirming that identity." Challenges to that identity lead inevitably to dramatic increases in the "rage quotient" in political life, "because to argue against my idea is to unhinge my private identity."[14]

Elshtain and others point out that this breakdown of the private and public spheres is not simply the invasion of privacy; it is also fatal for politics. The collapse of the distinction "is anathema to democratic thinking, which holds that the difference between public and private identities, commitments and activities are of vital importance" because they permit "different sorts of relationships—both the mother and the citizen, the friend and the official, and so on."[15]

THE LIBERTARIAN CRITIQUE

Libertarians are at the opposite end of the political spectrum. But even among libertarians, there are sharp differences in approach over whether and how privacy should be protected in the private sector. Virginia Postrel, the editor of *Reason* magazine, flatly rejects arguments that individuals own their own identity and should therefore have the legal right to control the sort of information that is available to others. "But this premise simply isn't true," Postrel argues. "The other party in any relationship—whether your former landlord, your boss, your ex-girlfriend, or Amazon.com— owns information about you as surely as you do. Gathering and sharing such information is as old as gossip and is absolutely essential to a free society. Neither speech nor commerce can function if such communication is illegal. Privacy advocates want to outlaw not only journalism but reputation." Postrel is especially critical of privacy advocates like Marc Rotenberg, who argue that privacy is a fundamental right. Testifying before

Congress on the need for regulations of marketing databases and other forms of electronic datawebs, Rotenberg had quoted Justice Brandeis, who argued that the Constitution's Framers "sought to protect Americans in their beliefs, their thoughts, their emotions, and their sensations. They conferred, as against the Government, the right to be let alone—the most comprehensive of all rights and the right most valued by civilized men." Postrel, however, insists that this "right . . . has nothing to do with infringing other people's freedom to communicate." The Fourth Amendment, she insists, "says not that you own every fact about yourselves but that the government cannot invade your home, your papers, or your life without an awfully good reason."[16]

As far as constitutional law goes, Postrel is correct. But, as we have seen, Brandeis did indeed have a far more comprehensive right in mind— a right so comprehensive that it would quite explicitly extend to limiting the right of others to communicate private facts about a person. But Postrel's point, which is echoed by other libertarians, is that privacy advocates are misguided by focusing on private violations of privacy, when they should instead be concentrating on "the government's police power, which is exercised without the check of competition, rather than working to suppress commercial speech."

Even more disdainful of concerns about commercial violations of privacy, the Cato Institute's Solveig Singleton dismisses the threats to privacy posed by private datawebs as relatively insignificant. "There is little reason," she says, "to fear the growth of private-sector databases." Like Postrel, she sees no justification for regulating the collection and use of data by anyone in the private sector. Specifically, she dismisses concerns about direct marketing as trivial; mere annoyance with junk mail or "spamming," she argues, does not rise to the level of a moral imperative.

On balance, rather, she defends the benefits of the free flow of information to start-up companies and to consumers. "Marketing to masses of uninterested people is expensive and wasteful," she explains. "Targeted marketing, by contrast, puts information about new products and services into the hands of the consumers for whom it is most useful. New firms and products spring into existence, using new understanding of consumer's preferences to identify new market niches." Singleton sees nothing at all "sinister about the explosion of wealth and efficiency that libraries of information about customers' buying habits will allow." In a world where such cheap, easily available information was not readily available, she writes, "another company like Land's End would never be born."[17]

Singleton also does not see much that is fundamentally new about the new technologies of surveillance. She argues that the collection and dispersal of information is a natural, common practice, which we simply take for granted. The only reason anyone now sees it as a threat, Singleton writes, is because the advanced technology makes this normal process more obvious. "It is a mistake," she cautions, "to view the collection of information as morally shocking because we have never noticed that it goes on."

Perhaps the most powerful argument she makes against privacy protections involves free-speech issues and what Singleton calls "the right of human beings to learn about one another." She argues that we naturally and constantly shed information about ourselves. "In the course of a single day, an individual collects an enormous amount of information about people he encounters—their age and appearance, their manner of speaking and dressing, and their actions and preferences. Except under rare circumstances, he will feel no obligation to ask anyone's permission before relaying the information he has collected to a third party, however embarrassing that might be to the subject of their conversation ("Did you notice that Bob Jones's suit was absolutely covered with dog hair?")

The same principle, she writes, should apply to speech about commercial transactions: "If you buy a hedge trimmer from a hardware store, there are two parties to the transactions: you and the hardware store. It makes no more sense to let you prevent the store from giving out your name and address in a list of hedge-trimmer buyers than it would to give the store the right to forbid you from telling *Consumer Reports* what you think of the trimmer."

Singleton regards the compilations of private databases as merely an extension of what once was mere gossip. "There is an obvious similarity between the information collected in databases about consumers and the information we regularly exchange with one another informally ("Mrs. Horton has a new car!") "For the vast majority of people, the casual exchange of this type of information—commonly called 'gossip'—is not an evil great enough to justify regulation." For Singleton, the new databases merely serve the same function that informal communications in small towns might have served: the local butcher knows that Mrs. Jones buys a ham every Saturday and tells the mustard merchant. In practice, Singleton insists, the collection of such information on a large scale in a database is actually less likely to have a negative impact on Mrs. Jones since it is (1) more likely to be accurate than mere gossip, and (2) "few of the people who have access to the information will particularly care about Mrs. Jones or have power over her, especially if Mrs. Jones is a typical resident of a large, anonymous community." She concludes: "If we do not regulate the exchange of personal information in private conversation, we cannot justify regulation of consumer databases." Like Virginia Postrel, Singleton sees the danger to civil liberties from government databases to be vastly greater than the commercial counterparts.

Such critics are correct in noting that the threat from a coercive government is far worse than anything even the largest business could contemplate. But their argument has several flaws. The first is the illusory nature of their distinction between public and private databases. There is more than a touch of naïveté in imagining that we can secure our privacy by locking the front doors of our privacy from invasion by the government, but leave our back doors ajar for invasion by nongovernmental snoops. More fundamentally, they ignore what has become the symbiotic relationship between personal data in the hands of private entities and in the hands of the government: No bright line between the two realms exists. The government-mandated Social Security number, for example, has become a de facto national identification number for business as well as government agencies and provides the key to vast stores of information to private hands. Information flows regardless of whether the entity coercing its release or disseminating it is the government or a mail-order house. Moreover, the private sector is actively mining and exploiting government databases and information, while the government has returned the favor, accessing the volumes of information gathered by the private sector and applying it to its own purposes. A dramatic example of this process was the involvement of the Secret Service in quietly bankrolling a private company that purchased millions of driver's-license photos to create a national-image database. Ostensibly, the database would be used by retailers to combat fraud, but it also promised to be a potent weapon of government surveillance. If there was ever a time when it was possible to build a wall between public and private, that time has long since passed.

Singleton suggests that she might support some limits on the right of business to require customers to provide them with their Social Security numbers as a condition of doing business with them. But her support is halfhearted, at best. If it is all right for gas stations to record license numbers of cars that purchase gas on credit, she writes, "it is arguably justifiable for credit reports, for example, to contain identifying information such as Social Security numbers." Her answer to this dilemma is that this would not be a problem, as we just privatized Social Security.

We would also make a ham sandwich, if we just had some ham. And some bread.

Singleton argues that the challenge for privacy advocates is they "must argue that gossip is fundamentally safer, more trivial, and of much less economic consequence than the new databases." The challenge is easily met: Gossip *is* safer and poses less of a threat that the modern datawebs because technology *does* matter. A horse and buggy and a jet airplane are both modes of transportation. A peashooter and an AK-47 are both projectile weapons. It is not a good idea to ignore the differences.

Having a neighbor watch you out of the back window is not the same as being monitored by video cameras, wiretaps, and hidden microphones. It is one thing to be gossiped about among your acquaintances; it is quite another to have the same information reported in the newspaper; and quite yet another to be broadcast on network television. These are not simply versions of the same thing, but dramatically different levels and types of violations. In only a few moments, even a novice information broker could access Solveig Singleton's name, address, Social Security number, sources of income, marital status, property ownership, legal status, as well as her tastes and habits. However this might be used, it is somewhat different from the fact that her local Starbucks knows she likes regular, not decaf.

Her attempt to dismiss the data-mining, data-crunching and dossier-creating new technologies as simply an updated version of old-fashioned gossip also fails to take into account the question of medical and genetic privacy. Although it's true that maladies, diseases, and disabilities have long been the subject of whispers, our society has traditionally recognized those as areas that deserve special protections of confidentiality. Having one's uterus on the Internet or one's psychological disorders in the hands of a managed-care company can hardly be written off as merely a new form of gossip or defended on the grounds that the dissemination of such information is a form of protected free speech. Having said that, however, it has to be noted that Singleton and others have a valid point when they criticize proposals to limit certain kinds of speech. As Eric Hughes declares: "Information does not just want to be free, it longs to be free." But this merely underscores why it is so important to control access to that information in the first place.

THE COMMUNITARIAN CRITIQUE

As a communitarian, Amitai Etzione approaches privacy from the opposite angle from Singleton. Where libertarians fear the expansion of the state at the expense of the individual, communitarians worry about excessive individualism. Thus, Etzione is relatively untroubled by government encroachments on privacy and believes the greatest threats to privacy come from the private sector, and what he calls the "privacy merchants."[18]

Indeed, Etzione insists that as far as the "public interest" and government is concerned, Americans have *too much* privacy. In a series of articles and a book arguing for limits on privacy, Etzione claims that in several important areas "the common good is being systematically neglected out of excessive deference to privacy."[19] Far from regarding privacy as under siege, Etzione argues that we should not "privilege"[20] the value of privacy over other needs. This is not a new idea of Etzione, whose philosophy, known as "responsive communitarianism," is a conscious reaction against the excessive individualism of the 1960s.[21] For years, Etzione has argued for the need to curtail a wide range of rights and liberties in the name of the public interest. But it is also clear that Etzione recognizes that privacy is a pivotal value and that it is central to debates over individuals versus the state and the freedom of individual choice versus the "social good."

In balancing the "public good" against personal privacy, Etzione not surprisingly tends to come down against privacy. Focusing on a relatively narrow range of issues, Etzione has little to say about the media culture, political issues, or the tell-all culture. In his book *The Limits of Privacy*, Etzione acknowledges the need for medical privacy, but argues against limits on the government's ability to decrypt communications, supports mandatory AIDS tests for newborns, and is especially enthusiastic about the prospect that Americans be required to carry a universal ID card which they would have to present to officials on demand.

Characteristic of much of his scholarly work, Etzione's case for a "balance" between privacy and public health and safety concerns sounds reasonable, but his critique is really quite radical. Of course basic rights—including privacy—are not absolute. Even the most fundamental rights can be abridged under extraordinary circumstances, when there is a compelling interest at stake. But Etzione would not set the bar so high. Rather than requiring a compelling interest, Etzione proposes a much more modest "balancing" test. But "balance" is not the same as "compelling interest."

Almost by definition rights tend to be awkward, even annoying to those in power. But Etzione takes an alarmingly constrained view of rights, especially those that are inconvenient or inefficient to those agencies, which believe they wield their power in the public interest. Arguably, public safety would be enhanced if police did not have to worry about limits on their ability to wiretap, stop, and search defendants. Arguably public health would benefit from mandatory routine tests for sexually transmitted diseases and cholesterol levels. But we do not simply "balance" the two values.

Etzione argues that he is simply righting the imbalance that occurred after the 1960s, but his views represent a rejection of the tradition of rights that traces back to the Magna Carta. That tradition recognized that fundamental rights could not simply be "balanced" against whatever the ruling authorities thought of as the social good. Etzione's use of language is revealing: repeatedly he warns against "privileging" privacy. That suggests strongly that he wants to shift our understanding of privacy from being a basic right to being a "privilege," a boon granted by a beneficent state, rather than a preexisting and fundamental value.

The peculiar genius of the American system has been that we do not let the government impose its view of social good on us without substantial restraints. Those restraints are not *privileges*, they are *rights*. At one point, Etzione refers to privacy as "societal license"[22] that exempts a category of acts from scrutiny. But licenses, by definition can be revoked. Rights are not so easily dismissed by politicians acting in "the public interest."

As if to illustrate the point, Etzione's own views of what constitutes the "public interest" are problematic at best. He assumes, for example, that the public would be better off if we had weaker protections on our communications, more government surveillance and tracking, and a national ID card.

Your papers, please

If Singleton is unconcerned about the growth of private databases, Etzione is positively blasé about the threats from government surveillance and tracking. He has no problem giving the government keys to electronic communications, insisting this would not affect "all Americans," simply those suspected by the government. This is not reassuring, especially since he proposes limiting the ability of every American to communicate privately. His faith in the benign intentions of government similarly leads him to support the introduction of national ID cards and biometric identifiers. Far from being squeamish about officials demanding our papers, Etzione insists that we all "pay a hefty price for this freedom."[23] He envisions an ID card which citizens "would be required to carry . . . with them at all times, and to present it when asked to do so by public authorities." Etzione likes the ID cards because they are efficient, especially when used to deal with criminals, child abuse, tax fraud, credit-card theft, and identity theft.

He also recognizes that the national ID would be the key to a central tracking database. "This card must be linked to a database that enables authorities both to verify the information that identifies the person and to link it to other information about that person—for instance to determine whether the person has been convicted of a felony and thus is not entitled to purchase a gun."[24] An alternative might be biometric identifiers—eye scans, handprints, and so forth—which would also be stored in central databases.

There is, Etzione confidently predicts, "no evidence or reason to assume that their implementation will set in motion a steady descent into even greater restrictions on privacy and autonomy." In fact, there *is* precisely such evidence: the spreading application of the Social Security number and the proliferation of databases that rely on its use. But Etzione sees no slippery slope. Etzione notes that in and of themselves, such cards "do not transform democratic societies into totalitarian ones." But he also sees no threat whatsoever that they might lead in that direction. "Totalitarian governments do not creep up on the tails of measures such as ID cards, they arise in response to breakdowns in the social order, when basic human needs, such as public safety and work opportunities, are grossly neglected."[25] Etzione ridicules suggestions that invasions of privacy could ever lead to a police state on the grounds that such measures historically have never done so. But historically, society has never faced the sort of challenges it confronts today. Etzione clings to a Big Bang theory, blind to the possibility that freedom may be lost not in a thunderclap, but eroded drip by drip.

In any case, Etzione argues, the national ID would not demonstrably enhance the government's tracking abilities, since the government already has pretty much all the information it needs. An irresponsible state would only need to consolidate data from the IRS, INS, FBI, and SSA, to get a comprehensive picture of its citizens. Basically, Etzione argues, we already suffer all the drawbacks of having an ID card, but get none of the benefits he envisions. This is also true of the data in the private databases.

Etzione acknowledges that a single National ID card would give government agencies access to much of the tracking data in the private datawebs. Far from being a troubling development, Etzione argues that we should grant law-enforcement officials access to the same information we already grant to private business. "To be realistic, the probability of returning the genie to the bottle is nil. Therefore, the real question is: Will this capacity [to invade our privacy and track our behavior] be available only for the profit makers or also for public protection and other social purposes?"[26] Since the private sector already tracks us, why not let the government track us as well?

And yet, Etzione worries about the "pro-privacy" bias in American life today. An excessive concern for privacy, he insists, has delayed "needed public actions" and chilled discussion of "public policies that would advance the common good."[27]

This, he says, is one of the consequences of the egoism, individualism, and rights-happy decade of the 1960s. But one suspects the pendulums of reaction and counterreaction now move too quickly for Etzione. In the late 1990s, Americans face little danger that they have too much privacy. Etzione's statements that we are "systematically" ignoring the public good in the name of privacy is at best an exaggeration, and at worst an absurdity. His concerns are akin to warning a drowning man of the dangers of dry land; a drunk of the dangers of excessive sobriety.

THE TRANSPARENT SOCIETY

Advocates of greater protections for privacy face a far different challenge from author David Brin, who also regards the encroachments on our privacy as both inevitable and possibly a very good thing. Brin agrees with Andrew Kantor, whose response to the growing threats to privacy is essentially to say: "There's no going back, and there's no hiding the information. So let everyone have it."[28]

For Brin, the age of surveillance is a given; what interests him is how we respond to it. Brin sees a future where the cameras are everywhere, watching the streets and public places. He proposes two alternatives: In one possible future, only the security authorities, the police, will control the cameras. In his alternative future, the cameras will still be everywhere, but the watchers will be . . . everyone. Every citizen will have access to every camera image. We will all be watched, but we will also be watchers.

Brin advances several provocative arguments: Given the impossibility of controlling or blocking the new technologies of surveillance, why not democratize them? Let everyone watch. The question Brin poses is: "Will average citizens share, along with the mighty, the right to access these universal monitors? Will common folk have, and exercise, a sovereign power to watch the watchers?" This approach has a decidedly populist tinge to it. "The rich, the powerful and figures of authority will have them," Brin argues, "whether legally or surreptitiously. And the contraptions will become smaller, cheaper, and smarter with each passing year."[29]

Brin is skeptical that moral precepts, the harangues of philosophers, or other legal and moral prescriptions will make people behave themselves with the new technology. So he proposes what he calls "a pragmatic tool more in keeping with our ornery nature. Accountability."[30] Forget about blocking or legislating them into good behavior. "Light *is* going to shine into nearly every corner of our lives."[31] For Brin, an open, transparent society, in which nothing is hidden, veiled, or secret is a society that can be held accountable. Rather than shutting down the flow of information, we should actually make the information flows *even wider.* "For instance, if some company wishes to collect data on consumers across America, let it do so only on condition that the top one hundred officers in the firm must post exactly the same information about themselves and all their family members on an accessible Web site," Brin proposes.[32] Put another way:

"[W]e may not be able to eliminate the intrusive glare shining on citizens of the next century, but the glare just might be rendered harmless through the application of more light aimed in the other direction."[33]

Brin rests his defense of transparency precisely on his belief that violations of privacy can be answered tit for tat. He argues that the transparent society will also create a balance of terror. Brin calls this "reciprocal transparency," the privacy equivalent to the military's Cold War doctrine of "mutually assured destruction." Just as an armed society "is a polite society," Brin argues that a society in which we all carried cameras, watching and recording everyone else, would be both a polite and an accountable society. For example, we are not too far away from a time when all police officers may wear cameras. What, Brin asks, if we all wore cameras, too, letting us watch the watchers? Would such a society not only be more secure, but also more civil? In his transparent society of the future, the flow of information will be more or less even; the most egregious violations of privacy will be tempered by the knowledge that the violator can easily be the victim. We will all live in glass houses; ergo, no one will throw stones.

As an analogy he offers the unspoken etiquette of the crowded restaurant. Most of us, he writes, feel free to hold intimate conversations even in a crowded public place, because we know that we are unlikely to be stared at or watched. "We don't achieve this confidence by wearing masks, or because laws require other customers to wear blinkers or blindfolds. Mutual civility and common decency play a role, but not alone."[34] Fellow diners are also deterred from staring at us, because they do not want to be caught in the act; voyeurism is frowned upon, and to be caught is embarrassing. "Aren't cameras just extensions of our eyes?" he asks. "What holds for a restaurant should apply when we have tomorrow's amplified senses, assuming that such powers are distributed evenly. If it is considered boorish to brandish your camera too openly, people will 'shoot back' at those with itchy trigger fingers, retaliating by spreading reputation-damaging evidence of their voyeurism. . . ."[35] But this is a poor analogy, because the very essence of the new surveillance is the fact that it is often hidden, surreptitious, anonymous, and quite unaccountable.

Brin repeatedly implies that privacy is objectionable because it is unegalitarian. But so is freedom. So is transparency. Secrecy, he argues, feeds the imbalances of power because the rich and powerful will always have the power to probe into our lives. One of the attractions of transparency is that it empowers the rest of us to peer back. But the transparency of society would actually do very little to right the imbalance of power. Even at its most utopian, it would simply shift the center of that imbalance. A society in which we all walked around naked would not be one that would emphasize our equality in any respect, except in God's eyes. Clothes enhance inequality, but a society of naked people would quickly demonstrate what true inequity was all about.

Elsewhere, Brin says that his transparent society stops at the doorstep of our homes, which he insists would still be sacrosanct. But why stop there? And why stop at cameras? Why not plant listening devices as well as cameras in our living rooms? Our bedrooms? Why not broadcast the activities of our bathrooms? Aren't we protected by "reciprocal transparency"? But Brin asks us to believe that a society of voyeurs will maintain its discretion intact when it comes to our homes. Others may not be so sanguine.

Nevertheless, Brin's argument is provocative. Brin is right when he says that transparency, openness, and accountability are essential to a free and open society. The principle that people in power should be watched is not only a powerful tradition, it simply makes sense. It was Justice Brandeis, the father of privacy law, who suggested that light was the best disinfectant. Brin's idea of "transparent reciprocity" is also tempting, especially when it comes to institutions such as the media, which thrive on the assurance that the flow of information goes only one way. From a practical point of view, it is unlikely that there are any legal means to restrain the press as it pushes back the lines of privacy even further. Constitutionally, the media can invoke the protections of a free press, while label and slander laws provide little or no protection at all for "public figures."

Would it make any difference if editors and reporters knew that the same spotlight shining on their targets would shine on themselves? Can we imagine a media watchdog organization that would monitor the private lives of the editors and reporters with the exact same diligence that they probed the private lives of others? What if every editor knew that every front-page story about the sexual indiscretions of the local alderman would be accompanied by publicity about the sexual indiscretions of members of the editorial board? If the divorces of editors were handled the same as celebrities? Or if the drinking habits of the pressroom were held to the same standard as the drinking habits of other citizens? Would this affect the media's attitude toward privacy issues? Would it change the way they made decisions about what they would pursue and what they would publish?

We can imagine the objections: Reporters and editors do not regard themselves as public figures. They would insist that they should be held to a different standard from the men and women who seek public office—and would have power over the lives and livelihoods of other citizens. But can anyone deny that full-blown "reciprocal transparency" would have a rather salutary effect on the media's sensitivity toward privacy issues?

ACCOUNTABILITIES

Brin also cautions against a society that promiscuously encourages anonymity. He rightly points out that although anonymity can assure privacy, it is hardly a guarantee of good conduct. In fact, the human experience suggests the opposite is often true. The man on a business trip in a strange city where he is unknown and unrecognized might use his new anonymity to visit the local art museum, but there is also a chance he will behave in ways that he would never attempt among his neighbors. Thus it has always been; the anonymity of the city has long been a magnet for unconventional behavior. "While a man remains in a country village," Adam Smith wrote in *Reputation*, "his conduct may be attended to, and he may be obliged to attend to it himself. . . . But as soon as he comes to a great city, he is sunk in obscurity and darkness. His conduct is observed and attended to by nobody, and he is therefore likely to neglect it himself, and to abandon himself to every low profligacy and vice." Perhaps even by ordering an X-rated movie in his hotel room.

A society of anonymous strangers, Brin points out, is not a particularly attractive prospect. He proposes this thought experiment. "Imagine a person in your neighborhood behaving bizarrely—"perhaps performing a strange dance, or erecting a mysterious device, or just mumbling to himself." Brin asks, what is more likely to arouse suspicions and perhaps attempts to restrain that person's behavior: If the man is wearing a ski mask and an overcoat, and refuses to identify himself or explain what he is doing; or if it is someone you know whose history and past quirkiness has long been known and tolerated?

"Which one will provoke mothers to call in their children, and fathers to gather in a wary, murmuring crowd? Which 'eccentric' is more likely to be let alone?"[36]

But this question again highlights the difference between privacy and secrecy. Much that we do is private, but hardly secret. The man performing the dance is not engaging in private behavior, even if he wants to keep his identity secret. But Brin's story reminds us what the loss of privacy would mean to other nonconformists. As Brin acknowledges, most societies punish nonconformity. One of the most powerful arguments for privacy is that it also protects us from social pressures, by permitting us to develop interests and a personality outside of the glare of the enforcers of social norms. Societies without much respect for individual autonomy invariably use gossip and public censure to enforce their standards of virtue and correctness. But, Brin says dismissively, "that was there. That was then." In contrast, he says, our society "refutes the images of relentless conformism."[37] He points to the way homosexuals have come out of the closet, the withering away of racial stereotypes, and the extraordinary tolerance of the eccentric and even the weird in our diverse society. Surely never before in human history has a society so accepted and even celebrated those who defy and challenge its traditional values.

But . . .

But this has hardly resulted in the disappearance of social pressures to conform. Ask any adolescent. Or any woman who struggles to conform to the body images in the media. Or an evangelical Christian working at a Hollywood production company. Or a Republican on the faculty of an Ivy League college. Or a homosexual on an NFL team. Or a housewife at a reunion of her feminist classmates.

True, many of the old stigmas have vanished. But our liberation from many of the old pressures has given birth to a myriad of new conformities. What else is political correctness? Society may no longer stigmatize illegitimacy. But what about smoking? Adultery may be winked at . . . Or is it? And what about the telling of ethnic jokes? Drug use? The new conformist pressures can be every bit as stifling, made even more powerful by the echo chamber of the media, the courtroom, and political action. Contemporary social norms are also less predictable than in the past, subject to shifts and sudden eruptions as the social agenda zigs and zags to conform to the passion or anxiety of the moment. Once, divorce was considered virtually disqualifying for a political figure; then, for decades, it was tolerated and even ignored. Might it again be stigmatized? What about single motherhood? Or the enjoyment of adult beverages? Today no one thinks of holding it against a couple who has chosen not to have children—but will that be true in the future? Will we have to reveal what medical procedures we have undergone; or explain and justify our choice of religion?

With the sort of honesty that is quite rare in debates of this sort, Brin admits that he might be badly mistaken about the consequences of a transparent society. He cites, for instance, the case of Vincent Foster, the deputy White House counsel who committed suicide, perhaps because he feared embarrassment and shame if the various scandals involving his friends, the Clintons, ever came to light. Indeed, the case highlights the flaw of reciprocity: it cannot account for variations in conscience and sensitivities.

Inevitably, people's secrets, like their nakedness, are not exactly proportionate. Reciprocity only works if there is a rough balance of reticence. But what happens if one part of society doesn't care? Does a transparent society work the same way for the sort of people who appear on the *Jerry Springer Show* and for the blue-hairs of the Moral Majority? Does privacy mean the same thing to a twenty-something free spirit and fifty-year-old man who suffers from heart disease and cares for an incontinent spouse? Would the bright light of accountability shine the same on both? Would it really be equivalent to maintain surveillance and dossiers on abortion doctors *and* pro-life activists? Would the consequences be the same?

Ultimately, the argument that we need to have transparency in order to be accountable begs the fundamental question: To *whom* are we accountable? And for *what*?

Moreover, aren't there multiple accountabilities? I am willing to be accountable to my children in a way that I am not willing to be accountable to, say, the news media, or to my neighbors.

Brin would have us believe that a society to which no one had any secrets would be more respectful of everyone's secrets. But he has perhaps missed the full significance of our society's diversity: There is no longer one standard or one set of rules. There are, in fact, many different communities, with different standards, requiring different levels of accountability from us. A young man may have no problem sharing his homosexuality with his family and friends—but not with his coworkers. Society as a whole may well have regarded the controversies about "Travelgate" that so consumed Vince Foster as—to use Brin's word—"picayune."[38] But Foster may have also held himself accountable to a smaller society, including his family, or perhaps his church, or simply a group of compatriots bound together by certain ideas of honor and rectitude not shared by society as a whole.

Many of us may not feel accountable to society as a whole, but feel a profound accountability to such smaller, discrete communities or groups. In some cases, those accountabilities may clash. Rather than withering away, those pressures may be intensifying, as the various groups enforce their new cultural norms without the benefit of the long-standing cultural support that helped bolster more traditional norms. Indeed, the new conformities are often enforced with the special ferocity that often accompanies attempts to create new values. As society becomes more diverse, it becomes increasingly difficult to be accountable to so many different possible sets of expectations, many of which may seem to be in conflict with one another. We no longer simply face the prospect of being held up to ridicule by the dominant society's values; we are constantly being weighed on innumerable scales, some that find us wanting, others that embrace us—sometimes at the same time, for the same things.

Even so, Brin's arguments are also interesting because they force us to confront the challenges in starker terms than we are accustomed to facing. Brin highlights this with his vision of a society not with one Big Brother, but with millions of Little Brothers, watching, checking, listening, and following us. Most of us would find that extremely creepy—even if none of the watchers carried a badge. Brin's utopia is for most of us a pure dystopia. Few of us would react to the news that a Peeping Tom is prowling our neighborhood by proposing that we all lift all of our shades or that we all go about naked all of the time.

Although it is not his purpose, Brin ultimately exposes the flaw of the libertarian argument that we should act only against government violations of privacy. The fact is that privacy is a seamless fabric; it is a value against the world, not just the state. Any definition of privacy that ignores the nongovernmental threats or the social dimension of privacy is unduly narrow. While it is true that most of us are far more likely to be concerned with the excessive power of the IRS than we are of Lands' End, it is also true that on a day-to-day basis, we are much more concerned about what sorts of information might fall into the hands of our enemies, our boss, our ex-wives. For many of us, it is more worrisome that an embarrassing personal detail will appear in the local newspaper than that it will become known to the FBI.

But once information is available it is almost impossible to control. The reality is that it is more important than ever for individuals to somehow maintain control over information about their own lives.

14

■

"It's None of Your Business"

So how do we restore a culture that respects privacy? We can begin to give individuals that control by creating a *presumption of privacy* as the default setting of the Information Age. Our presumption of privacy should be as strongly held—and jealously guarded—as our presumption that we have free speech, freedom to worship, the right to own private property, and equality of opportunity, all values that are deeply ingrained in our culture, law, and politics. Those presumptions can be rebutted, of course, in specific cases, but the burden of proof should be on others to explain why any of those rights should be abridged. In the case of the presumption of privacy, the burden should be on others to say why they have any right to know about our lives. Absent that, the presumption should be that each of us has control over such information. In practical terms, that means that we should not be required to "opt out" of a system that invades our privacy; the presumption of privacy would dictate that no one is allowed into our zone of privacy without our specific choice to "opt in."

This also means that we no longer presume that anyone has a right to pry into the intimacies of our life and no longer assume that we are under any moral or political obligation to join in the public disemboweling that has become so much a part of our culture of exposure.

We will not, of course, get there through legislation. But there are areas where Congress, the courts, consumers, and business can change the climate for privacy. This will require significant changes in the political and legal dynamics.

CYBERSTALKERS

As difficult as protecting medical privacy has proven to be, the issue of protecting consumers from marketers, information brokers, direct mailers, and the new generation of "cyberstalkers," is even more problematic. Congress is understandably reluctant to create the regulatory regime and accompanying bureaucracy that a private-sector Privacy Act would entail. But the United States is under heavy pressure from the European Union, which has taken a hard line on the issue of data protection. The EU's demand that the United States take action to protect the privacy of European citizens adds urgency to the problem already facing consumers in this country on a daily basis.

Privacy advocates themselves are divided on the role of legislation, with some, such as the Electronic Privacy Information Center pushing for tighter legal restrictions on the use and dissemination of personal information without a consumer's permission. But other advocates, like Esther Dyson, are skeptical of European-style regulations.[1] Rather than focusing on the question of who "owns" information, Dyson suggests that the real question is who *controls* that information. Dyson opposes sweeping laws that regulate the dissemination of information because "even if we passed a thousand pages of airtight laws, there's no way to enforce them." But she also avoids simply relying on industry self-regulation. Instead, she proposes a "third way"—neither relying on government nor industry, but an environment "where consumers themselves can exercise their power and control their own data." They would do so through a combination of new technology, contract law, and a minimum of regulation.

Dyson begins by distinguishing between different kinds of personal information, which require different sorts of handling. She draws a distinction, for example, between information offered voluntarily to commercial enterprises as opposed to information forced from us by government fiat or from a monopoly.

Dyson would place tough limits on the dissemination of "information required in tax returns, information for driver's licenses, health insurance or medical care, and other such benefits" because this data is "not negotiated by individuals," and therefore should be subject to special legal protections.

The key for Dyson is empowering the consumer himself. The problem now is that though some consumers are deeply concerned—perhaps even paranoid—about their privacy, many others are careless, even reckless with their personal information. "No one knows what is known and what isn't," Dyson remarks. "It's the one-way mirror effect that makes people so uneasy." This could be remedied if the government passed legislation requiring business and Web sites to disclose their privacy policies (but not dictating the content of those policies). Such government-mandated disclosure could then create a market for privacy policies, as companies begin to compete for customers by offering them greater levels of security and marketing their own reliability and credibility. A model for this is the so-called TRUSTe trademark, which certifies that the business not only agrees to disclose its privacy policies, but that the credibility of those policies is backed by a trusted third party. Ideally, those privacy policies would clearly spell out how personal information will be handled and by what means consumers can limit its disclosure, provide clear recourse for violations, and describe the means by which consumers can verify that the business is living up to its promises.

Expanding the ability of consumers to protect their privacy, Dyson argues, would merely follow that same pattern of high-tech companies like Microsoft that have built their industries by empowering individuals in the Information Age. Moreover, Dyson is hopeful that business would respond positively to such an environment, because they would recognize that their loyalty should be to their customers, not to other companies that want to vacuum their data.

Given the poor record of industry-self-regulation to date, however, even the skeptical Dyson may prove to be a tad naïve about the response of industry. But foremost among the reasons for optimism is the fact that privacy makes good business sense. Companies that can assure consumers that their data will be protected and held in confidence will have a significant competitive edge in the era of electronic commerce, especially as consumer awareness increases. In contrast, the cardinal sin of the Information Age may be the obtuse decision by companies to sacrifice their own customer's privacy. A basic principle of business is that customers do not tend to reward betrayal with loyalty.

Unlike some of the cypherpunks, Dyson has a healthy respect for the limits of mere technical fixes to protect privacy. For examples, she notes that solutions like the World Wide Web Consortium's P3P (Platform for Privacy Preferences) lets users define and manage their own data. But, as

Dyson notes "it also makes it easier for Web sites, servers and database managers to aggregate, manipulate, distribute, trade or sell such data." Rather than limiting technology, Dyson argues that we continue to develop better systems and concentrate on discouraging their abuse. Whether through legislation or voluntary action, the key for the future of electronic commerce will be the adherence of organizations and businesses alike to what has become known as the Code of Fair Information Practices. The underlying principles of these practices are that:

- Only the minimum essential information should be collected in any transaction.
- Ideally, information should be collected directly from the subject individual, as opposed to using second- or thirdhand information.
- Whenever information is gathered, individuals should be told why the information is needed.
- The information collected should be used only for the purpose for which it was collected and should not be used for any other purpose without the individual's permission.
- Individuals should have the right to see their personal information and correct any errors they might find.

REINING IN BIG BROTHER

Much of the debate over privacy has often focused on the private sector, however, it is both naïve and disingenuous to suggest that we can cleanly separate private data from the data held in the hands of the government. Government data and identifiers have become the backbone of electronic dossiers.

Rather than expanding the use of government identifier numbers—including the Social Security number—Congress should be trying to limit its contributions to the dataweb. Rather than expanding the permitted uses of the Social Security number, for instance, Congress needs to consider placing sharp limits on its use outside of the specific purposes for which it was designed. But government threats to privacy run much deeper.

Alarmed by the prospect of an omniscient single government database in the 1960s, Congress moved with some decisiveness to block the chilling prospect of a single global record-keeping system. But that original nightmare pales beside our current reality, and Congress needs to recognize its own role in expanding and facilitating the dataweb. Many of the politicians who have complained loudly about invasions of privacy when it is to their political advantage have been responsible for privacy intrusions that would have been unimaginable even to the more paranoid futurists of the Sixties.

Unfortunately, the courts have been notably laggard in applying constitutional protections to many of the new technologies that have brought surveillance and intrusion to levels of sophistication and artistry. Dating back to the 1928 decision in *Olmstead,* in which the Court had refused to extend Fourth Amendment protections to wiretapping, the justices have been slow to recognize the changing shape of the threats to the "right of the people to be secure in their persons, houses, papers, and effects." As a matter of law, any electronic communication or private conversation should be constitutionally protected.

Specifically, the federal government has no business having a trapdoor into the computers, telephones, or any other aspect of the information superhighway. The Fourth Amendment places sharp limits on the government's ability to search our homes or listen into our conversations. Under certain limits, government can execute searches; but its agents have never been assured of the absolute right to find what they are looking for. A nation that took privacy seriously would not even entertain the suggestion that law enforcement, in effect, be given the keys to every door, every file cabinet, and the code to every private communication in the electronic age.

New technologies, such as encryption and digital telephones, actually make it possible for individuals to reclaim some of the privacy that has been eroded by other technologies. Neither Congress nor the courts should allow the government to take away these protections or render them vulnerable.

Undoubtedly, this would be somewhat inconvenient for law enforcement. But police agencies can hardly claim that the balance of the new technologies of surveillance does not weigh heavily in their favor. They can still deploy highly sophisticated listening and monitoring devices against those who are legitimately suspected of criminal activity, and for whom they have obtained warrants. However, they do not need and should not be given carte blanche to listen in on everyone's conversations. In any case, many of the protections of the Bill of Rights are admittedly unhelpful to the police, but it is an inconvenience that a free society has decided it can live with.

Besides limiting the government's capacity for snooping, there are also other opportunities for refining constitutional privacy protections. Since its ruling in *Whalen* v. *Roe* in 1977, the Court has recognized that the constitution protected two types of privacy: the individual's independence in making highly personal decisions and the interest in "avoiding disclosure of personal matters." In *Whalen,* the Court ruled that despite the right to control such personal information, the state of New York could continue to maintain a database listing all of the patients receiving certain kinds of legal narcotics through prescriptions. Even so, Justice Brennan acknowledged that the "central storage and easy accessibility of computerized data vastly increase the potential for abuse of that information" and wrote that he was not prepared to say "that future developments will not demonstrate the necessity of some curb on such technology." This seems to raise the possibility that the Court might be willing to revisit the issue of medical databases in light of the dramatically increased scope as well as the advances in technologies. Would the Court feel the same about a federally mandated cradle-to-grave database that included every contact with a doctor? Might it find that laws requiring doctors to reveal details of their treatment of individual patients violate the constitutional right of informational privacy?

Similarly, privacy advocates ought to pursue the implications of the Court's doctrine of "practical obscurity," in addressing the proliferation of government databases and computerized records.

FREEDOM OF INFORMATION

One of the more difficult privacy dilemmas is balancing "freedom of information" with the need to protect personal privacy. In many states, some records are routinely open to the public, even those that deal with highly personal matters. This includes divorce files, criminal records, assessment records, tax liabilities, and a host of other documents and records that government requires and which have fueled the creation of highly revealing personal dossiers. With the exponential growth of public databases—including those dealing with medical issues—the issue takes on special urgency. Advocates of open-records policies argue persuasively that free access to such records is essential to keep government accountable. The Founding Fathers, according to historian Henry Steele Commager, "thought secrecy in government one of the instruments of Old World tyranny and committed [themselves] to the principle that a democracy cannot function unless the people are permitted to know what their government is up to." But how can this be squared with the individual's interest "in avoiding disclosure of personal matters"—which the Supreme Court has also recognized as a constitutionally protected right? In other words, are we forced to choose either between a transparent and accountable government on the one hand and protecting personal privacy on the other? Is there an irresolvable conflict between the two values?

The Supreme Court has provided a novel—and overlooked—answer. One of the high Court's most notable decisions on the issue came in a case known as *U.S. Department of Justice et al.* v. *Reporters Committee for Freedom of the Press*,[2] in which the Court propounded the rather extraordinary doctrine of "practical obscurity." The case involved a request under the Federal Freedom of Information Act by CBS News for the rap sheet on a man named Charles Medico.

Some years earlier, the Pennsylvania Crime Commission had identified the family's business, Medico Industries, as a legitimate business "dominated by organized crime." There were also allegations that Medico Industries had used a cozy relationship with a crooked Congressman to obtain defense contracts. CBS asked the FBI for the record of any and all arrests, indictments, acquittals, convictions and sentences of any of four members of the Medico family. At first, the FBI denied the requests, but later released the rap sheet information on three of the Medicos who had died. CBS persisted, demanding the rap sheet for Charles Medico, the remaining family member. The FBI again refused, saying that it had no record of any financial crimes involving him, but declined to confirm or deny whether it had a record of any other crimes. CBS sued.

The core of the issue was the balance between the need for openness and transparency on the part of the government and Mr. Medico's interest in privacy. On the surface, the law seemed to favor the media's request. Much of the information the reporters sought was in public records—open and available to the public in various offices and courthouses around the country. The FBI rap sheet was merely a compilation by a public agency of other public actions. Indeed, that was how the Court of Appeals saw the matter, ruling that "an individual's privacy interest in criminal history information that is a matter of public record was minimal at best."

But at least one appeals court judge did not see it so simply. In a dissent, Judge Kenneth Starr (who would later become the independent counsel who would plague President Clinton) rejected the argument that individuals had no privacy rights in their criminal records. Specifically, Starr wrote, the use of computerized databanks had changed the privacy landscape. "We are now informed that many federal agencies collect items of information on individuals that are ostensible matters of public record. For example, Veterans Administration and Social Security records include birth certificates, marriage licenses, and divorce decrees (which may recite findings of fault); the Department of Housing and Urban Development maintains data on millions of home mortgages that are presumably 'public records' at county clerks' offices. . . ."

If the courts upheld the reporters' request for the federal printouts of such records, Starr warned, the "federal government is thereby transformed in one fell swoop into the clearinghouse for highly personal information, releasing records on any person, to any requester, for any purpose." This is not at all what Congress had in mind. The FOIA was designed to keep government honest; it was not designed to turn it into the ultimate gatherer and disseminator of information about private citizens. The law was designed to open windows onto the government, not turn the government into a microscope.

The Supreme Court agreed with Starr. The attorneys for the media argued that because the events summarized in the rap sheets had previously been disclosed to the public, Mr. Medico's "privacy interest in avoiding release of a federal compilation of these events approaches zero." But the high court rejected what it called that "cramped notion of personal privacy."

Roaming widely over the law and theory of privacy, Justice John Paul Stevens wrote that the Court had already recognized two distinct types of privacy rights. The first protected the "independence in making certain kinds of important decisions." The second right of privacy was the interest "in avoiding disclosure of personal matters"—a right he also found in the common law and in the common understanding of what privacy entailed. Because the right of privacy included the right to control personal information about oneself, Stevens wrote, the Court had to draw a "distinction, in terms of personal privacy, between scattered disclosure of the bits of information contained in a rap sheet and revelations of the rap sheet as a whole."

The issue, Stevens wrote, "is whether the compilation of otherwise hard-to-obtain information alters the privacy interest implicated by disclosure of that information. *Plainly there is a vast difference between the public records that might be found after a diligent search of courthouse files, county archives, and local police stations throughout the country and a computerized summary located in a single clearinghouse of information."* (*Emphasis added.*)

This is what the Court would come to call "practical obscurity." The documents were public, but the very difficulty in finding and accessing them made it impractical to search them all out.°

Critics, including David Brin, gibed that, in effect, Stevens was saying that the "First Amendment is great, as long as there is no efficient means of carrying it out." That is, of course, unfair. But with due allowances for hyperbole, the Court was essentially saying that the government had no obligation to make the practice of First Amendment rights more convenient. With a sense of practicality and common sense rarely found in such cases, the Court had recognized one of the elements of privacy enjoyed in the past was precisely the "practical obscurity" of personal information. The Court not only found that individuals had a genuine privacy interest in keeping their criminal past out of the public domain, but they also had an interest in the "practical obscurity" of a precomputerized age.

Focusing its ruling on the exemption in the Freedom of Information Act, which allowed agencies to delete identifying information "to the extent required to prevent a clearly unwarranted invasion of personal privacy . . ." the Court drew a strikingly bright line between information about government operations and decisions, and information the government had collected about private citizens.

"The privacy interest in maintaining the practical obscurity of rap-sheet information will always be high," the Court ruled. "When the subject of such a rap sheet is a private citizen and when the information is in the Government's compilation, rather than as a record of 'what the government is up to,' the privacy interest" protected by the exemptions in the

---

° The very fact that federal funds have been spent to prepare, index, and maintain these criminal-history files," Steven wrote for the Court, "demonstrated that the individual items of information in the summaries would not otherwise be 'freely available' either to the officials who have access to the underlying files or to the general public."

FOIA "is at its apex while the FOIA-based public interest in disclosure is at its nadir." The Court ruled that as a "categorical matter," such requests for personal nongovernmental information were "unwarranted."*

The Court not only had reiterated the constitutional right to informational privacy; but, by balancing the need for transparency and accountability with the need to keep government from becoming surrogate snoop, it had also established a useful guideline for resolving other disputes about open records and privacy. Government, it argued, can be kept accountable, without turning it into an instrument of surveillance of fellow citizens.

Although it may be difficult as a practical matter to regulate private information brokers and marketers, the Court has set out the constitutional parameters for sharply limiting both the government's information-gathering abilities and its right to disseminate such personal information to others. This could be helpful in any attempt to scale back, limit, or abolish the many government databases, which threaten to undermine personal privacy. At minimum, such databases should be limited to using personal information strictly and exclusively for the purpose for which it was gathered.

The other area ripe for development is privacy as a cause of *civil* action. The tort of privacy invasion has not fared especially well, and its enforcement has been spotty, at best. In large measure the development of tort law will depend on society's general willingness to tolerate invasions of privacy by individuals, the media, employers, organizations, and businesses. As early as 1971, privacy expert Arthur Miller warned of the gradual numbing effect that increased intrusions might have on such community attitudes. "The danger is that widespread computerization of personal data coupled with continuous demands for data by society's information managers will slowly narrow the community's conception of what is private, which in turn will gradually reduce the effectiveness of the privacy

---

* Nor did the media have any special right to learn about Medico's past. The Court declared, "Medico may or may not be one of the 24 million persons for whom the FBI has a rap sheet. If [the media] is entitled to have the FBI tell them what it knows about Medico's criminal history, any other member of the public is entitled to the same disclosure—whether for writing a news story, for deciding whether to employ Medico, to rent a house for him, to extend credit to him, or simply to confirm or deny a suspicion."

action," he wrote. Just as "constant exposure to scenes of war and squalor have caused many to grow callous about human life and the destruction of the environment, the public may lose its sense of the private if large-scale transfers and dissemination of personal information become common. . . . people accustomed to the revelation of sensitive personal data eventually may define most information as public and place it beyond the law's protection."[3]

There are no easy solutions to the problem posed by an increasingly sensationalistic and competitive media. But there are signs that media overreaching and excess are breeding their own backlash, especially when they involve the invasion of privacy. Unfortunately, as the law is now interpreted, there are few realistic restraints on the media for invasion of privacy or libel, especially in the case of persons deemed to be "public figures." As a result, anyone who becomes involved in public debates forfeits many of his or her legal protections against invasions of privacy and even false reporting. This has already become a formidable deterrent to the exercise of the duties of citizenship. Legislation can go some distance toward righting the balance between the media and individuals in the area of "intrusion" (intruding upon one's solitude in a highly offensive manner), the publication of "private facts" (offensive private information of no legitimate public concern), and "appropriation" (the use of a person's likeness or name without permission.) Each of these areas is recognized as a tort—an injury in civil law—however, the law is, at best, confused, inconsistent, and in need of clarification.

Miller has noted that because the Constitution's protections of privacy are greater than the protections against loss of reputation, the courts should consider having a different standard for invasion-of-privacy cases than for cases of liberal and slander. Miller and other commentators have also suggested that privacy protections against the appropriation of one's name or likeness for commercial advantage could be used to protect consumers from marketers who use personal data without either consent or compensation. If an individual can sue a marketer for using his or her picture for advertisements without their permission, why not allow suits against those same marketers for using detailed dossiers that arguably paint a far more personal and intimate picture than any photograph?[4]

RECLAIMING OUR PRIVACY

The reclamation of privacy does not, however, begin with the courts, politicians, or even celebrities. Instead, its beginnings are more modest, a single cloud on the distant horizon.

The privacy revolution will ultimately be decided by the attitudes of individuals, reflected in our general culture. Until individuals, as citizens and consumers, take privacy more seriously in their daily lives, there is unlikely to be the critical mass necessary for change. This not only means taking practical steps to protect our own privacy (by not giving out our Social Security numbers or refusing to do business with companies that market our names), but also rejecting the assumption that there is something wrong with keeping our private lives private. Our attitude toward the culture of relentless self-exposure will inevitably shape the debate over what should be kept private and what opened up for public scrutiny. The key to the revolutions will be our willingness to confront the culture of exposure by recognizing that there are some things that others (including the public) not only do not have the right to know, but which it is right that they not know. As long as we measure "sincerity" by our willingness to engage in conspicuous emotionalism, as long as we applaud acts of exhibitionism as signs of mental health, as long as we tolerate the ratcheting down of media standards and devour the sordid details of other people's failings, it is unlikely our society will grow more respectful of privacy.

Indeed, a measure of the recovery of privacy will be the day when we feel comfortable saying "It's none of your business," without hesitation, explanation, or apology to the busybodies intent on snooping into our lives.

Who knows? They might even blush.

This may also require us to rethink the reach of the therapeutic state. Slogans such as "It takes a village to raise a child," for example, tend to blur the differences between intimate communities—such as households and neighborhoods—and the largely anonymous society as a whole, including government. This blurring of the lines has become especially alarming in social-welfare bureaucracies and public schools, where members of the "helping professions" often act as if they had a mandate to be substitute parents. Appealing to anxieties about drug use and child abuse, some edu-

cators have taken it upon themselves to probe into intimate family relationships and, occasionally, even to intervene. Parents who complain about
such intrusiveness are often regarded with suspicion. In some cases the in-
terventions are, indeed, justified, but too often the privacy of *all* families is
placed at risk because of the dysfunction of a relative few.

A society that takes civil liberties and family values seriously will recognize that there is a fundamental interest in the right of families to be let
alone and to be able to resist the imposition of the dominant culture's values. By invoking that right of family privacy, we can help restore some of
the lines between public and private that have come under such persistent
attack.

But respect for the privacy of the individual and of the family is only a
first step. Respect for privacy will be at the heart of any renewal of a civil
society. For it is privacy that gives us control over our lives, enables us to
be individuals, and thus allows us to fulfill our public as well as our private
duties.

Notes

Prologue and Introduction

1. E. L. Godkin, "The Rights of the Citizen," quoted in Rochelle Gurstein, *The Repeal of Reticence* (New York: Hill and Wang, 1996), p. 58.
2. James B. Twitchell, *For Shame: The Loss of Common Decency in American Culture,* (New York: St. Martin's Press, 1998), p. 199.

2. Why It Matters

1. Janna Malamud Smith, *Private Matters* (Reading, Massachusetts: Addison-Wesley, 1997), p. 66.
2. Ibid. See discussion, 70 ff. Notes Smith, "People today live with a greater feeling of daily privacy, but in many ways it is a illusion—a kind of virtual privacy. No one knows you very well, but many strangers hold pieces of your life."
3. Primo Levi, "If This is a Man: Remembering Auschwitz" (New York: Summit Books, 1985), p. 329.
4. Quoted in Ellen Alderman and Caroline Kennedy, *The Right to Privacy* (New York: Vintage Books, 1997), p. 14.
5. See discussion in Judith Decew, *In Pursuit of Privacy* (Ithaca: Cornell University Press, 1997), pp. 41ff.
6. Quoted in Ben Brantley, "'Jackie': Enter Smiling but Elusive, as Always," *The New York Times,* November 11, 1997.
7. Carl D. Schneider, *Shame, Exposure, and Privacy* (New York: W. W. Norton and Co., 1992), p. 45.
8. Hannah Arendt, *The Human Condition* (Chicago: The University of Chicago Press, 1958), p. 51.
9. Ibid., p. 64.
10. Quoted in Jean Bethke Elshtain, *Democracy on Trial* (New York: Basic Books, 1995), p. 45.

3. Trapped in the Dataweb

1. Carole A. Lane, *Naked In Cyberspace* (Wilton, CT, Pemberton Press, 1997), p. 3.
2. Robert Pear, "Social Security Closes Online Site, Citing Risks to Privacy," *The New York Times,* April 10, 1997.

3. Matt Rosoff, "Net Confidential," CNET, 1998.

4. Jeff Pelline and Courtney Macavinta, "Billionaires Left Exposed," CNET, January 14, 1997.

5. Nina Bernstein, "High-Tech Sleuths Find Private Facts Online," *The New York Times*, September 15, 1997.

6. Source: "The Cat," The CAT Midwest, downloaded from *www.spytaps.com*, last updated February 1998.

7. Thomas Goetz, "Using Government Data, Web Sites Track Highflying Execs in Their Jets," *The Wall Street Journal*, October 29, 1998.

8. "Fact Sheet #11: "From Cradle to Grave: Government Records and Your Privacy," Privacy Rights Clearinghouse, 1997.

9. Ashley Dunn, "The Fall and Rise of Privacy," *The New York Times*, September 24, 1997.

10. Nina Bernstein, op. cit.

11. Iver Peterson, "State Government Agencies Turn Data Base Records Into Cash Cows," *The New York Times*, July 14, 1997.

12. *The Politics of Privacy* (Washington, D.C., The Center for Public Integrity, 1998), p. 6–7.

13. "Mistakes Do Happen," Public Interest Research Groups, 1998.

14. Jeffrey Rothfelder, "Is Nothing Private," *Business Week*, September 4, 1989.

15. Rose Aguilar, "Research Service Raises Privacy Fears," CNET, June 10, 1996.

16. Laurie J. Flynn, "Company Stops Providing Access to Social Security Numbers," *The New York Times*, June 13, 1996.

17. Robert Pear, "Government to Use Vast Database to Track Deadbeat Parents," *The New York Times*, September 22, 1997.

18. Ann Cavoukian and Don Tapscott, *Who Knows: Safeguarding Your Privacy in a Networked World* (New York, McGraw-Hill, 1997) p. 83.

19. John Markoff, "Deals to Move Global Positioning Technology Toward Everyday Use," *The New York Times*, August 11, 1998.

20. Robert Suro, "FCC Proposes Rules For Cellular Wiretaps," *The Washington Post*, October 23, 1998.

21. David Banisar, *CAQ* 56, Spring, 1996.

22. Ibid.

23. "An Appraisal of the Technologies of Political Control," Omega Foundation Report for the European Parliament, September 1998.

24. Bill Gates, *The Road Ahead* (New York: Viking, 1995), p. 269.

25. David Banisar, "Big Brother Goes High Tech," *CAQ* 56, Spring, 1996.

26. Rick Crawford, "Techno Prisoners," *Adbusters Quarterly*, Summer 1994, pp. 21–22.

27. "Civil Liberties Implications of Airport Security Measures," Statement by Gregory T. Nojeim, American Civil Liberties Union, Before White House Commission on Aviation Safety and Security, September 5, 1996.

28. David Banisar, op. cit.

29. Peter Wayner, "Closed-Door Policy and Key Cards at Princeton," *The New York Times*, November 12, 1998.

30. Nadine Strossen, "Everyone Is Watching You," *Intellectual Capital*, May 28, 1998.

31. Tom Heinen and Meg Kissinger, "Refusal to Wear Hidden Camera Costs Job," *The Milwaukee Journal-Sentinel,* February 14, 1999.

32. Robert O'Harrow Jr., "Posting a Privacy Problem?" *The Washington Post,* January 22, 1999.

33. Robert Windrem, "Spy Satellites Enter New Dimension," MSNBC.com, August 8, 1998.

34. Peter H. Lewis, "Forget Big Brother," *The New York Times,* March 19, 1998.

35. "Lawsuit Over Taped Call Appealed," *The New York Times,* August 14, 1998.

36. Rene Sanchez, "Abortion Foes' Internet Site on Trial," *The Washington Post,* January 15, 1999.

37. Alan Westin, Michael Baker, *Databanks in a Free Society: Computers, Record-Keeping and Privacy* (New York: Quadrangle Books, 1972), p. 3.

38. Arthur Miller, "The Surveillance Society," in *Uncle Sam Is Watching You* (Washington, D.C.: Public Affairs Press, 1971), p. 31.

39. Ibid., p. 21.

40. Aryeh Neier, *Dossier: The Secret Files They Keep on You* (New York: Stein and Day, 1975), p. 12.

41. *The Politics of Privacy* (Washington, D.C.: The Center for Public Integrity, 1998), p. 14.

42. "Your Right to Privacy," An American Civil Liberties Union Handbook (Carbondale, Illinois: Southern Illinois University Press, 1990), p. 13 and p. 127.

43. *Privacy Times,* January 20, 1988.

44. *The Politics of Privacy* (Washington, D.C.: The Center for Public Integrity, 1998), pp. 15–17.

45. Ibid., p. 23.

46. Simon Davies, "Europe to U.S.: No Privacy, No Trade," *Wired,* May 1998.

47. Joint Letter from American Civil Liberties Union, Electronic Privacy Information Center, U.S. Public Interest Research Group," November 15, 1995.

48. "Privacy, Open Records and the Trade-Off of Values," The Wisconsin Data Privacy Project, April 1998.

49. Bob Whitby, "Data Dragnet," *Isthmus,* May 16, 1997.

50. "EPIC Alert 5.10," July 20, 1998, Electronic Privacy Information Center.

51. See Declan McCullah, "Congress Divided Over National ID cards," *Netly News,* August 7, 1998.

52. "Your Right to Privacy," op. cit., p. 61.

53. "National Identification Cards," The American Civil Liberties Union, 1996.

54. See: "Civil Liberties Implications of Airport Security Measures," Statement by Gregory T. Nojeim, op. cit.

55. Letter to Vice President Al Gore, February 11, 1997, Source: Electronic Privacy Information Center; see also "Civil Liberties Implications of Airport Security Measures," Statement by Gregory T. Nojeim, op. cit.

56. Declan McCullah, "Al Gore, Reborn as Privacy Advocate, Has Sinned Before," *Netly News,* August 7, 1998.

57. Declan McCullagh, "Fear of Flying," *The Netizen,* September 12, 1996.

58. Charles Simonyi, "I Fit the Profile," *Slate,* May 24, 1997.

59. Tod Robberson, "Plan for Student Database Sparks Fears in Fairfax," *Washington Post,* January 9, 1997.

4. Big Brother at the Mall

1. *California Bankers Association* v. *Shultz,* 416 U.S. 21 (1974).

2. *U.S.* v. *Miller,* 425 U.S. 435 (1976).

3. James Glave, "AI Technology Watches What You Read, Sells Accordingly," *Wired News,* December 2, 1996; see also R. Colin Johnson, "Surfing the Web Gets New Smarts—Neural-Learning and Fuzzy-Logic Tools Add Intelligence to Internet Advertising," *EETimes,* January 5, 1998, Issue 987.

4. David Banisar, op. cit.

5. Robert O'Harrow Jr., "Posing a Privacy Problem? Driver's License Photos Used in Anti-Fraud Database" *The Washington Post,* January 22, 1999.

6. Robert O'Harrow Jr. and Liz Leyden, "U.S. Helped Fund Photo Database of Driver Ids," *The Washington Post,* February 18, 1999; see also Robert O'Harrow, "ACLU Cites Photo Flap, Seeks New Privacy Laws," *The Washington Post,* February 19, 1999.

7. Andrew Kantor, "Privacy Replaces Censorship as #1 Concern of Users," *Internetnews .com,* March 26, 1998.

8. "E-Commerce & Privacy: What Net Users Want," A Survey of the American Public Conducted by Louis Harris & Associates, Inc. and Dr. Alan F. Westin, June 23, 1998.

9. "A Little Net Privacy, Please," *Business Week,* March 16, 1998.

10. Nina Bernstein, "Personal Files Via Computer Offer Money and Pose Threat," *The New York Times,* June 12, 1997.

11. Ibid.

12. Ibid.

13. Andrew L. Shapiro, "Privacy for Sale: Peddling Data on the Internet," *The Nation,* June 23, 1997.

14. Nina Bernstein, op. cit.

15. "Case Study: Blue Cross and Blue Shield of North Carolina," Source: Acxiom Corporation, "Case in Point," 1997.

16. "Case Study: AT&T Corporation," Source: Acxiom Corporation, "Case in Point," 1998.

17. "Case Study: MCI," Source: Acxiom Corporation, "Case in Point," 1997.

18. Bruce Horovitz, "Playboy May Tell All About Customers," *USA Today,* November 12, 1998.

19. EPIC Alert 6.09, The Electronic Privacy Information Center, June 10, 1999.

20. "SelectCast for Commerce," Source: Aptex Corporation, August 1998.

21. Ibid.

22. Chip Bayers, "The Promise of One on One," *Wired,* May 1998.

23. "Aptex Technology," Source: Aptex Corporation, August 1998.

24. Ibid.

25. Craig Bicknell, "For Sale; Your Tastes, Interests," *Wired News,* June 24, 1998.

26. Saul Hansell, "Big Web Sites to Track Steps of Their Uses," *The New York Times,* August 16, 1998.

27. Frank James, "Intel Chip Fires Up Privacy Debate," *The Chicago Tribune,* January 1999.

28. Jeri Clausing, "Intell Pentium III Processor Makes Its Debut," *The New York Times*, February 27, 1999.

29. Jeri Clausing, "After Intel Chip's Debut, Critics Step Up Attack," *The New York Times*, February 19, 1999.

30. Ibid.

31. Joel Brinkley, "FTC Says GeoCities Violated Privacy Rules," *The New York Times*, August 14, 1998.

32. Jeri Clausing, "Self-Regulation of Internet Companies Is Poor, Says FTC," *The New York Times*, June 5, 1998.

33. "Privacy Online: A Report to Congress," The Federal Trade Commission, June 1998.

34. Pamela Mendels, "Sites Aimed at Children Collect More Than Just Hits," *The New York Times*, June 29, 1998.

35. "FTC Urges Congress to Guard Children's Privacy On-Line," *The Wall Street Journal Interactive*, June 4, 1998.

36. "Surfer Beware," Electronic Privacy Information Center, 1997.

37. Marc Rotenberg quoted in David E. Kalish, "Web Users Seen as Unprotected," washingtonpost.com, June 9, 1997.

38. Katharine Q. Seelye, "A Plan for Database Privacy, But Public Has to Ask for It," *The New York Times*, December 18, 1997.

39. Philip Shenon, "Navy Case Combines Gay Rights and On-Line Privacy," *The New York Times, January 17, 1998.*

40. Letter to John Dalton, Secretary of the Navy from David L. Sobel, Electronic Privacy Information Center, January 14, 1998.

41. Lisa Napoli, "Sailor's Case Becomes Privacy and Rights Cause," *The New York Times*, January 14, 1998.

42. Ibid.

43. Philip Shenon, "On-Line Service Accuses Navy of Deception in Inquiry About Sailor," *The New York Times*, January 22, 1998.

44. Memorandum Opinion, U.S. District Judge Stanley Sporkin, *McVeigh* v. *Cohen, et al.* (Civil Action 98-116, D.D.C.).

45. *Tucker* v. *Waddell, U.S. Court of Appeals for Fourth Circuit,* 1996; see also Carl S. Kaplan, "Navy Case Likely to Clarify Loopholes in Privacy Law," *The New York Times*, February 5, 1998.

46. Philip Shenon, "Sailor Victorious in Gay Case of On-Line Privacy," *The New York Times*, June 12, 1998.

47. Carl S. Kaplan, "Law That Helped Sailor in Privacy Case Has Major Loophole," *The New York Times*, June 19, 1998.

5. Losing Ground

1. Linda Greenhouse, "High Court Curbs Claim On Privacy in a Home," *The New York Times*, December 2, 1998.

2. *Howard* v. *Des Moines Register* (283 N.W. 2d 289, 1979).

3. *Waters* v. *Fleetwood* (91 S.E. 2d 145, S.C. 1986).

4. *Howell* v. *New York Post Co.* (612 N.E. 2d 699, 596 N.Y.S. 2d 350, 1993 N.Y LEXIS 658, N.Y. 1993).

5. *Degregorio* v. *CBS, Inc.*, 473 N.Y.S. 2d 922 (N.Y. Sup. Ct. 1984).

6. *Cape Publications, Inc.* v. *Bridges*, 423 So.2d 426 (Fla. 1982).

7. Ellen Alderman and Caroline Kennedy, *The Right to Privacy* (New York, Vintage Books, 1997), p. 171 ff.

8. Quoted in Ellen Alderman and Caroline Kennedy, *The Right to Privacy* (New York: Vintage Books, 1997), p. 58.

9. John H. F. Shattuck, *Rights of Privacy* (New York, National Textbook Company, 1976), pp. 15.

10. *Pierce* v. *Society of School Sisters* 268 U.S. 510, 1925.

11. *NAACP* v. *Alabama* (357 U.S. 449, 1958).

12. *Talley* v. *California* (362 U.S. 60, 1960).

13. *Olmstead* v. *United States* (277 U.S. 438, 478, 1927).

14. *Griswold* v. *Connecticut* (381 U.A. 479, 1965).

15. Robert Bork, *The Tempting of America: The Political Seduction of the Law* (New York, Macmillan, 1990), p. 246; see also pp. 110–17.

16. *Loving* v. *Virginia* (388 U.S. 479, 1965).

17. *Stanley* v. *Georgia* (394 U.A. 557, 1969).

18. *Eisenstadt* v. *Baird* (405 U.S. 438, 1972).

19. *Roe* v. *Wade* (410 U.S. 113, 1973).

20. *Moore* v. *City of East Cleveland* (431 U.S. 494, 503, 1977).

21. *California Bankers Association* v. *Schultz* (416 U.S. 21 1974); *U.S.* v *Miller* (425 U.S. 435, 1976); *Smith* v. *Maryland* (442 U.S. 735, 1979); *California* v. *Greenwood* (486 U.S. 35, 1988).

22. *Bowers* v. *Hardwick* (478 U.S. 186, 1986).

23. Kevin Sack, "Georgia's High Court Voids Sodomy Law," *The New York Times,* November 24, 1998.

24. Samuel Warren and Louis Brandeis, "The Right to Privacy," *Harvard Law Review,* 1998.

25. *Cooley on Torts,* 2d ed., p. 29, cited in Samuel Warren and Louis Brandeis, op. cit.

26. Rochelle Gurstein, *The Repeal of Reticence* (Hill and Wang, 1996), p. 148.

27. Arthur Miller, *The Assault on Privacy* (Cambridge: Harvard University Press, 1971), p. 172.

28. *Pavesich* v. *New England Mutual Life Insurance Co.* (1904).

29. see Prosser, *Law of Torts,* 829 et. Seq., 3d edition, 1964.

30. Arthur Miller, op. cit., p. 173.

31. David Rosenzweig, "Celebrities Lose Nude Photo Cases," *Los Angeles Times,* November 3, 1998.

32. *Hall* v. *Post* (N.C.Super.Ct. April 21, 1986).

33. *Arrington* v. *New York Times Co.* (434 N.E.2d 1319, 449 N.Y.S.2d 941, N.Y. 1982).

34. *Atkinson* v. *Doherty* (1899), cited in Rochelle Gurstein, op. cit.

6. Medical Privacy

1. Harris Equifax, "Health Information Privacy Survey," 1993.

2. ACLU, "Live and Let Live," 1944.

3. Nothing Sacred, op. cit.

4. Craig Palosky and Doug Stanley, "Privacy Laws Allow Leaks," *Tampa Tribune,* February 15, 1997.

5. Noah Robischon, "Rx for Medical Privacy," *Netly News,* August 29, 1997.

6. John Markoff, "Patient Files Turn Up in Used Computer," *The New York Times,* April 4, 1997.

7. Maggie Scarf, "Keeping Secrets," *The New York Times Magazine,* June 16, 1996.

8. *The Politics of Privacy* (Washington, D.C., The Center for Public Integrity, 1998), p. 1.

9. "Cases from the Privacy Rights Clearinghouse Hotline, October 1995–September 1996," Privacy Rights Clearinghouse, San Diego.

10. Warren E. Leary, "Panel Cites Lack of Security on Medical Records," *The New York Times,* March 6, 1997.

11. Joan Biskupic, "Justices Shield Therapist-Patient Communication," *The Washington Post,* June 14, 1996.

12. Arthur Allen, "Exposed: Computer Technology, Managed Health Care Are All Undermining The American Tradition of Medical Privacy, In the Name of Progress," *The Washington Post,* February 8, 1998.

13. "How Managed Care Can Change a Therapist-Patient Relationship," *The Boston Globe,* October 16, 1998.

14. Arthur Allen, op. cit.

15. Alison Bass, "Conditions Turning Harsh for Psychotherapists," *The Boston Globe,* October 16, 1998.

16. Denise Grady, "Hospital Moves to Secure Patient Records," *The New York Times,* March 12, 1997.

17. Mark Siegler, "Confidentiality in Medicine—A Decrepit Concept," *New England Journal of Medicine,* 307 (1995).

18. Craig Palosky and Doug Stanley, "Privacy Lost," *Tampa Tribune,* February 15, 1997.

19. John Riley, "Open Secrets: Changes in Technology, Health Insurance Making Privacy a Thing of the Past," *Newsday,* March 31, 1996.

20. Ibid.

21. Doug Stanley and Craig Palosky, "Health Information Industry Embraces Technology," *Tampa Tribune,* February 17, 1997.

22. Laura M. Litvan, "How Private is Your Health?" *Investor's Business Daily,* May 28, 1998.

23. Palosky and Stanley, op. cit., "Privacy Lost."

24. Sheryl Gay Stolberg, "The Numbering of America; Medical I.D.'s and Privacy (Or What's Left of It)," *The New York Times,* July 26, 1998.

25. "Minnesota Takes the Lead on Agreement to Protect 41 Million Americans," PRNewswire, October 25, 1997.

26. *Whalen* v. *Roe* (429 U.S. 589, 1977).

27. Letter from John D. Riesch to Joe Leean, Secretary, Department of Health and Family Services, October 29, 1998.

28. "PCASSO with a Mouse," *American Medical News,* October 13, 1997.

29. Milt Freudenheim, "Privacy a Concern as Medical industry Turns to Internet," *The New York Times,* August 12, 1998.

30. *The Politics of Privacy* (Washington, D.C.: The Center for Public Integrity, 1998), p. 8.

31. Robert Pear, "Plan Would Broaden Access Of Police to Medical Records," *The New York Times,* September 10, 1997.

32. Sheryl Gay Stolberg, "Health Identifier for All Americans Runs Into Hurdles, *The New York Times,* July 20, 1998.

33. Alissa J. Rubin, "Medical ID Plan Ignites Privacy Debate," *The Los Angeles Times,* July 21, 1998; Sheryl Gay Stolberg, "Health Identifier for All Americans Runs into Hurdles," *The New York Times,* July 20, 1998.

34. *The Politics of Privacy* (Washington, D.C.: The Center for Public Integrity, 1998), p. 34.

35. Bernadine Healy, "Hippocrates vs. Big Brother," *The New York Times,* July 24, 1998.

36. Robert Gellman, "Feel Like a Number," *Intellectual Capital,* August 27, 1998.

37. "Congress Prepared to Strip Away Your Privacy Protections," *USA Today,* July 31, 1998; see also EPIC Alert 5.11, Electronic Privacy Information Center.

38. Quoted in Arthur Allen, op. cit.

7. Genetic Privacy

1. Lawrence O. Gostin, "Genetic Privacy," *Journal of Law, Medicine and Ethics,* 23 (1995).

2. Larua F. Rothstein, "Genetic Information in Schools," in Mark A. Rothstein, *Genetic Secrets: Protecting Privacy and Confidentiality in the Genetic Era* (New Haven: Yale University Press, 1997), p. 317 ff.

3. "Genetic Information in the Workplace," US Department of Labor, January 20, 1998.

4. Ibid.

5. Eugene Pergament, "A Clinical Geneticist Perspective of the Patient-Physician Relationship," in Mark Rothstein, op. cit., p. 95.

6. S. A. Cummings, "DNA Testing: A Comparison of Opinions Between the Public and Health Care Providers" (M.S. thesis: Northwestern University, 1995).

7. Eugene Preferment, op. cit., pp. 96–97.

8. Jean E. McEwen, "DNA Data Banks," in Mark Rothstein, op. cit., pp. 232–233.

9. Ibid., p. 234.

10. Nicholas Wade, "FBI Set to Open its DNA Database for Fighting Crime," *The New York Times,* October 12, 1998.

11. Jean E. McEwen, op. cit., p. 236.

12. Nicholas Wade, op. cit.

13. Ibid.

14. Jean E. McEwen, op. cit., p. 239.

15. Ibid. pp. 245–246.

16. Ibid., p. 246.

17. Mark A. Rothstein, "The Law of Medical and Genetic Privacy in the Workplace," in Mark Rothstein, op. cit., p. 281ff.

18. Ibid., p. 290.

19. George J. Annas, "Privacy Rules for DNA Databanks: Protecting Coded Future Diaries," *Journal of the American Medical Association,* 270 (1993).

20. Franklin M. Zweig, Joseph T. Walsh, and Daniel M. Freeman, "Courts and the Challenges of Adjudicating Genetic Testings's Secrets," in Mark Rothstein, op. cit., p. 335.

21. George J. Annas, Leonard H. Glantz, and Patricia Roche, "Drafting the Genetic Privacy Act: Science, Policy and Practical Considerations," *Journal of Law, Medicine, and Ethics,* 23 (1995).

22. Ibid.

23. Thomas H. Murray, "Genetic Exceptionalism and 'Future Diaries': Is Genetic Information Different from Other Medical Information?" in Mark Rothstein, op. cit., pp. 71–72.

24. Ibid., p. 71.

25. Mark A. Rothstein, "Genetic Secrets: A Policy Framework," in Mark Rothstein, op. cit., p. 490.

26. Ibid., p. 461.

27. John R. Lumpkin, "Finding a Balance Between Privacy and Safety," *Intellectual Capital,* August 27, 1998.

28. "MMS Policy: Patient Privacy and Confidentiality," Massachusetts Medical Society, 1998.

29. From: "Principles for Federal Privacy Protection of Medical Records," Electronic Privacy Information Center, October 30, 1995.

8. Big Brother at the Office

1. Sabra Chartrand, "What Your Employer Knows About You," *The New York Times,* May 19, 1996; see also "Employee Monitoring: Is There Privacy in the Workplace," Utility Consumer's Action Network, 1997.

2. Walter Olson, *The Excuse Factory* (New York: The Free Press), p. 223.

3. Lewis Maltby, testimony to House Education and Labor Subcommittee on Labor-Management Relations, June 30, 1993.

4. Stuart Silverstein, "Survey Shows Surveillance of Workers Is Growing," *The Los Angeles Times,* May 23, 1997.

5. Charles Piller, "Bosses with X-Ray Eyes," *Macworld,* July 1993.

6. Chartrand, op. cit.

7. *Nothing Sacred: The Politics of Privacy* (Washington, D.C.: The Center for Public Integrity, 1998), p. 49.

8. Silverstein, op. cit.

9. *Shoars* v. *Epson Am., Inc.,* (No. SWC 112749, Cal. Super Ct. December 8, 1992).

10. Patrice Duggan Samuels, "Who's Reading Your E-Mail? Maybe the Boss," *The New York Times,* May 12, 1996.

11. Ibid.

12. *O'Connor* v. *Ortega* (480 U.S. 709, 1987).

13. Samuels, op. cit.

14. Ibid.

15. Walter Olson, p. 74.

16. Chartrand, op. cit.

17. *Norman Bloodsaw* v. *Lawrence* (U.S. 9th Circuit Court of Appeals, 1998).

18. "Many Companies Fail to Protect Confidential Employee Data," University of Illinois at Urbana-Champaign News Bureau, April 22, 1996.

19. *Nothing Sacred,* op. cit., pp. 43–44.

20. *Soroka* v. *Dayton Hudson, Corp.* (I CalReptr.2d 77, 1991 Cal. App).

21. *Hill* v. *National Collegiate Athletic Association* (865 P.2d 633, 1994).

22. Judith Decew, op. cit., p. 137.

9. The Government's War on Privacy

1. See Testimony of Dr. Whitfield Diffie, Before Senate Judiciary Committee on Technology and Law, May 3, 1994.

2. *Olmstead* v. *United States* (277 U.S. 438, 478, 1927).

3. Brock Meeks, "The End of Privacy," *WIRED,* April 1994.

4. John Perry Barlow, "Jackboots on the Infobahn," *WIRED,* April 1994.

5. Brock Meeks, "Electronic Privacy—A Call to Action," WIRED Online, 1994.

6. See General Accounting Office, IRS Systems Security: Tax Processing Operations and Data Still at Risk Due to Serious Weaknesses (GAO/AIMD-97-49, April 8, 1997); "Bill Would Tell I.R.S. Workers Not to Snoop." *The New York Times,* April 8, 1997; John Broder, "Acting Commissioner Apologized for I.R.S. Abuses," *The New York Times,* September 26, 1997; Statement of Margaret Milner Richard, IRS Commissioner, Before Senate Appropriations Subcommittee on Treasury and General Government, April 15, 1997).

7. Quoted in Declan McCullagh, "Archive: The Privacy Snatchers," *The Netly News,* December 30, 1997.

8. Vance Packard, *The Naked Society* (New York, David McKay Company, 1964), p. 12.

9. Alan Barth in *Uncle Sam Is Watching You: Highlights From the Hearings of the Senate Subcommittee on Constitutional Rights* (Washington, D.C., Public Affairs Press, 1971), p. v.

10. Aryeh Neier, *Dossier: The Secret Files They Keep on You* (New York, Stein and Day, 1975), p. 14.

11. Ibid.

12. David Banisar, "An Overview: Pre-Wiretapping Telephones: Operation Root Canal," July 1996, in Bruce Schneier and David Banisar, *The Electronic Privacy Papers* (New York, John Wiley & Sons, 1997), pp. 138 ff.

13. "Back to Smoke Signals," *The Washington Post,* March 26, 1992.

14. Memo by Wm. R. Loy, General Services Administration, May 5, 1992.

15. David Banisar, "Behind the Curtain: Operation Root Canal, op. cit., p. 148.

16. Speech by Louis J. Freeh, at American Law Institute, May 19, 1994.

17. David Banisar, "Behind the Curtain," op. cit., p. 151.

18. Letter from Ira Glasser and Laura Murphy Lee to Congressman Jack Brooks, September 25, 1994.

19. Letter from Marc Rotenberg and David Sobel to Senator Malcolm Wallop, October 6, 1994.

20. "Keep Snoops Off-line," *USA Today,* March 7, 1994.

21. "A Keyhole for Washington? Don't Require Communications Networks to Build in a Way for the Government to Eavesdrop," *Charlotte Observer,* March 7, 1994.

22. Letter from Ira Glasser and Laura Murphy Lee to Congressman Jack Brooks, September 22, 1994.

23. See Testimony of Dr. Whitfield Diffie, Before Senate Judiciary Committee on Technology and Law, May 3, 1994.

10. Breaking the Code

1. David Kahn, *The Codebreakers* (New York, Macmillan, 1967), p. 84.

2. Carol M. Ellison, "Who Owns Cryptography," in Bruce Schneier and Avid Banisar, *The Electronic Privacy Papers*, op. cit., pp. 271–272.

3. Eric Hughes, "A Cypherpunks's Manifesto," in Bruce Schneier and David Banisar, op. cit., pp. 285–287.

4. Bruce Schneier, "Cryptography Primer," in Bruce Schneier and David Banisar, op. cit., p. 259.

5. Ibid.

6. "An Appraisal of the Technologies of Political Control," European Parliament: Scientific and Technologies Options Assessment, January 6, 1998.

7. Patrick S. Poole, "ECHELON: America's Spy in the Sky," Free Congress Research and Education Foundation, 1998.

8. Ibid.

9. Patrick S. Poole, op. cit.

10. Vernon Loeb, "NSA Admits to Spying on Princess Diana," *The Washington Post*, December 12, 1998.

11. M. Fletcher, "Cook Faces Quiz on Big Brother Spy Net," *Financial Mail on Sunday*, March 1, 1998.

12. Tom Bowman and Scott Shane, "Battling High-Tech warriors," *Baltimore Sun*, December 15, 1995.

13. Patrick S. Poole, op. cit.

14. "Cracking DES," Electronic Frontier Foundation Press Release, July 17, 1998. See also, Will Rodger, "Group Cracked DES Data Security Code," *Inter@ctive* Week, July 17, 1998.

15. Bruce Schneier and David Banisar, op. cit., pp. 295–296.

16. Ibid., p. 297.

17. Ibid.

18. Ibid., p. 309.

19. Ibid.

20. Ibid., pp. 310–312.

21. Philip Elmer Dewitt, "Who Should Keep the Keys?" *Time*, March 14, 1993.

22. "Clipping Privacy," *The Christian Science Monitor*, February 24, 1994.

23. "Don't Let Washington Play 'I Spy' On You," *Business Week*, March 24, 1994.

24. William Safire, "Sink the Clipper Chip," *The New York Times*, February 14, 1994.

25. Bruce Schneier and David Banisar, op. cit., pp. 316–317.

26. Ibid., p. 320.

27. Brock Meeks, "Jacking in from the Narco-terrorist Encryption Port," *CyberWire Dispatch*, May 12, 1995.

28. *Your privacy is at stake*, Americans for Computer Privacy, 1998.

29. "National Research Council Report: Cryptography's Role in Securing the Information Society" (Washington D.C.: National Academy Press, 1996).

30. Jeri Clausing, "Support for Encryption Is Less Than U.S. Claims, Study Says," *The New York Times*, February 9, 1998.

31. "EC Rejects Key Escrow Encryption," EPIC Alert 4.15, November 10, 1997.

32. Brock Meeks, "Jacking in from the Narco-terrorist Encryption Port," *CyberWire Dispatch*, May 12, 1995.

33. CDT Policy Post Volume 2, Number 29, August 1, 1996.

34. Jeri Clausing, "House Committee Casts Wide Net with Encryption Vote," *The New York Times*, September 12, 1997.

35. Ibid.

36. Peter Wayner, "Mockery and Fear Greet Encryption Plan," *The New York Times*, September 12, 1997.

37. Jeri Clausing, "House Panel Rejects FBI Plan on Encryption," *The New York Times*, September 25, 1997.

38. Jeri Clausing, "FBI Halts Its Push for Encryption Access Legislation," *The New York Times*, March 18, 1998.

39. John Markoff, "Encryption Issue Threatens Silicon Valley Rapport with Clinton," *The New York Times*, February 27, 1998.

40. Peter Wayner, "FBI Plan Would 'Deputize' Sector Companies," *The New York Times*, July 11, 1997.

41. Ashley Dunn, "Governments and Encryption: Locking You Out, Letting Them In," *The New York Times*, October 8, 1997.

11. The Tell-All Society

1. James B. Twitchell, *For Shame; The Loss of Common Decency in American Culture* (New York: St. Martin's Press, 1997), p. 31.

2. Carl D. Schneider, *Shame, Exposure, and Privacy* (New York: W. W. Norton and Co. 1992), p. 5.

3. Ibid., p. 42.

4. Cynthia Crossen, "In This Tell-All Era, Secrets Just Aren't What They Used to Be," *The Wall Street Journal*, March 31, 1998.

5. Quoted in Kenneth Turan, "His Show of Shows," *The Los Angeles Times*, June 5, 1998.

6. "Are 'Net Virgins' for Real?" *Reuters*, July 16, 1998.

7. Frederick Exley, *Pages from a Cold Island* (New York: Random House, 1974), p. 37.

8. Wendy Shalit, "Have You No Shame," *The Wall Street Journal*, July 27, 1998.

9. Kevin Reichard, "Look at Me! Webcams and the Internet Unite Voyeur and Exhibitionist," *Isthmus*, August 7, 1998.

10. Edward Rothstein, "Tuning In to Timothy Leary's Death Bed," *The New York Times*, April 29, 1996.

11. Quoted in Vicki Abt and Leonard Mustazza, *Coming After Oprah: Cultural Fallout in the Age of the TV Talk Show* (Bowling Green, Ohio: Bowling Green State University Popular Press, 1997), p. 101.

12. "Too High A Price For Fame," *Newsweek*, September 15, 1997.

13. Ibid.

14. Christopher Lasch, *The Culture of Narcissism* (New York: Warner Books, 1979), p. 117.

15. Sarah Lyall, and Robin Pogrebin, "Diana's Hunters: How the Quarry Was Stalked," *The New York Times,* September 10, 1997.

16. Andrew Morton, *Diana: Her True Story,* Revised Edition, (New York: Pocket Books, 198), p. 17.

17. "Why Do the Young Mourn Her?" *The New York Times,* September 3, 1997.

18. Ibid.

19. Andrew Morton, op. cit., p. 10.

12. Clinton's Bedroom

1. Quotes taken from "The Starr Report: The Official Report of the Independent Counsel's Investigation of the President."

2. Text of Clinton Speech, August 17, 1998.

3. Quoted in Janna Malamud Smith, *Private Matters,* op. cit., p. 198.

4. Ibid., p. 199–200.

5. Jeffrey Rosen, "The End of Privacy," *The New Republic,* February 16, 1998.

6. Jeffrey Rosen, "TRB from Washington: Take the Fourth," *The New Republic,* September 7, 1998.

7. Adam Bryant, "Companies Watch Scandal for Clues to own Policies," *The New York Times,* February 16, 1998.

8. Philip Weiss, "The Sexual Revolution: Sexual Politics on Campus," *Harper's,* April 1991.

9. Tamar Lewin, "Debate Centers on Definition of Harassment," *The New York Times,* March 22, 1998.

10. Quoted in James Taranto, "The Real Sexual McCarthyites Back Clinton," *The Wall Street Journal,* December 22, 1998.

11. Report of the Senate Ethics Committee.

12. Jonathan Rauch, "Washington Diarist: High Lying," *The New Republic,* April 20, 1998.

13. Jean Bethke Elshtain, "The Hard Questions: Going Public," *The New Republic,* March 23, 1998.

14. John Kass, "Sure Clinton's Tryst is a Private Matter—Just Like War Is," *The Chicago Tribune,* September 15, 1998.

15. Quoted in Jean Bethke Elshtain, *Democracy on Trial* (New York: Basic Books, 1995), p. 45.

16. "Gays Playing the Name Game," *Insight,* September 17, 1990.

13. Privacy and Its Critics

1. *Bowers v. Hardwick* (478 U.S. 186, 1986).

2. Robert Bork, op. cit., pp. 121–122.

3. Hannah Arendt, *The Human Condition* (Chicago: The University of Chicago Press, 1958), p. 61.

4. Ibid., p. 71.

5. Rochelle Gurstein, op. cit., p. 58.

6. Ibid. p. 71.

7. Ibid. p. 91.

8. Catherine MacKinnon, *Toward a Feminist Theory of the State* (Cambridge: Harvard University Press, 1989), p. 194.

9. Ibid., pp. 190, 191.

10. Quoted in Judith Decew, *In Pursuit of Privacy,* op. cit., p. 88.

11. Quoted in Jean Bethke Elshtain, *Decocracy on Trial* (New York: Basic Books, 1995), p. 48.

12. Jean Bethke Elshtain, op. cit., p. 43.

13. Patricia Boling, *Privacy and the Politics of Intimate Life* (Ithaca: Cornell University Press, 1996), p. ix.

14. Ibid. p. 42.

15. Ibid. p. 39.

16. Virginia Postral, "No Telling," *Reason,* June 1998.

17. Solveig Singleton, "Privacy As Censorship," Policy Analysis, No. 295, The Cato Institute, June 22, 1998.

18. Amitai Etzione, *The Limits of Privacy* (New York: Basic Books, 1999), p. 9.

19. Ibid. p. 4.

20. Ibid., p. 3 and throughout.

21. Ibid. p. 198.

22. Ibid., p. 196.

23. Ibid., p. 111.

24. Ibid. p. 113.

25. Ibid., p. 127.

26. Ibid. p. 313.

27. Ibid. p. 8.

28. David Brin, *The Transparent Society: Will Technology Force Us to Choose Between Privacy and Freedom?* (Reading, Massachusetts: Addison-Wesley, 1998), p. 1.

29. Ibid. p. 7.

30. Ibid. p. 26.

31. Ibid. p. 9.

32. Ibid., p. 81.

33. Ibid. p. 23.

34. Ibid., p. 14.

35. Ibid., p. 256.

36. Ibid., p. 217.

37. Ibid., p. 257.

38. Ibid., p. 295.

14. "It's None of Your Business"

1. Esther Dyson, "Privacy Protection: Time to Think and Act Locally Globally," Release 1.0, April 1998.

2. *U.S. Department of Justice et al; v. Reporters Committee for Freedom of the Press* (489 U.S. 749, 1989).

3. Arthur Miller, op. cit., p. 180.

4. Ibid., p. 174 ff.

Index

databases (corporate and commercial), 59–79
  closing the data circle, 72–75
  consumer surveys, 63, 64
  credit bureaus, 30
  customer databases, 64–66
  cyberspace, loopholes in, 75–79
  direct-marketing lists, sale of, 60
  driver's license pictures, sale of, 60–61
  information, price of, 29
  list of resources, 28n
  Metromail, 63, 63–64, 72, 74
  prison inmates and data entry, 63–64
  private investigators and, 26–27
  selling private information, 32–33
  volunteer regulation, 74–75
databases (government), 25–58
  abuses, 44–50, 45–46n
  accessability of, 26
  creation of a dataweb, 5
  employees misusing, 25–26
  list of resources, 28n
  new databases, 50–55
  private investigators and, 26–27
  selling information to commercial interests, 29
  Social Security numbers, distribution on the
    Internet, 25
  social-welfare databases, 9
  state agencies and medical information,
    111–12n
  students, electronic profiles of, 55–58
  surveillance technology, 34–35, 35–39
databases (social-welfare), 9
  creation of a dataweb, 5
  employees misusing, 25–26
  Social Security numbers, distribution on the
    Internet, 25
dataweb
  creation of, 5
  medical dataweb, 111–15
  state agencies and, 111–12n
Davida, George, 173
Davies, Simon, 50
Davis, Richard Allen, 63
DBT-Online, 26
DCS Information Systems, 74
DEA (Drug Enforcement Administration)
  direct-marketing lists, purchase of, 60
Decew, Judith, 148, 149, 149n
DeGeneres, Ellen, 188, 195
Dennis, Beverly, 62–63
Department of Motor Vehicles
  driver's license pictures, sale of, 60–61
  Driver' Privacy Protection Act, 48–49
Department of Transportation
  Social Security number encoded in driver's
    licences, 52
Des Moines Register, 80
Diana, Princess of Wales
  NSA surveillance of, 172
  paparazzi and, 190, 191n
  personal revelations, 9, 190–93

Diffie, Whitfield, 169
digital telephony (FBI wiretap bill), 155–56,
  163–66, 166n, 174n.2
Dimensions International, 27
Direct Marketing Association, 74n
DNA
  CODIS (Combined DNA Identification
    System), 126
  forensic DNA typing, 126–28
  Human Genome project, 120, 125
  See also medical privacy (genetic informa-
    tion)
DNA Identification Act, 126
DNA Specimen Repository (U.S. military), 128
Douglas, William O., 59, 84, 86
  FBI wiretapping of, 159
Driver' Privacy Protection Act, 48–49
Drudge Report, 198
drug investigations and wiretaps, 163n
drug testing
  Americans with Disabilities Act and, 149–50
  constitutional protections and, 148
  and employees rights, 137, 142, 147–50
  error rates, 149n
Dunn, Ashley, 28
Dyson, Esther, 247–49

Echelon (NSA surveillance system), 170–73,
  171n
Edwards, George, 161–62
Eisenhower, Dwight D., 199
Eisenstadt case, 87, 88, 90
electric key systems and collages, 39
Electronic Communications Privacy Act
  (ECPA), 48, 77, 78, 79, 140
electronic monitoring of employees, 6
Electronic Privacy Information Center
  (EPIC), 71, 73–74, 74n, 77, 78, 247
  guidelines for medical privacy legislation,
    135–36n
Ellison, Carl, 167–68
Elshtain, Jean Bethke, 211, 228–29
e-mail
  Electronic Communications Privacy Act,
    48, 140
  employer access, 3–4, 6, 137, 140, 141
  Timothy McVeigh and the U.S. Navy, 75–79
  privacy of, 3–4
employee files
  accuracy and confidentiality of, 142
  sharing information with creditors and gov-
    ernment agents, 138
Employee Polygraph Protection Act, 144
employees
  secretly taping coworkers and managers,
    138
employers (and employee rights), 137–51
  Americans with Disabilities Act, 129,
    149–50
  computer keystroke monitoring, 137
  computer monitoring, 137

employers (*cont.*)
  corporate paternalism, 138
  credit reports access, 137
  drug testing, 137, 142, 147–50
  e-mail access, 3–4, 6, 137, 140, 141
  employee files, accuracy and confidentiality
    of, 142
  employee information, sharing with credi-
    tors and government agents, 138
  Employee Polygraph Protection Act, 144
  employees secretly taping coworkers and
    managers, 138
  Federal Privacy Commission, 141, 144
  legal and regulatory protection, 140–41,
    141–44, 143–44n, 150–51
  medical records access, 137
  polygraph testing, 46, 138, 144
  psychological testing, 144–47
encryption
  AT&T's Surity 3600 (encryption device), 175
  Clipper Chip, 159–60, 174–77
  cypherpunks, 168
  Data Encryption Standard (DES), 173–74,
    174n.1
  encryption products, 178n
  European Commission and restrictions on
    encryption, 179
  government limitation of, 155–56
  history of, 167–69
  key escrow, 159–60, 177–78
  McCain-Kerrey proposal (encryption re-
    striction), 181–82
  National Security Agency and, 170–73
  PGP (Pretty Good Privacy), 140, 178n
  public key/private key, 169–70
  Safety and Freedom through Encryption
    Act (SAFE), 180
Engage (CMG Information Services), 69–70
Entick, John, 83
Equifax (credit bureau), 30, 30n, 48
Erikson, Erik, 209
European Commission
  and restrictions on encryption, 179
European Union
  and privacy protection standards, 49–50, 74,
    116, 247
Ervin, Samuel James, Jr., 162
Ervin Committee (Senate Subcommittee on
  Constitutional Rights), 161–62
Etzione, Amitai, 234–38
Excuse Factory, The (Olson), 149–50
Exley, Frederick, 187
Experian Information Systems, Inc., 48

facial thermograph, 38
Fair Credit Reporting Act, 47, 48, 66
Falwell, Jerry, 214
Family Educational Rights and Privacy Act,
  47
Farber, Celia, 206
Fayed, Dodi al-, 190, 191n

FBI, 66
  CODIS (Combined DNA Identification
    System), 126
  digital telephony (wiretap bill), 155–56,
    163–66, 166n, 174n.2
  direct-marketing lists, purchase of, 60
  and encryption restrictions, 179, 181
  and key escrow systems, 177–78
  National Crime Information Center
    (NCIC), 45–46n
  "Operation Root Canal" (telecommunica-
    tion trapdoor), 162
  phone calls, intercepting and deencrypting,
    71
  surveillance of individuals, 160
  See also intelligence agencies; law enforce-
    ment
Federal Communications Commission
  and cell-phone tracking, 34
Federal Deposit Insurance Corporation (FDIC)
  "Know Your Customer Rule," 33–34
Federal Privacy Commission, 141, 144
Federal Trade Commission (FTC), 72–73
feminism and the right to privacy, 226–29
Financial Crimes Enforcement Network
  (Treasury Department), 66
financial data
  private information, price of accessing, 29
  Right to Financial Privacy, 48
First Data Solutions, 65
Flynt, Larry, 198, 214
Ford, Henry, 138
Ford Motor Company and corporate paternal-
  ism, 138
forensic DNA typing, 126–28
Fortas, Abe, FBI wiretapping of, 159
Forward Looking InfraRed (FLIR), 37
Foster, Vince, 244
Fraser, Jason, 191n
Free Congress Foundation, 170
Freedom of Information Act, 47, 116
Freeh, Louis, 71, 163, 165, 179–80
function creep, 51

Gates, Bill, 36
Gattaca (film), 120–21
Gellman, Robert, 118–19
genetic information. *See* medical privacy
  (genetic information)
Genetic Privacy Act, 130–31
Geneva Declaration, 98
GeoCities, 72–73
Geographic Information Systems (GIS), 64
Georgia Tech, 61
Gingrich, Newt, 42
Glantz, Leonard, 130–31
Global-position satellites, 34
Godkin, E. L., 8, 189
Goodlatte, Bob, 180
Gore, Al, 53
  and key escrow, 159–60, 177–78, 178n